APPROACHES
TO
SEMIOTICS

edited by

THOMAS A. SEBEOK

Research Center for the Language Sciences
Indiana University

28

THE LANGUAGE
AND
TECHNIQUE OF THE FILM

by

GIANFRANCO BETTETINI

1973

MOUTON

THE HAGUE - PARIS

Translated by David Osmond-Smith

LIBRARY OF CONGRESS CATALOG CARD NUMBER: 72-94443

Printed in The Netherlands by Mennen, Asten

TRANSLATOR'S PREFACE

Although most problems of translation are dealt with in the appropriate footnotes, two general points should be noted:

(1) *Significato* has been translated as 'meaning', except when the author refers to the Saussurian opposition between *significante* and *significato*, in which case it has been translated as 'signified'. (See also Part I, note 3.)

(2) Since *montaggio* is almost always used to indicate the physical process of cutting up and joining together pieces of film, it has been translated as 'cutting' rather than 'montage', which can also imply more specific and elaborate technical processes. (Naturally, when such processes are referred to, 'montage' is used.) It should however be noted that in the various quotations from R. Arnheim and S. M. Eisenstein, 'montage' is used to indicate the general process elsewhere referred to as 'cutting'.

D.O.-S.

TABLE OF CONTENTS

THE FILM AND ITS SIGNS

PREMISES

During the last few years a particular type of approach to the film has become established in Italy. Its basic outlines are derived from a number of French studies, but all the same it shows increasing evidence of a clearly defined speculative autonomy, and could well find application as an effective basis for programs of empirical research.

Structuralism has had a lively impact on western thought as a model for synthesis between differing ideological universes whose variances ought to have been overcome through moving right away from the traditional conception of 'ideology'. It has also stimulated the interest of students of the film, encouraging the foundation of an approach that is by now widespread, and, regarding its consequences, not entirely predictable.

In France, Roland Barthes, Claude Bremond, A. J. Greimas, Tzvetan Todorov, Jules Gritti, and other researchers have for some time been attempting a rigourous restructuring of literary criticism so as to render more clearly 'scientific' the use of its tools, and to completely divorce it from any impressionistic or traditionally ideological tendencies – which is, indeed, precisely the approach made possible by the philosophical and linguistic implications of structuralism. The basic material that the Barthes group take as a starting-point for their semiological and aesthetical observations is not their own; it has its origin in the work of a number of philologists: above all E. Benveniste, L. Hjelmslev, and L. J. Prieto, who in turn have developed the principles and methods of Ferdinand de Saussure.

The critical work of these researchers has rapidly shifted from verbal language to areas of communication that do not so evidently lend themselves to codification, in particular the field of moving images. A notable example is Christian Metz's study on the hypothetical linguistic functions of the cinema (see issue No. 4 of *Communications*), which has opened up the possibility of serious discussion on cinematic communication within .the scientific terms of a structuralist outlook.

In Italy, interest in the work of this group was transformed into autonomous investigation by P. P. Pasolini, who gradually developed a poetic of
film-as-reality (into which a prospective semiology of the film ought, by
its very nature, to be absorbed), by the editors of *Filmcritica*, and by
other tenacious champions of the critical canons suggested by this new
mode of research. The reports presented at the Round Tables of three
International Exhibitions of the New Cinema at Pesaro – at the most
recent of which, from 27 May to 4 June 1967, the principal speakers included Galvano Della Volpe, Umberto Eco, Pier Paolo Pasolini, Antonin
Sychra, Emilio Garroni, Christian Metz, Pio Baldelli, Gianni Toti, and
Vittorio Saltini – have fostered the evolution of two currents of thought
which, although they share the same intellectual precedents, differ widely
in their provisory conclusions and in the methodologies that they derive
from them. Some talk of a universal semiotics, capable of including within
itself all aspects of the film as sign-system by virtue of a mystical acceptance of the specular nature of a photographic mode of reproduction;
others, instead, move confidently toward the concept of an autonomous
semiology of the film. But in both cases research is still too strongly linked
to the precedents of linguistics, from which it has borrowed intuitions
and methods of procedure without, however, having yet had the chance to
establish its own experimental basis in the form of a series of analyses
concerned strictly with a science of the film.

Hence the need to clarify a scientific definition of the problem by carefully distinguishing between the two linguistics: the old, which is by now
codified, and the new, which can only be guessed at by comparing and
transposing work that has preceded it in other areas of human communication. It is undoubtedly desirable to eliminate all equivocal similarities
and to prevent reckless transpositions and deductions before confronting
the language of the film, as an autonomous phenomenon, within the terms
suggested by the most recent semiological speculation.

It is with this in view that the following pages are written, and they
would seem confirmed by the latest developments in film production,
whose best directors are becoming increasingly engaged in a metalinguistic critique within the body of their work – they are reinventing, that
is, the basic forms of their language, absorbing them into the stilemes of
their audio-visual narrations. The principal names may be easily identified: Bertolucci, the most recent Bergman, Antonioni, and above all Jean-
Luc Godard.

We shall return to the critics and directors who merit further attention
later on. For the moment, however, it would seem more appropriate to

begin the analysis of so complex a subject by proposing a series of definitions that will serve to avoid possible interpretive misunderstandings.
There exists a certain confusion in the use of terms recently coined by
semiologists, and in the attribution of meanings to the terms themselves,
so that it is appropriate that one should start by making clear, by means
of a sort of lexicon adapted to the text, the semantic area of the words that
will most frequently be met with. The whole study will be conducted with
a view to establishing a semiology of the film, understanding by semiology
the science of signs, or better, as Umberto Eco puts it, the scientific
discipline that seeks to interpret and study every phenomenon in which
the free action of man is involved (Eco would say every CULTURAL phenomenon) as a system of signs and thus as a communicative event.[1]
Semiology is based on the hypothesis "...which has already proved very
fruitful, that all cultural phenomena ARE communicative phenomena and
may therefore be described and catalogued as SYSTEMS OF SIGNS".[2]

But by SIGN one means everything taking the form of a communication
between a SENDER and a RECEIVER that simultaneously obeys two functions: that of acting as the bearer (or one of the bearers) of the message,
and that of representing something else and, for the purposes of cognition, replacing it. Thus every sign presents two aspects: one direct, the
other, derived from its capacity for signification, indirect. As is well
known, Ferdinand de Saussure maintains that each linguistic sign is "a
psychic entity with two faces", the combination of a concept and an
acoustic image. To make his attitude the clearer, he defines as a SIGNIFIED
the concept subtended by the sign, and as a SIGNIFIER the complex of
sounds that expresses it.[3] But it may be maintained that the functional
ambivalence of the sign should be extended beyond the isolated area of
linguistics. Any sign, the iconic type included, acts by virtue of an intellectual content, a signified that must never be confused with the so-called
'referent', the real object to which the sign makes reference.

---

[1] Umberto Eco, *Appunti per una semiologia delle comunicazioni visive* (Milano, Bompiani, Per l'Università di Firenze, Facolta di Architettura, 1967a), 7-8.

[2] Gianfranco Bettetini, *Il segno, dalla magia fino al cinema* (Milano, 1964), 41.

[3] Ferdinand de Saussure, *Cours de linguistique générale* 5th ed. (Paris, 1955), a text
put together by Bally and Sechehaye on the basis of notes taken by pupils during the
three courses in general linguistics given by Saussure at Geneva, as well as a number
of autograph notes found after his death (1913). English translation: *Course in General
Linguistics*, trans. W. Baskin (London, Peter Owen Ltd., 1959), 66-67. (Baskin's inele-
gant but inevitable anglicization of *signifié* and *significant* has been retained here. One
should however note the more coherent, if less faithful version: "meaning" and "sign
vehicle", that is now coming into use. See, for instance, Umberto Eco's "A Semiotic
Approach to Semantics", *Versus* I [1971]. Translator's note.)

An ICONIC SIGN is the type of sign that stimulates in the receiver of the communication a perceptive scheme very similar to the one that would have been directly stimulated in him by contact with the real object, or natural referent. We shall have occasion to pause over the concept of iconicity and its distinguishing features a number of times during the course of this book. But for the moment, suffice it to observe that signs of this type also have a signifier and a signified, and that a semiology of the film must discover a means of passing from the first level to the second, from that of expression to that of content. (As in the work of Roland Barthes, who borrows the idea from L. Hjelmslev, the LEVEL OF EXPRESSION will indicate that of the signifiers, and the LEVEL OF CONTENT that of the signifieds.)[4]

Lévi-Strauss also points out the ambiguous nature of signs when he writes that they "resemble images in being concrete entities", which, however, resemble the concept "in their powers of reference. Neither concepts nor signs relate exclusively to themselves; either may be substituted for something else."[5]

A particular type of sign is the SYMBOL, which may be considered as the result of an inventive act and as an instrument of communication. It aims not only at representing a thing, but also at substituting for it completely within the area of its values and functions.[6]

In more complex systems of signification, along with signs and symbols, one must take into account, as does Luis J. Prieto, the so-called 'semas' – that is, signs whose signifieds correspond to a verbal proposition.[7] The term 'SEMA' is also used by A. J. Greimas, but with a very different meaning; in this case it is a matter of the semantic properties of one "*terme-objet*" by virtue of which it can enter into relationship with another (so that it contributes to the semantic content of a relation between two *termes-objects*).[8] To sum up, we shall say that in a sign the SIGNIFIER is the formal aspect of the communicative function. It is the element, or elements, or groups of elements "... that make possible the

---

[4] Roland Barthes, "Éléments de sémiologie", *Communications* 4, (1964a). English translation: *Elements of Semiology*, trans. Annette Lavers and Colin Smith, (London, Jonathan Cape, 1967), 39.

[5] Claude Lévi-Strauss, *La pensée sauvage* (Paris, Librairie Plon, 1962). English translation: *The Savage Mind* (London, Weidenfeld and Nicolson, 1966), 18.

[6] Bettetini (1964), 190.

[7] Luis J. Prieto, *Messages et signaux* (Paris, P.U.F., 1966). See also the same author's *Principes de noologie* (The Hague, Mouton, 1964).

[8] A. J. Greimas, *Sémantique structurale* (Paris, Larousse, 1966a), 21-22. (There being no satisfactory equivalent for *terme-objet* in English, Greimas' original terminology has been retained. Translator's note).

appearance of signification at the level of perception, and that are recognised in precisely this moment as being exterior to the perceiver";[9] it is
"form as generator of sense".[10]

The SIGNIFIED, on the other hand, is the ideological content of the communicative act, the goal that the perceiver's cognitive act arrives at by
means of the signifier.[11] Furthermore, every sign fulfills its communicative
function in two distinct and complementary modes: DENOTATION and
CONNOTATION. We shall say that a sign (or a system of signs) DENOTES
when its significative function is limited to the relationship between a
signifier and its primary and direct signified; but that a sign (or system of
signs) CONNOTES when its level of expression (the signifier) is composed of
another significative system – that is, of a simple relationship between
signifier and signified.[12] Denotation is the generic and primitive function
of the sign, whose capacity for connotation, on the other hand, derives
from its history and development its context, its expressive richness, the
social tradition that characterizes it, the mental capacity of the communicator and the receiver, and everything that can contribute to those of
its semic components that transcend the basic level of signification.

Articulated communication implies the formation of a DISCOURSE within which the message is structured. The discourse can equally well reveal
its sphere of action to be the level of elementary and unitary signs (the so-
called PARADIGMATIC level), or the complimentary combinatorial level, in
which the smallest units are complexes of elementary signs bound together
as a unit so as to signify something (the SYNTAGMATIC level).[13]

We shall have to further examine this fundamental distinction later on;
but having indicated it, it will for the moment be sufficient to bear in mind
that every message, and thus every discourse, can communicate to the
receiver a certain amount of information. According to the cybernetic
theories of Norbert Weiner, C. E. Shannon, W. Weaver, Colin Cherry,
etc.,[14] INFORMATION is not to be identified with how much is communicated, but with the "measure of the possibility of choice in the selection of a

[9] Greimas (1966a), 10.
[10] Eco (1967a), 39.
[11] Eco (1967a), 35.
[12] Barthes (1967), 89.
[13] Greimas (1966a), 41.
[14] Norbert Weiner, *Cybernetics* (Cambridge, M.I.T. Press, 1961); J. R. Pierce,
Symbols, Signals, and Noise (New York, 1961); André Martinet, *Éléments de Linguistique Générale* (Paris, A. Colin, 1960), English translation: *Elements of General
Linguistics*, trans. Elisabeth Palmer (London, Faber and Faber, 1964); Roman
Jakobson, *Essais de Linguistique Générale* (Paris, Minuit, 1963). For a more complete
bibliography, see notes 2, 4, 11, 12 and 13 from Eco (1967a).

message".[15] The concept of information thus occupies an area of possibility that is more basic than that of the communicative act. But unless otherwise specified, the term INFORMATION will here be used on the semantic level of notional communication, of the quantity of primary signifieds contained in the message and transmitted to the receiver. In this sense, INFORMATION will almost always manifest itself on the denotative level of the sign-relationship. We shall therefore call EXPRESSION the redundancy that the message presents with respect to its designative function; that is, the connotative richness with which it establishes itself as a significative form. A work of art, for example, will be composed of a complex of messages that are, generally speaking, only modestly informative (in the sense defined above; because, according to information theory, the value of a poetic message is proportional to the ambiguity of its structure with respect to expectations and hence with respect to the code – so that it is "extremely informative"),[16] but rich in connotations and semantic resonances. Any communicative act functions by virtue of a general aim to which all the elements that compose it emerge as subordinate, so that in the body of the message one may always trace out a scheme of reference, a STRUCTURE. We may adopt Michel Foucault's definition of a STRUCTURE or SYSTEM as "a set of relations that maintain themselves and transform themselves independently of the things that they link";[17] Greimas is more concise, and perhaps more pertinent – structure for him is the presence of two terms and the relationship between them.[18] This is certainly not the most appropriate point for analyzing and selecting adequate and universally valid definitions for the much-discussed concept of STRUCTURE. For our purposes, it is enough to say that STRUCTURE is the ideological frame of reference that presides over the formation of the message, and that it may, at a limit, be identified with the ultimate code of the message itself.

Structure is the way in which the communicator forms his signs, thus revealing to the receiver (often unconsciously, especially when their frames of reference coincide and the structure is extremely socialized) the ways in which he interprets the world around him.

[15]   Eco (1967a), 25.
[16]   Eco (1967a), 62-63.
[17]   M. Foucault, "Entretien", La Quinzaine littéraire (15 May, 1966); on this subject, see also Esprit (May 1967), which is dedicated to Structuralism, with essays by Y. Bertherat, P. Burgelin, J. Conith, J. Cuisenier, Jean-M. Domenach, M. Dufrenne, J. Ladrière, and P. Ricoeur.
[18]   Greimas (1966a), 19. On page 28, he gives a further definition of structure that is even more synthetic from a semantic point of view, but at present useless as far as this enquiry is concerned.

At this point, our list of definitions comes up against the problems that really concern us – those of LANGUAGE and CODE.

Since some definitions of the type put forward above could appear excessively vague, and give rise to facile transpositions and dangerous misunderstandings, it will be better to spread out an analysis of the themes and problems implied by these terms over the whole length of this chapter, which will attempt to single out a bridge between the general universe of signs and the specific area of a semiology of the film.

In the field of traditional criticism, there is still a certain opposition to this mode of research. But although greatly impeded and conditioned by its industrial obstacles, film production is taking possession of a linguistic autonomy that becomes continually more evident and less easily dealt with by the canons of traditional analysis. What do most of the articles and studies that are published in review columns or specialized magazines tell us about a film by Resnais, or Godard, or Antonioni? Withering disparagements and giddy eulogies appear simultaneously, without the remotest attempt to provide a foundation for valid and stable aesthetic judgements. The producer's political beliefs, as revealed by the film, become a target for criticism; but no one bothers about analyzing their poetic sublimation within the work, or their effect as straightforward external conditioning. This problematic lack of attention is hardly surprising, since the application of a new method would involve a real revolution, not only in film criticism, but in all spheres of the film world – and, even more crucially, in the intellectual life of the men who work there. Cultural revolutions have always developed very slowly and, above all, with the radical and constant opposition of those generally recognised as figureheads.

It is easier to pigeon-hole films by evaluating their content and to hazard extemporary stylistic hypotheses instead of discovering the roots of a general organization of images, above and beyond the contingencies of the individual work, which may perhaps be structured along lines that are in some way analyzable. Consequently it is not a matter of perceiving beyond the moving images a single and unequivocal meaning (such as the signs of a scientific discourse always ought to reveal), but of searching for a method of investigation at various and numerically endless semantic levels – all, however, deriving from a critical reading of the work. One is in fact concerned with an attempt to found a science of the cinematographic language, the philological aspect of which is the first important datum. "Rien n'est plus essentiel à une société que le CLASSEMENT de ses langages", Roland Barthes wrote in a recent polemical essay confined to literary criticism.

Changer ce classement, déplacer la parole, c'est faire une révolution... La philologie a en effet pour tâche de fixer le sens littéral d'un énoncé, mais elle n'a aucune prise sur les sens seconds. Au contraire, la linguistique travaille, non à réduire les ambiguités du langage, mais à les comprendre, et, si l'on peut dire, à les INSTITUER.[19]

The delicacy and humility displayed by Roland Barthes' proposals for the foundation of a possible linguistics of symbols, or science of literature, ought to weigh heavily on the enthusiasm of someone preparing for a parallel investigation among the forms of a language that has not yet found a precise philological ordering, if indeed it is ever destined to find one. But this does not mean that the undertaking is doomed to failure, or, above all, that it is useless.

At the 1965 Pesaro Festival, Pier Paolo Pasolini put forward several suggestive hypotheses in a talk on the "cinema of poetry", directing his research towards the tracing of possible semantic constants in a language composed of images in movement. The same argument re-appeared in the first paragraph of a study of his that was published in *Filmcritica*.[20] The hazards of this type of linguistic approach are very evident (and they are pointed out by Armando Plebe in the same number of *Filmcritica*); searching out and establishing an operative method in the field of expressive communication can introduce grave compromises of a formalistic nature, can obscure the origin and scope of a message in signs, and can, above all, fossilize the work in a state of painful communicative impotence. But the danger of such a methodological degeneration lies not so much in the scientific attitude that would become characteristic of the scholar's approach to his task of analysis, as in the potential and all too comfortable regression that the dogmatic application of a few partial fictions could engender. This, however, would be a defect to be attributed to the sparse human, cultural, and sociological awareness of the scholar, rather than to the characteristics of the method that may be applied and, in part, invented during a reading of the work.

Pasolini distinguished the possibility of a technical language of poetry in the "subjective, the free, and the indirect",[21] and so came to concen-

---

[19] Barthes, "Critique et vérité", *Collection "Tel Quel"*, (Paris, Seuil, 1966a), 45 and 53.
[20] "In calce al 'cinema di poesia'", *Filmcritica* XVII: 163 (January 1966a), 8. Pasolini's text is preceded by an essay by Edoardo Bruno and followed by contributions by Armando Plebe and Christian Metz.
[21] "It is however certain that free and indirect discourse is also possible in the cinema: let us call this operation (which, with respect to its literary analogue, can be a great deal less articulated and complex) 'free and indirect subjectivity'. And in view of the fact that we have established a difference between the 'free and indirect' and 'interior monologue'. we shall have to see which of the two operations the 'subjective, free, and in-

trate the whole autonomous capacity of the cinematographic language, from the poetic point of view (this definition is not a model of literary style, but it seems reasonably clear), on "making the cine-camera aware" – to some extent the technical and stylistic orientation behind the *nouvelle-vague*. Eric Rohmer then replied to Pasolini in No. 172 of the *Cahiers du cinéma* (Nov. 1965), maintaining the autonomy of the object translated into images, and thus proposing the contrasting hypothesis of a "cinema of prose".[22] The polemic was remarkably interesting and worthy of careful attention on the part of the more alert critics.

It cannot be maintained that this sort of approach within the field of film-criticism is absolutely new, since Léon Moussinac had already contrasted the theory of a 'descriptive' cinema with that of a poetic cinema, even talking in terms of a film-poem in connection with the extraordinary suggestive and expositive (or expressive in the widest sense of the term) power of the visual image free from all musical or verbal additions – and *Naissance du cinéma*, his basic work, dates from 1925.[23] But perhaps the time is riper nowadays. The struggle to gain recognition for the film as an art has now been accepted for some time (for it was in that context that Moussinac's studies were produced), and, more crucially, film-criticism feels with particular force the need for cultural integration with other forms of the criticism of expression, as well as a clear-cut and solidly based methodological autonomy; a need to insert itself as a qualified component within the universe of that total communication, the product of artistic and technical messages, both written and visual, which forms a guide-line for some of the most astute contemporary thinkers.

THE METALANGUAGE OF LINGUISTICS

The difficulty that has most obstructed the semioticist's work would seem to have been that of searching out and formulating a metalanguage with

---

direct' is nearer to…. The fundamental characteristic of the 'subjective, free, and indirect' is that of being not linguistic, but stylistic. So it can therefore be defined as an interior monologue deprived of its conceptual and explicitly philosophical and abstract element." Pier Paolo Pasolini, "Introduzione alla Tavola Rotonda sul tema: Critica e nuovo cinema", *Prima mostra internazionale del Nuovo Cinema, Pesaro, 29 May-6 June 1965* (Roma, Istituto Nazionale dello Spettacolo, Via degli Uffici del Vicario 33) (text cyclostyled by the Print Office, Ufficio Stampa).
[22] See also Adriano Aprà's lucid analysis of the positions taken up by Pasolini and Rohmer in *Filmcritica* XVII: 163 (January 1966), 19-21.
[23] Léon Moussinac, *Naissance du cinéma* (Paris, J. Povolozky, 1925).

which to discuss the various linguistic systems that were to be studied.

According to Hjelmslev, one must make a distinction between scientific and non-scientific metalanguages. Greimas agrees with him, maintaining that a non-scientific metalanguage is "comme la langue objet qu'elle explicite, 'naturelle' ", while a scientific one is constructed. For example, an art-critic would use a non-scientific metalanguage, "un sous-ensemble déjà existant", while a technical discussion on phonology would use terms that together constituted "un corps de définitions cohérent". To formulate a scientific metalanguage covering the semiology of the film, one would have to postulate a complex series of definitions and relationships between the various terms, and thus the existence of a 'meta-metalanguage' or 'tertiary language'.[24] For Roland Barthes, a metalanguage "is a system whose plane of content is itself constituted by a signifying system; or else it is a semiotics which treats of a semiotics". It is basically a matter of a function which, within the area of semantic relations, is the opposite of the one that we have already noted as defining the process of connotation.[25]

Morris maintains that semiotics provides such a 'metalanguage' for linguistics, and that "the terminology of linguistics is to be defined by linguists on the basis of the terms of semiotics. In this way, one could describe all the languages of the world in a uniform terminology which would make possible a scientific comparative linguistics."[26] The signs of semiotics ought, therefore, to constitute the elements of a discourse that is also valid for audio-visual language – all the more so in that the images of such a language may, without excessive strain, be brought within the definition of a 'sign' put forward by the behaviourist theory. Usually, when Morris is talking about images, he uses the definition "iconic sign" – that is, one that has the characteristic property of being more or less similar to the signified referent – but in the case of the cinema it is undoubtedly dangerous to generalize this term when there are so many possible modes of ASYNCHRONIC sonic integration which are not linked to the visual image by any relationship of cause and effect (or by aiming at a reproductive likeness), and when, in any case, dubbing and the addition of a musical sound-track can remodel the relation between image and

[24]   Greimas (1966a), 15-16.
[25]   Barthes (1967), 90.
[26]   Charles Morris, *Signs, Language and Behaviour* (New York, 1946; reprinted in Charles Morris, *Writings on the General Theory of Signs* [*Approaches to Semiotics* 16] The Hague, Mouton, 1971), 221 and note D on page 279. Morris mentions the names of several linguists who have moved in this direction, such as Edward Sapir, Alan Gardiner, Leonard Bloomfield, and Manuel J. Andrade.

object, reducing the iconic power of the image itself.[27] For the moment, it is more convenient to consider the moving image of the cinema as one would a sign, without further qualification, and to utilize this particular point of view to articulate a general discourse on cinematographic and, as far as possible, televisual communication.[28]

THE FILM

A film is composed of a number of significant elements, or sources of stimuli for the hypothetical perceptor. However knowledgeable a spectator may or may not be, he will be aware that, when going into a cinema, he is placing himself in contact with a certain reality that communicates something to him. He may make contact with the images on the screen by directly identifying himself with the characters and the situations in which they are involved, he may be aware of the scenic fiction presented to him and know how to judge it objectively, or he may spontaneously take up one of the innumerable standpoints that lie between these two extremes, but in every case he will come out knowing more than when he went in, and aware of having received something, maybe completely passively, from his relation with the screen. The spectator at a film is thus the target for a one-way solicitation by means of signs, in which the stimulus induced by the message triggers off an immediate response, plus other responses at further points in time, none of which can make any impact upon the objective, formal configuration of the moving image – the cinematographic sign, unlike the theatrical one, does not in any way have to take into account such characteristics as a reply from a chorus or a single interlocutor. The cinematographic work of art is complete and definitive before being projected, and it only regains an open dimension within the receptive universe of the perceiver, as a result of his interpretive freedom.[29]

[27]   Eco has subjected Morris' theories to some lively criticism, transforming the relation between iconic sign and thing into a relation between two perceptual conditions (See Eco [1967a], 101-113).

[28]   For a definition of 'sign' see Charles Morris, (1946) and C. K. Ogden and I. A. Richards, *The Meaning of Meaning* (London, Routledge and Kegan Paul Ltd., 1923). See also Stephen Ullmann, *Semantics: An Introduction to the Science of Meaning* (Oxford, Basil Blackwell & Mott Ltd., 1962); and, as well as the many books listed in the bibliographies and notes of these two books, my own *Il segno dalla magia fino al cinema*, which refers, among others, to the definitions of Morris, Masure, Maritain, and Tromp. As will be seen further on, Christian Metz's theory is based on reducing the cinematographic image to a 'sign', whereas Mitry's denies the possibility of such an identification.

[29]   Perhaps it is because of this that the film has always had within it a dimension of

Furthermore, the cinematographic message does not consist of a straightforward sequence of elementary signs, but resorts to significant elements at various levels (direct, indirect, symbolic, etc.), and coordinates them into a structured form that constitutes its communicative corpus. Between screen and spectator a certain discourse unfolds, constructed by means of signs that reproduce in mirror-fashion and of signs that hint at more obscure meanings, of signs that spontaneously represent something and of signs that are conventionally figurative, all composed according to certain norms of coordination dictated by the sender's intentions.

The cinema, therefore, communicates with the spectator through the use of a language that, by the very nature of its signs (at any rate when considered from a quantitative point of view), is not easily generalized or reduced to abstract or somehow classifiable formulas for the purposes of study. The cinema makes use of a language that may be thought of as coinciding with the cinema itself, because the one forms the other in the process of forming itself; so that every linguistic analysis, if undertaken with care, will become transformed into an investigation at the very heart of the cinematographic phenomenon, into a complete and unreserved study of the nature of the contingent cinematographic message and of the whole range of audiovisual expression permitted by the cinema.

LANGUAGE

It is above all necessary to formulate as exhaustive and polyvalent a definition as is possible of the reality to which we refer when speaking or writing the word 'language'. In this instance, points of view can vary noticeably, and thus lead to dangerous confusion as to the method, and indeed, every so often, the object referred to. A very useful definition, and one that embraces a wide area of significative reality, is that put forward by Carla Schick in her precise and well documented study *Il linguaggio – Natura, struttura, storicità del fatto linguistico*.[30] Distinguishing the dual

tragically closed form, and has discovered its natural epic tendency so late. See Jean Mitry, *Esthétique et psychologie du cinéma*, II: *Les formes* (Paris, Éd. Universitaires, 1965), 308; also Christian Metz, "Problèmes actuels de théorie du cinéma", *Revue d'esthétique* 2-3 (1967c), 204-205; for the epic aspect of film narrative, see Peter Szondi, *Theorie des modernen Dramas* (Frankfurt am Main, Suhrkamp Verlag, 1956); and for the relations between theatre and its film version, see also my *La regia televisiva* (Brescia, La Scuola, 1965), and my "La regia teatrale alla T.V.", *La rivista del cinematografo* (January 1966), 58 et seg.
[30] Carla Schick, *Il linguaggio – Natura, struttura, storicità del fatto linguistico* (Torino, Einaudi, 1960), 26-27.

aspects that characterize the manifestation of a language – the subjective and the objective – Carla Schick defines LANGUAGE as "the verbal expression of an intuition, obtained by means of the act of a subject who reworks traditional material, handed down to him as a result of an infinite number of previous creative acts, so as to render it capable of manifesting a moment of his spirituality". The idea expressed here refers to verbal language, and is not easily translated into the terms of a general semiotics, so as to be equally valid for signs that reproduce in mirror-fashion (photographically, that is) a certain physical reality. On the other hand, the duality pointed out by Carla Schick in her rigorous attempt at a definition constitutes one of the basic elements of any linguistic research, above and beyond the nature of the signs that are the objects of analysis.

As is well known, Ferdinand de Saussure had already contrasted the concept of LANGUE with that of PAROLE in his definition of language. The *langue* is a potential instrument, the *parole* its translation into action; the first is a system of "sound-impressions left behind by the actual sounds that we have ourselves pronounced or heard from others",[31] and the second is the result of a personal operation of choice and of adaption to the expressive needs of the specific situation, the "use of the *langue* by one person in a specific situation".[32] The *langue* is therefore only a part of the language – it is language minus *parole*.[33] Its existence is not limited to a single individual, even if potentially it lies within his communicative capacities, but is extended to the traditional usage of a number of individuals, together constituting a social group, who have recourse, in their internal communicative exchanges, to the words invented and built up upon the corpus of their language. The *langue* is not complete in any individual, but reaches perfection in the mass alone.[34] The *langue* thus coincides with the objective aspect of verbal language, and the *parole* with its subjective aspect. These coincide with each other when the speaker (or writer) fossilizes his expression into an impersonal repetition of models that have been taken over without any original re-elaboration, or, at the opposite extreme, when his linguistic invention becomes so completely rooted in the cultural sources and social traditions of the community as to engender a gradual, but real mutation in the traditionally conserved linguistic corpus; in the first instance one is concerned, for instance, with stereotyped manifestations of bureaucratic prose, and in the second with a successful poem.

[31]   Ullmann (1962), 19; see also de Saussure (1959), 11 et seg.
[32]   De Saussure (1959), 20.
[33]   De Saussure (1959).
[34]   Ogden and Richards (1923), 5.

This is not perhaps the moment for lingering over the theoretical and practical importance of Saussure's distinction and its polemical fruitfulness – but even today, almost fifty years after its formulation, linguists in every country argue over it, continually discovering new interpretations for it, or raising doubts as to its fundamental validity.

Following up Morris's suggestion, which has been confirmed by the many contacts being realized between linguists and students of other disciplines concerned with communication, such as electrotechnics and electronics,[35] we shall therefore try turning to general semiotics in order to deduce from it a definition that is in harmony with what has been stated above, but that is, at the same time, more elastic and universal. For Morris, the term LANGUAGE is rather vague, and of ambiguous application; he prefers to make use of the formula "system of linguistic signs" which we shall now try to define in the light of his precise exposition. A linguistic system is evidently made up of a number of signs; these must possess an interpersonal significance – they must, that is, mean the same (or almost the same) thing to all the members of the community that makes use of them for its internal communicative exchanges, even though a certain margin of idiosyncrasy may be tolerated (the question of *langue-parole* comes into evidence once more). Furthermore, these signs must be produced without excessive difficulty by their users, must conserve a constant signified in differing situations (and therefore be amenable to a reasonably acceptable abstract generalization), and must finally be able to combine in certain ways but not in others. Thus, for Morris, a language is "a set of plurisituational signs with interpersonal significata common to members of an interpreter-family, the signs being producible by members of the interpreter-family, and combinable in some ways but not in others to form compound signs"; or, more simply, "a language is a set of pluri-situational consigns restricted in the ways in which they may be combined".[36]

Morris himself, having formulated this definition, points out certain of its limitations, and above all that it is particularly well adapted to those languages that are easily codified into semantic schemes, and into a series of grammatical or syntactical norms. For languages that do not so easily lend themselves to a generalization of their component signs, and of the structural norms that regulate their combinations, insertion into the universe sketched out by Morris's researches becomes somewhat forced

---

[35]   See, for example, the fertile development of Information Theory; see also Ullmann (1962), 18.
[36]   Morris (1946), 35-36.

and dangerous. The definition set out above, in spite of the general validity and universal application within the field of semiotics that its author claims for it, is basically oriented towards the analysis of those languages that may readily constitute the object of a scientific investigation, and that are, therefore, furnished with an ample series of studies and classifications – above all the verbal languages and all others derived through a similar mode of reproduction (phonetic script, alphabetic scripts, the Braille system, etc.).

The metalanguage of semiotics may, in this instance, constitute a notable step forward with respect to previous definitions, but one suspects that the proposition's powers of designative generalization derive more from a formal artifice, from a fortunate choice of words, than from any real applicability to cases such as the cinematographic language. One could then attempt a further process of generalization, making use of a terminology closely related to Morris's, but at the same time looking for a formula that could successfully exclude some of the implications of his definition that are not easily brought within the limits of a language which cannot be divided into more or less monosignificant elements. Yet even if one allows that LANGUAGE is "a group of signs so organized that they are adapted for certain exchanges within a social group",[37] one simplifies the problem, and at the same time one loses all reference to the many studies that have been dedicated to the verbal language. One cannot, furthermore, avoid considering two fundamental aspects of the signs that are involved in this behaviourist outlook (however generalized one may care to imagine it) if one is to be able to view them as capable of combining among themselves to articulate the forms of a language – their SOCIALITY and their PLURISITUATIONALITY (the latter characteristic coinciding with Morris's definition).

SOCIALITY

A language is used by the individuals belonging to a certain community, and its elementary signs must conserve their significative relationship in an almost constant form during the passage from the linguistic reserves of one member of the group to those of another. This is to say that on the basis of the definitions put forward up to now, there must be a collective linguistic corpus to which all members of the social group may refer no matter what mode of speech they may adopt, and, above all, no matter what the basic intentions behind the communicative gesture

[37]   Bettetini (1964), 231.

may be. The transmitter of the message may want to convince or command someone, or he may simply want to set out the elements of a scientific demonstration, but in every case he will (according to the previous definitions) have to refer to a single corpus of signs, and then bring to bear upon it his own creative liberty regarding the choice and organization of such signs as are best adapted to his purpose. A word from a verbal language, however refined, uncommon, or harmonious to the ear it may be, does not of itself bring into play considerations of expressive intent, structure, or style; unless it takes on the functions of an entire expressive phrase by itself (although even in this case the general orientation of the speaker's argument, the particular situation in which a word is placed, the writer's punctuation, or other rhetorical or cryptographical devices imply a syntactic construction that is normally more spread out, but has in this case been compressed), it may be integrated into scientific texts or poetic ones, into an advertisement or the spiritual testament of a philosopher. The point of reference in such a case is a single system of signs which could, according to Saussure's definition, be considered as the LANGUE, and thus as the dynamic basis of the language (but one is here concerned with a slow, long-term dynamism).

Leaving aside all aesthetic considerations, and limiting the problem to its semantic aspects, the word *sound* as used, for example, by T. S. Eliot in the verses "if there were the sound of water only/Not the cicada/And dry grass singing/ But sound of water over a rock"[38] must be considered as identical with the one employed by the aeronautical engineer when he calculates the resistance of materials suitable for crossing the sound barrier. The sign-reserves of a language whose elementary components are characterized by a social consistency of meaning is a system that is itself open to analysis according to the canons of classical research; its signs and symbols exist in a sort of syntactic and pragmatic amorphism because, although standing in a defined relation to their meaning (which in itself is sometimes ambiguous, and can be modified in the construction of the message), they acquire life, and actually complete their process of signification – that is, they acquire significative form – only after being chosen and inserted into the communicative universe in which the sender's intentions channel themselves.[39]

[38] T. S. Eliot, "The Waste Land, V. What the Thunder Said", from *Selected Poems* (London, Faber and Faber, 1954), 65.
[39] Referring to verbal signs, Greimas singles out within every *terme-objet* a positive semic content, which is permanent and unvarying, to be called the SEMIC NUCLEUS, and a complex of semic variables which depend upon the context, the CONTEXTUAL SEMAS.

Thus for the sort of language that the definitions proposed up to this point are concerned with, there exists a set of signs and symbols that may be analyzed even before one proceeds to use them, a rationally organized (or, in most cases, organizable) group that one may approach in order to take up contact with the linguistic universe that is concentrated there. The study of an institutionalized language usually begins with an investigation on the lexical level followed by and integrated with others on the grammatical-syntactic level, and, finally, on the literary level. In the case of a language that has not yet been perfectly analyzed by its own particular science, an approach is usually made along different lines, even though the habit of a particular type of research can condition (sometimes mistakenly, since the linguistic corpus that is being studied is by nature highly individual) the choice of method and its application.

THE SOCIALITY OF CINEMATIC SIGNS

In the case of the cinema it is not at all easy to establish a parallel between the theories set out above and the theory of a language consisting of moving images. Film-makers may come into contact with finished and linguistically definite works, but they do not have at their disposal a system of signs with almost constant references; they do not possess signs that may be easily inserted into every cinematic project that they undertake, whatever their expressive intentions and however the tone and aim of their discourse may be defined. A sensitive and well-prepared director will choose different images to convey the same thing (but only apparently the same, because meaning is a relationship that changes notably when one varies the characteristics of the object referred to) or, better, what could conceptually appear as the same thing – let us say an object that may be verbally translated with the same words – when he wishes to articulate discourses with various different ends in view. His creative intentions are made clear in the images, conditioning their form, their figurative composition, their internal and external rhythms, and all the other additional properties that normally define them. This process comes about in an apparently direct and total way, so that the perceiver does not have to mediate his analysis by means of an abstract and mono-significant instrument.

The CONTEXT "...constitue un niveau original d'une nouvelle articulation du plan du contenu" (Greimas [1966a], 52).

The choice of a certain image on the director's part[40] – for example the choice of a shot or a certain relationship within the cutting – and its consequent realization within the narrative span of the film coincide in all cases with a creative process that is unaided by a potential recourse to signs that are, by convention, valid for all the spectators. The director, spurred on by what he is concerned to express (which may, in many cases, be conditioned by the same reality that is to be analyzed by the film-camera), conceives the events of his film-to-be and is able to translate his inspiration and his plan of action into the code of a language whose signs are far removed from those of the work towards which he is aiming; he can describe in detail, within the terms of a verbal language, the future images of his film, thus constructing an intermediate object of considerable practical utility, but with no expressive autonomy – and yet, despite this, so ambiguous in its more thorough realizations (as in the case of a particularly detailed scenario) as to have frequently given rise to intense polemics with regard to its possible literary value.[41]

The images of a film can be described before or after their realization; their formal content can be summarized and narrated; but receiving a description, however precise, of a cinematographic work or of some part of it, can never substitute for the direct perception of its images, which may be accomplished without recourse to an abstract and generalized medium. Even if whoever conveyed the information were to include among his remarks appreciative descriptions aimed at convincing others or indicating his own particular mode of aesthetic enjoyment, the receiver would never succeed in perceiving the real heart of the communication in question. A cinematographic work expresses something in a certain way – if you change that way of expressing things, you change the substance of the message as well, so that its verbal translation may be considered as a key, but nothing more.[42]

---

[40]   As will be made clearer later on, the word IMAGE is always used in its widest and most generic sense, as 'the reproduction of a certain reality' (which, in the case of the cinema, is a dynamic reality) – so that its meaning is not limited to relations with elements of film technique, such as the frame or shot.

[41]   Indeed Eisenstein, in his *The Film Sense* (London, Faber and Faber, 1952), recalls a Renaissance example of scenario, a series of notes that Leonardo da Vinci took for a pictorial representation of the Flood. Eisenstein points out that the piece "was not intended by its author as a poem or literary sketch.... The description is not a chaos but is executed in accordance with features that are characteristic rather of the 'temporal' than of the 'spatial' arts.... Unquestionably, though, Leonardo's exceedingly sequential description fulfils the task not of merely listing the details, but of outlining the trajectory of the future movement of the attention over the surface of the canvas" (32-33).

[42]   Galvano della Volpe, *Critica del gusto*, 2nd ed. (Milano, Feltrinelli, 1964). Here is developed, from a Marxist-materialist point of view, the theory of a "concrete intellec-

Working with a fictional reality that is capable of reproducing, mirror-fashion, a phenomenal reality, the film-director is compelled to express himself by means of concrete acts that can be credibly and truthfully inserted into this reality which, although false, is so similar to the true one that it is almost tangible.[43] Every choice and intervention that he, as author, makes will coincide with the manipulation of a reality which, although artificially constructed, is presented to the spectator with the characteristics of being almost completely true to life. The spectator is confronted by the objects of the film, and the direction consists, precisely, in the composition of these 'photographic' objects, in the construction, for example, of a time and a space that, however fictional, are the time and space of the reality that the spectator comes up against.

The receptor of a verbal communication, irrespective of the level of socio-cultural awareness at which he lives, is always aware that he is confronted by an indirect instrument which refers him to a reality that is different from the words he has perceived (or at any rate his response to the stimulus of verbal signs is spontaneously directed towards the reality that the words represent, and not towards the words themselves – only in the case of an irrational and magical confusion between name and object signified can ambiguous reactive behaviour arise, but this will occur more on the appreciative and formative level than on that of conscious information and thus of active commitment). On the other hand, the spectator at a film hardly ever manages to perceive the indirect character of the images, and reacts to the fictional reality on the screen as if it were a concrete universe, able to involve him directly.

In his article "À propos de l'impression de réalité au cinéma", Christian Metz, referring to the writings of Jean Leirens (*Le cinéma et le temps*, éd du Cerf, 1954), Rosenkrantz (in *Esprit*, 1937), and Giradoux (*Théâtre et Film*, preface to *Le film de "La Duchesse de Langeais"*, Grasset, 1942),

---

tuality", a "logical-intuitive complex" present within the poet's expressive intentions and work – the theory, that is, of a "discourse" formulated by the poem. In the case of the cinematographic work of art, the poetic 'discourse' can be extracted and verbally formulated, but with a fundamental reduction in its semantic power, a depreciation of the audio-visual metaphors that compose it (as long as the film is a valid one, naturally). See also, by the same author, "Il verosimile filmico" in *Filmcritica* 121, where he talks of the impossibility of translating "a film image into a literary one". This topic is taken up again by Edoardo Bruno in No. 163 of the same publication ("Prospettive del cinema diretto in relazione al linguaggio filmico").

[43] "...les symboles doivent avoir l'air 'naturel'", writes Christian Metz, paraphrasing Jean Mitry, "ils doivent donner au spectateur l'impression d'être inscrits dans la diégèse même, et non d'y avoir été artificiellement surajoutés par une intention cinéaste sensible comme telle" (1967c), 219.

proposes a theory that differentiates between the attitude of the average
spectator towards the theatrical actor, and towards the film actor. At the
theatre he is, in fact,

> forced to take up a position with respect to real actors rather than to identify
> himself with the characters that they represent. Their physical presence opposes
> the temptation, always present during a performance, to see them as protago-
> nists within a fictional universe, since the theatre cannot be anything other than
> a game that is freely accepted and played out between accomplices.[44]

At the cinema, the illusion of reality that the screen creates by suggestion
induces in the spectator a tendency towards facile self-projection into the
world of the images, and a process of identification with the characters
and events of the film. A spectator at the theatre finds himself confronted
by real men, and does not believe, unless indirectly and by virtue of a
certain 'cultural' awareness, in their dramatic games, thereby opposing
himself dialectically to what is happening on stage. A spectator at the
cinema finds himself confronted by images of men and things (that are
'true' in their reproductive falsity), and believing what he sees, gradually
integrates himself with what is happening in the film. This apparent paradox is, in fact, determined by the unique and unrepeatable expressive
character of each cinematographic sign. The director's creative intentions are brought to life in the images, and having been made clear in this
concrete fashion, infiltrate directly into the receptive universe of the
spectator. The Phantasms on the screen realize the author's creative
dream, and present it to the public with all the limitations and the richness
of their existence as real entities within a world that is conceived and
structured in relation to certain expressive interests, certain ideological
beliefs, and certain poetic choices. The cinema therefore communicates
by means of sign-objects, connected in such a way as to form a universe-
object that is bounded by the limits of the work – as Peter Szondi has
written, the cinema is an "epic and autonomous form of art. This epic
character ...is based upon the juxtaposition of film, camera and object, on
the SUBJECTIVE REPRESENTATION OF OBJECTIVITY AS OBJECTIVITY";[45] the
epic character that is 'immanent' in the language of moving images is the
basic cause of its congenital incapacity for formulating interior states of
mind, or indeed subtle conceptual invective, or for creating an atmosphere
of refined rationality. A film lives by the elements that its author has

[44] "À propos de l'impression de réalité au cinéma" appeared in *Cahiers du cinéma*
166-167 (May-June 1965), 75-82.
[45] Szondi (1956); as regards the cinematographic language's immanently epic nature,
see also Mitry (1965), 281-368.

managed to compose by photographing spontaneous or conveniently arranged realities; even the integration of the various sound-events is linked to the visual stimuli and, in cases where it takes on the role of a misjudged and over-emphatic definitive complement to the object, the average perceptor should not notice its unpleasant and excessive dominance over the visual aspect of the work, but should instead encounter the audio-visual reality in its entirety, however peculiarly deformed and unadapted to the mode of existence suggested by the visual aspect of the film it may be.

Reviewing all the previous observations, one could say that the director's expressive intentions are hypostatized in the images on the screen, which communicate them by involving in their development the attention and participation of the spectator; while the expressive intentions (or in a wider sense, the communicative intentions) of the author of a verbal message are translated into words which convey them to the receiver.

It therefore seems fairly evident that the concept of 'sociality' deduced from the definitions of Morris and others, and considered as a basic property of the signs of a language, would seem to be completely useless, or at any rate of episodic and laborious application in the case of cinematographic signs. It is true that after fifty years of film-making examples of images with a single meaning for different perceivers do exist, images that are used above all to solve fairly common problems of narration that even occur in differing types of film – the rotating hand of a clock signifying the passage of a certain length of time, the gradual or sudden increase in the number of cigarette ends in an ash tray which conveys the same temporal variation (with a tenser atmosphere in this case), the cross-fade to signify the passage of time or change of place (either one or the other, or both – but the variation of space alone is rarer), and so on. Yet even in these cases the signs do not equal each other in their various realizations, but are instead re-created every time in the style of the individual work – the only thing that remains constant is the verbal translation of their signification, which in almost all cases may be considered incomplete or indeed inadequate.

A CERTAIN DEGREE OF SOCIALITY

But a consideration of these strange linguistic constants of the cinema can guide one's attention towards an aspect of the film that is usually overlooked, and that may, perhaps, offer fruitful material for study. A cinematographic work is formally defined, and cannot be altered while it is being viewed, but unlike the theatre or a painting it can be repeated in different and potentially simultaneous viewings, and is not limited to a single specimen. Instead, it may be reproduced in a theoretically unlimited number of copies, all equal to one another. Like lithography and photography (from which it borrows this characteristic), cinematic production always ends up by forming repeatable objects, by virtue of a basic negative that can generate all the copies that one may wish to print off.

The film's adaptability to reproduction constitutes an extremely stimulating subject of research for the sociologist and the psychologist,[46] but it can also aid the investigations of those who work in the field of language and style. The traditional art-object takes up its own unique and unrepeatable position in human history – every indirect enjoyment of it, every contact with a reproduction of it, for example, is no more than an intellectualistic expedient in order to avail oneself of certain elements of its overall meaning. When a work of art is brought into being according to the classical canons of art, it can only be directly enjoyed by integrating oneself as far as is possible with the cultural tradition of the analyzed object. In the case of a picture, for example, the depth of contact with the work must achieve that level of interpretation which Erwin Panofsky defines as "iconological", and which can only be realized by studying "the way in which, in different historical conditions, the FUNDAMENTAL TENDENCIES OF THE HUMAN SPIRIT are expressed through specific THEMES AND CONCEPTS".[47] True appreciation of the work lies in a multi-level approach to it and to its author, a theoretically interminable study of all the cultural implications inherent in the brush-strokes that compose it. Thus the traditional art-object may only be approached by the alert and expert connoisseur who will, however, always perceive the gap between his cultural universe and that of the work; on the other hand a reproduceable art-object (such as a film) comes directly and spontaneously into contact with a much larger number of people, without in any way losing its expressive uniqueness, yet at the same time acquiring a complete capacity for general display and dispensing with the cultural aspect of the atmosphere in which the unique and essentially unrepeatable work exists.[48]

---

[46] See Walter Benjamin's essay, "Das Kunstwerk im Zeitalter seiner technischen Reproduzierbarkeit" (from *Schriften*) (Frankfurt, Suhrkamp, 1965). English translation: *The Work of Art in the Age of Mechanical Reproduction* (from *Illuminations*), trans. H. Zohn (London, Cape, 1970). This essay dates from 1936.

[47] Erwin Panofsky, *Meaning in the Visual Arts* (New York, Doubleday, 1955), 40. The essay from which this quote is taken dates from 1939.

[48] It is from these presuppositions that Benjamin develops his theories in the essay referred to in note 46.

In theory, everyone can go to the same film secure in the knowledge that they are capable of judging such a work of art, and of understanding it at the semantic level to which they spontaneously limit their analysis; the cinema provides a form of communication in which, more than in any other in use today, the gap between transmitter and hypothetical receiver is to some extent reduced, because the transmitter becomes hidden by the objects themselves, photographing them and restoring their movement to them,[49] and can thus communicate through them. The most successful films in the history of the cinema have been seen and appreciated by innumerable spectators all over the world: even today the most important of them are viewed and studied by enthusiasts, researchers, and the considerable number of people who interest themselves in such matters (even if these almost always enjoy a fairly high level of general culture). The various copies of the film thus allow a direct viewing of the work, without limits in space or time, because, even if watching a film that was made years before demands a cultural awareness that will suffice to permit a thorough appreciation of it (for basically, even though it is reproduced in a number of copies, the work preserves a certain original 'aura' to which it may bear direct witness), the photographic nature of the medium, the movement, and everything else that contributes to the illusion of reality encourage the spectator to involve himself spontaneously with the events on the screen. The images of certain films are therefore imprinted in the mnemonic reserves of millions of people who usually carry, along with their memory of the film, a significative process conditioned by the impressions received while viewing it – which is to say that, for each spectator, these images may possess a meaning that is conditioned by his personality and by the particular conditions in which he came into contact with the film, but it does not seem far-fetched to allow the existence of a certain degree of coincidence between signifieds amongst the innumerable stimuli to which the perception of the images could give rise (even if they are disconnected from the original work) when a film is recalled by several people. When translating into elements of the verbal language the images that they had in mind, they would use words that have more or less coincidental signifieds.

One may thus risk the hypothesis of the potential SOCIALIZATION of a few particularly pregnant cinematographic images whose realization has been notably successful, images that could conserve the unchanging (and thus universal) aspect of their meaning even when transposed into other contexts (see the section on plurisituationality below). One is not, of

[49] "Movement brings relief and relief brings life", from Metz (1965) (see note 44).

course, concerned with shifting the same images from one film to another (although this could possibly occur when realizing in the new film a scene concerned with the showing of the old one, or when using images from an old film as material for an impasto or a montage, together with excerpts from documentary and other sources – in the second instance the 'cited' film must be of sufficient historical importance to spontaneously justify its insertion as documentation of an epoch, ideology, or person[50]), but with the possibility of repeating in the new film figurative compositions, actions, internal and external movements, or features of the sound-track that the public may easily relate to others with which it is already acquainted. In fact, one is concerned with a basically stylistic operation that can only achieve a more or less linguistic value by means of choosing elements that have had an almost universal appeal throughout the history of the film, and therefore by turning to films that are popular, or else have generated general interest, and a widespread acquaintance with their images. After all, one may presume that behind every shot, and the director's every decision during shooting and cutting, there lies some historical comparison or critical relationship; but here we are concerned with something far more explicit and intentional, a choice that establishes in certain pre-existing values a fixed significative function on which general agreement has been reached, taking note of the results of some possible historicization (of judgement or value) so as to use them to create an exceptional linguistic convention.

But would the degree of sociality thus arrived at by the signs of the cinema suffice to constitute a system potentially corresponding in some way to the definition with which we began? And even if this desirable coincidence were realized, would we be faced with some real form of 'cinematographic language', or would it not rather be a one-sided form of metalanguage whose use would lead the cinema into facile and regressive procedures and expressive aridity, through an excessive preoccupation with semantic clarity (which would not, in the present situation, be scientifically verifiable), thus deviating from some of its most basic interests?

It is possible to reply to these two questions in a variety of ways, according to the outlook that may condition the investigation, or the ends im-

---

[50] For an example of the first case, see Godard's *Les carabiniers* (1963), where the director reconstructs several scenes from the first films of the brothers Lumière, picturing them as if projected in a hall. For the second case, see Tinto Brass's *Chi lavora è perduto*, where several images from Roberto Rossellini's *Paisà* are used as material for montage (Rossellini's images are rendered objectual in their new position) in a re-evocation of the partisan war.

posed upon it. But one can, however, establish that the sociality that these cinematic signs possess is weak, ambiguous, and undoubtedly inferior to that possessed by the words of any language – weak, because it only extends quantitatively to the members of that group of human beings who have at least seen the original film and profited from it; ambiguous, because variations in taste and semantic attribution may always arise among the members of such a community. And then, as far as the second question is concerned, it is by no means easy for a film conceived along the lines of our hypothesis to avoid, at the present moment and for some time to come, a tendency towards intellectualization in its formation and the provocation of an analogous and indispensable cultural sufficiency on the part of the spectator. Such a work could easily come to use a language comprehensible to a few initiates alone, and thus be formed through the evolution of a metalanguage (one might almost coin the term 'super-language') which would only be really useful within the limits of a laboratory experiment or an extremely restricted program of research.[51]

For the signs of such a cinema to diffuse themselves autonomously and freely, the vast majority of the public would have to arrive at so deep an understanding of the film, so widespread and spontaneous a historical awareness of it, as to be able to semantically qualify a particular image without any intellectual effort. Much as one may hope for the advent of a cinematographic society so naturally disposed to thinking in images, and above all so sure in its iconic tradition that it can refer to its own audio-visual memory almost as if it were a lexical synthesis for immediate consultation, a linguistic corpus that is globally transmitted to every component of the community, such a desire, even though to some degree justified by the cultural evolution of the past few years, comes within the category of realities that may be foreseen, but cannot be determined; we are concerned with a phenomenon that has not, up to now, come into evidence, and is not likely to do so in the immediate future, but that, nonetheless, is not impossible.

PLURISITUATIONALITY

Considerations analogous to those put forward with respect to sociality may also be brought to bear upon a hypothetical plurisituationality of cinematographic signs. If it proves difficult to assign to an image that re-

---

[51]   On the problems of metalanguage and 'meta-*langue*', see Greimas (1966a), 13-17. And Henri Lefebvre, *Le languge et la société* (Paris, Gallimard, 1966), 12-15.

produces a certain reality photographically a meaning that is valid for several people, it seems reasonable to consider the conservation of a significative relationship while shifting the same image from one situation to another almost impossible.

One may, after all, bear in mind that a certain socialization is immanent in the signs of the cinema, being implied by their photographic nature, and their external adhesion to the object; even if one is aware of the semantic limits of this primitive relationship, one cannot in fact forget that a child or an uneducated adult can understand a film with reasonable ease, if only at a level of total passivity and continuous personal projection. Without knowing of any of the conventions in which they had their origin, a man can make contact with the images on the screen and can even understand them in certain cases, because their relation of specular similarity with the object aids contact on a primitive and superficial level. One might thus be tempted to try and make out an analogous, implicit immanence for plurisituationality, since, basically, the image represents an object, and always the same object, in different contexts; but in this case a primitive form of signification is not enough, because the possibility of placing the same sign in differing cinematographic structures implies some consideration of the relationship between the various signs of the message, and thus raises the semantic level of the communication (from the point of view that is in this case relevant) to more complex and mediated values. In fact, the exact semantic orientation of an image (or, more specifically, of a shot) can only be established after the process of cutting has created various syntactic and structural relations between the images of the film – an elementary image may be significatively integrated in various ways, and in itself usually turns out to be confused in meaning. This semantic transience is not to be ascribed to the single shot and, obviously, the single frame alone, but also to more complex images, generated by the composition of several shots (which may nevertheless be absorbed into the concept of a linguistic unit – see below), since one can only attribute a real meaning to them after having considered the way in which they combine, linguistically and structurally, with all the other parts of the work.[52] As concerns these composed images, it is possible to make out a relationship of reasonably straightforward meaning and unitary value with a certain expressive intention or generic referent, if

[52] Jean Mitry is even more rigorous in this respect. "Non seulement l'image n'est pas comme le mot un signe 'en soi', mais elle n'est pas le signe d'aucune chose. Elle MONTRE, c'est tout. Elle n'est chargée d'un certain sens, d'un 'pouvoir de signifier' que par relation avec un ensemble de faits dans lesquelles elle se trouve impliqué" ("D'un langage sans signes", *Revue d'Esthétique* 2-3 [1967], 141).

they are compared to the semantic aspect of the whole work (usually, these images coincide with a complete action within the body of the scene: the action that an actor performs, or that the shot or the cutting makes him perform, the action of a static or dynamic object, even if the dynamism is conferred upon it by cinematographic techniques, etc.), but it is not possible to conceive of a constancy of signification without macroscopic exceptions above and beyond the contingent situation in which the images were produced and put together. The cutting composes the signs of a film according to semantic coordinates that are theoretically unrepeatable, precisely because of the objectual nature of the cinematic narration (apart, naturally, from audio-visual transpositions and syntheses that may be easily differentiated by the interpreter because they are constructed according to elementary logical principles). The image–assign is rendered concrete within the universe that absorbs the attention of the spectator, acquiring its definitive form from the contributions of the entire film; plurisituationality, as defined by Morris, would imply that the sign had renounced its roots within the work and that it had lost a substantial part of its contingent hypostatisation, succumbing to a process of abstraction with which the image could not keep up.

Even if one were to leave the expressive signification of the cinematographic sign out of consideration, and to give up any concern for symbolism when evaluating it, limiting one's interests to the direct signified of the image alone (which would already be enough for the formation of a theory of cinema as language), one could hardly help noting how assigning it to different contexts always involves it in a more or less profound semantic alteration. In the opening sequence of J. L. Godard's *Les carabiniers* a jeep is seen crossing an uncultivated and desolate piece of ground in search of two youths who have been called up for military service; after a while the jeep stops and two carabiniers get out. Towards the end of the film, the same jeep is seen crossing the same ground once more (it is the same image as the one at the beginning, or a very similar one), and one immediately understands that the two carabiniers are returning to the shack that was the goal of their original search. In both cases the verbal translation of the primary signified of the scene-image is simple – a jeep crossing a certain piece of ground; but the position assigned to the second by the cutting and the narrative situation within which it is placed naturally allow it a more complete signified – a jeep with two carabiniers crossing a certain piece of ground.[53] The image's primary and material signified is established by its photographic nature (the jeep and the ground)

[53]   With reference to film cutting, Mitry talks of a "logic of implication" (1965) Vol. I.

– but can one speak of signification in this case, or is it not rather a matter of a simple, specular representation, whose primary signification can only be brought to light in the context?[54]

Were one able to limit oneself to the value of the image as representation, then perhaps one might be able to introduce the plurisituational argument for cinematic signs – no matter what context it was inserted into, the image considered above would always represent a jeep moving across an incongruous and squalid landscape. But within these limits one would never succeed in formulating an autonomous linguistic hypothesis for the cinema, because its link with the photographed object would imply a semantic fragmentariness that could well reduce cinematic communication to an extremely primitive level. One could however propose that the choice of reality destined to be translated into images, the choice of angle, the choice of lens, and in fact all the technico-stylistic operations that precede the realization of a shot lead to a semantic tendency within the image, so that, even when considered by itself, it would always enjoy the privilege of a signification that is, however, neither particularly elastic nor easily manipulated. One could take the well-known paradigms of the high-angle shot and the low-angle shot in this way (roughly equivalent in the first case to mortification, and in the second to exaltation of the photographed object), as one could all the other contrivances allowed by an appropriate use of the medium; but someone would merely have to employ the first device with the intention of demonstrating some positive characteristic of the person or object filmed, that could not be seen from another angle, or use the second to bring to light some negative aspect, in order to invalidate the generalization (not to speak of all the implications of a SUBJECTIVE nature, either direct or indirect, that this type of shot implies).

A plurisituationality that is limited to the value of the image as representation will not therefore suffice or prove adapted to the process of institutionalizing cinematographic signs in a linguistic system; for the

---

[54] With reference to this, see Husserl's theory on meaning and object. "Between the MEANING and the WHAT IS MEANT, or what it expresses", writes J. Geyser, a disciple of Edmund Husserl, in *Neue und alte Wege der Philisophie*, "there exists an essential relation, because the MEANING is an expression of the MEANT through its own content (Gehalt). What is meant (dieses Bedeutete) lies in the 'object' of the thought or speech. We must therefore distinguish these three – Word, Meaning, Object." The translation is taken from Ogden and Richards' *The Meaning of Meaning*, and the two authors add the following comment: "The OBJECT is that about which the expression says something, the MEANING is what it says about it" (303). In the case of the cinema, the representative relation between image and object would thus be the primitive embryo of a real semantic relation.

impossibility of deducing from it a free and polyvalent generalization, the re-elaboration that takes place within the cutting process, and the semantic subordination to the whole span of the cinematic discourse that results from this will all oppose it. One could then consider some potential form of cinematographic language whose principle images were mediated by the history of the cinema itself, and thus conditioned in the formation of its signs by the possibility of reproducing one work in another. The considerations put forward above with regard to the sociality of linguistic signs would also apply here, when one bears in mind that the relations with the 'cited' film will be all the more unstable in that the various works that cite it have different linguistic aims.

THE INADEQUACY OF TRADITIONAL LINGUISTICS

The plurisituationality of cinematographic signs may thus be (cautiously) reduced to their capacity for immediate representation; their sociality, as we have observed, can be immanent in the specularity of their reproductive function. In the first case there is no possibility of inserting the sign into every type of situation (unless one has recourse to well-established cultural references), nor is there that of a semantic stability which is valid for the community as a whole in the second. The definitions of the linguist and the semanticist are thus revealed to be rather ill-adapted in the case of the cinema, and despite the fact that they offer enticing glimpses of a potential area of research (at least from the methodological point of view), it turns out that the results are not easily transposed from a verbal linguistic system to one composed of moving images, even resorting to Morris's metalanguage.

The fact is that all the linguistic studies that have been undertaken up to now have been dedicated to the scientific definition of a sector of human communication that has in itself already arrived at abstraction, generalization, and classification – Saussure, Ogden and Richards, Hjelmslev, Morris, Ullmann, and the various other specialists in this field have been working upon a system that is in itself already scientific, because it has been brought spontaneously into existence as a result of the needs of formal logic, whose accelerated philosophical progress and, during the last century, gradual regression it has in turn favoured. The relationship between logic and verbal language is very close, because the operations of the former (the science of sciences for classical culture) are conducted by virtue of elements of the latter and, vice versa, words are organized and

structured, above all in scientific or simply designative discourse, in relation to the fundamental principles of logic. Words are linked to an object
to which, in signifying, they make reference, but their relationship with
the thing is indirect, and passes through an intermediate reference to the
idea about the thing itself that the speaker (or listener) conceals behind
the word used. And it is precisely this reference, this intermediate
'thought', that allows a process of general abstraction, so that no word
can ever be confused with the object to which it refers, but can only be
placed in relation to concepts derived from an analysis of things. The
linguist may completely disregard the relation between thought and
thing, limiting his research to the relation between word and thought, so
that he comes to find himself in the happy position of having to analyze a
universe composed of objects (words and ideas) that spontaneously tend
towards classification and scientific arrangement according to fairly conventional methodological canons.

Traditional logic has in fact discovered a double world of signification,
implicit in every relation between verbal sign and object, such that every
word denotes a thing, and connotes the properties due to which the symbol may be applied to the thing (as regards Husserl's outlook on this
subject, see footnote 54) – more specifically, Ogden and Richards write
that:

the term Connotation has been adopted by those logicians who follow Mill in
the practice of discussing as though they were primary and paramount two
senses in which a SYMBOL may be said to mean: (1) It means the set of things to
which it can be correctly applied; and the members of this set are said to be
denoted or indicated by the word, or to be its denotation. (2) It means the
properties used in determining the application of a symbol, the properties in
virtue of which anything is a member of the set which is the denotation; these
properties are said to be the connotation of a symbol, or sometimes simply its
meaning.[55]

For the logician, the signified coincides with the connotation, and the relations of signification are therefore grasped by virtue of a process of
abstraction. The properties mentioned in the definition set out above are
selected by virtue of a process of adjectiving which (even if Ogden and
Richards invalidate the final phase of its substantivization) is always the
fruit of mental invention and classification. In any case, even if it does not
share the theories of the logicians regarding ways of signifying, and refers, for example, to a signified-as-essence such as was proposed by the

[55] Ogden and Richards (1923), 187-188. On the concepts of denotation and connotation, the reader is referred back to the first pages of this book, which in turn refer to the
definitions of Hjelmslev and Barthes.

critical realism of Santayana,[56] linguistic study is always aided, in the case of verbal language, by an ontological predisposition on the part of the material under examination towards generalization. One might say that the instrument of analysis and its material are commensurable, because they can be reduced to the same rational dimensionality. None of this occurs in the case of the cinema, for the various reasons listed above and for others that may be easily guessed – the entity that is in this case the object of research manifests itself according to paradigms that do not always coincide with the principles of classical learning and that may not be easily brought within the limits of a universal generalization.

THE LINGUISTIC UNIT

Up to this point our research has been oriented towards the possibility of extrapolating elements from one linguistic universe to another. The results have proved awkward and, above all, unsound and easily invalidated. However, the definitions that initiated it may be traced back by implication to a linguistic unit, an elementary sign whose possible modes of association with other similar signs they investigate. This component sign may, in the case of a verbal language, be superficially equated with the word; but linguistic research has brought to light even more elementary subdivisions of the analyzed elements, in relation to the phonetic, syntactic, or semantic interests of their authors. This further subdivision can be pursued *ad infinitum*, as in the field of the physical sciences, but if it were to penetrate into new stages of dismemberment, the resultant elements would be the fruit of an abstraction that was ever further removed from the living context of a spoken language. With the word, the cinema conventionally matches the image; with the phoneme, the morpheme, or the moneme (see below) the cinema still matches the image, perhaps divided up into some of its basic components, such as the shot, the sound-track, the angulation, etc., but in the case of the verbal language this subdivision into elementary parts favours the formation of free and polyvalent entities, whereas in the case of the cinema the search for linguistic units that contribute to the composition of the image reveals only their close link to the specific instance, and their contingent and very limited applicability.

---

[56] George Santayana, *The Sense of Beauty, being the outlines of aesthetic theory* (London – Norwood, Mass., Black, 1896); *The Realm of Essence* (London, Constable, 1928); *The Realm of Matter* (London, Constable, 1930).

Perhaps in this type of comparative study one sets one's sights too fixedly upon the concept of an elementary image whose realization is sought (perhaps mistakenly) in an audio-visual sign with a signification that can be translated into a minimal number of words – one, in the most felicitous cases. So that, from this point of view, cinema and verbal discourse are entirely incommensurable. Not even the unmoving image of a single object could be translated by the word corresponding to the photographed object, because in its definition one would have to take into account the lighting, the figurative relations between the object and the outline of the image, the angulation, the deformation that results from the use of a certain lens, and all the other technical elements that are open to the director. The cinematographic image always involves some significant intention on the part of its author, an intention that is at one with the image itself, and which one cannot leave out of consideration (even if in the process of cutting it is possible to effect substantial alterations in the signified). The definition of a word, on the other hand, always leaves out of consideration its contingent use, and seeks to isolate the relations of its signified within the limits of a generic and rigid functionality. The word really is a polyvalent *tessera* of the linguistic mosaic, and it is the result of a lengthy analytical operation upon a pre-existing language – in fact no verbal language comes into existence already broken down into words, but is instead structured in significant phonetic emissions that have a direct relation with reality (or with the impression that it leaves in the mind), its principal aim having almost always been persuasive or appreciative, rather than merely descriptive.[57]

The advancement of man's rational attitudes, the necessity of an ever more developed socialization of communication and the desire to recover a commensurability between the external world and the subjective universe, between phenomenon and mind, favoured a subdivision of the spontaneous and collective linguistic flux into elements that were as stable as possible. And words were born – but "the ancient Greeks wrote without interruption, and it was only the Romans who began to indicate with a dot the division between words".[58] Once the word had been understood as an element that is operatively convenient, and that is only occasionally capable of sustaining a complete communicative or expressive intentionality by itself, the linguist's analytical approach shifted to a deeper level (singling out the units comprising the words themselves), thus arriving at the PHONEME, considered as a distinctive unit of a language – the

[57] See Bettetini (1964), 231-280.
[58] Schick (1960), 30.

number of such 'phonemic segments' being discrete and determined;[59] like-wise the MORPHEME, the smallest unit within speech that is capable of con-serving a meaning[60] – Martinet prefers to call it a MONEME, and considers it as "the smallest segment of speech that has some meaning attached to it";[61] and finally the SENTENCE, which is derived from the combination of several words (in certain cases, as was noted above, it may be elliptically reduced to a single word) and which fulfills a complete and unitary ex-pressive intentionality. Consideration of these analytical elements has given birth to the various branches of linguistic science: phonology de-rives from the phoneme, lexicology from the word (the morpheme being in itself too "heterogeneous to form the subject-matter of a special branch of linguistics"),[62] and syntax from the sentence. On the border between lexicology and syntax lies grammar, which studies the more general as-pects of language.[63]

The phoneme, the morpheme, and the word (to which the morpheme may frequently be reduced) are thus the result of research oriented in a strictly analytical direction. They are units of the *langue*, that is, of a system of signs which will correspond perfectly to the characteristics that were singled out by our original definitions, and these, as we have already decided, are not particularly adapted to the ends of cinematographic communication and expression. But these linguistic units do not limit themselves to an embryonic existence on the margins of a language. Each enters into relation with the others, and this habitual interweaving of their forms, which constitutes the true linguistic reality, must also be studied and analyzed as a whole, in the contingency of a communication or an expression, and in relation to the general aims imposed upon it by the intentions of the speaker.

The SENTENCE is indeed the result of this approach, which concerns it-self with the relationships occurring between the various units.[64]

THE SENTENCE

But what exactly is a sentence? The question should not appear particu-

[59]   André Martinet, *A Functional View of Language* (Oxford, Clarendon Press, 1962), 6.
[60]   Ullmann (1962), 26.
[61]   Martinet (1962), 22.
[62]   Ullmann (1962), 33.
[63]   I refer to Stephen Ullmann's subdivisions, which seem to me exceptionally useful for didactic purposes.
[64]   Ullmann (1962), 23.

larly far-fetched, since an adequate definition could again allow us to open up the dialogue between linguistics and the semiology of the film, and could also aid the formation of a new method of approach. For a philologist such as A. H. Gardiner, a sentence is "a sonic and articulated symbol, in that it incorporates a volitional attitude on the part of the speaker with regard to the listener";[65] for a linguist such as Martinet, it is "an utterance all the elements of which are linked to a single predicate or to several coordinated predicates"[66] – a definition which allows one to eliminate the concept of intonation, considered by the author to be linguistically weak, and therefore more pertinent to a more extended structure. For Schick, the sentence is "the minimal unit of our expression that presents a unitary sense, intentionally formulated, and generally contained within a single breath".[67]

All the authors quoted here stress two fundamental characteristics of defined object: the intentionality of its author and, derived from this, the specific contingence of the signification. The sentence, writes Schick, is "endowed with a complete signified and refers to a determinate situation",[68] and is thus a unit of the language, but not of the *langue*, because it is excessively subordinate to the personality of the speaker and to the conditions within which the communication is generated.[69] Using the concept of 'sentence' as a focus for one's research implies, as was indicated above, that one's work is to be conducted along syntactic, and to some degree grammatical, lines.

One is thus no longer concerned with abstract semantics, which tends to be oriented towards a process of universalization (the semantic implications of phenomena, the study of the signifieds of words and of their parts), but with compound (but unitary) signs that are not easily abstracted from the human, social, and phenomenal context in which they have been used (as opposed to: are usually used). No longer a unit of the *langue*, therefore, but a unit of intentional communication or of expressiveness – but always, however, a unit of language.

---

[65] A. H. Gardiner, *The British Journal of Psychology* XII, Part IV (April 1922). See also Ogden and Richards (1923), 259 et seg.
[66] Martinet (1960), 122.
[67] Schick (1960), 41.
[68] Schick (1960), 32.
[69] As regards the CIRCUMSTANCES in which the communication takes place, Eco individuates their function as that of anchoring the abstract vitality of the systems of codes and messages to the "context of everyday life". Circumstances alter the choice of code, the message's sense, its function, and its informative quota (Eco[1967a], 54-55).

THE SENTENCE AND THE FILM

In the light of these observations, we may now resume our discussion on the cinema. The photographic and objectual nature of the cinema always results in the image being subordinated to the contingency of a situation which is concretely materialized on the screen. Shooting and cutting techniques allow the reality which has taken place in front of the lens to be translated into images according to a mode of distortion intended by the director, who recreates it in similar forms (for the sign is always iconic) which are nevertheless new and directed towards certain ends. We are thus concerned with situational contingence and creative intentionality in the cinema, just as we are in verbal language, considering the latter as it normally appears, and without reference to research concerned with language as *langue*. The cinematographic image may thus be brought within the limits defined for the verbal sentence, even if its unitary aspect has not yet been individuated. The term 'image', on the other hand, is too generic, and habitually sustains a large number of significant functions that tend to cover up its wide range of application – from static to dynamic reproduction, from sonic to visual reproduction, or from metaphorical translations to the most direct of scientific applications.

The image represents something in a manner that is true to life, but signifies more than the thing represented;[70] indeed, one could say that a consideration of its signified could leave out of account its relation with the thing and limit itself to the analysis of the image as an entity (in this case no longer representative, but instead significant) that is in itself capable of entering into dialogue with the perceiver. "What we are presented with when watching a film is a reality", says Cesare L. Musatti;[71] and this reality, organized so as to communicate or express something, must of necessity lend itself to an analysis capable of singling out

[70]   Panofsky (1955). See also Nazareno Taddei, *Trattato di teoria cinematografica – I – L'immagine* (Milano, 1963).
[71]   Cesare L. Musatti, "La visione oltre lo schermo", from *I problemi dell'informazione e della cultura di massa*, a series of lectures organized by the Istituto "A. Gemelli" for the academic year 1964-1965, 117. Prof. Musatti's lecture takes up, and treats to some courteous criticism, several statements from a previous lecture of mine which was published in the same issue (G. Bettetini, "Immagine cinematografica e immagine televisiva") – unfortunately without my having had a chance to correct the proofs. In any case, my argument is limited to an analysis of the technical procedures that form the images for cinema and television, leading towards a general orientation of a linguistic nature and a potential semiotic differentiation between the two media – the problems of interpretation are only hinted at in their most basic form.

its minimal unit, on which the author of the cinematographic discourse bases his construction. So we shall define as the linguistic unit of the film the smallest significant element of its expositive process, which is to say that complex of audio-visual signs which make up an imaginary entity with an autonomous and intentional signified (lending itself in almost all cases to the ends of some proposed action), and which may be divided into further analytical elements which, were they detached from their context, would come to lose the significant quality belonging to the specific corpus in which they are included. Thus not the frame, nor, when all is said and done, the shot (although in some types of cutting the shot can coincide with the unit thus defined) – the linguistic fragment as it is here conceived can extend to a number of shots, can coincide with an entire scene, or indeed can be understood as one part of a shot. The minimal significant element of a verbal language is the moneme (or morpheme) while that of the cinematographic language borrows its characteristics from the definition of a SENTENCE rather than from that of a WORD (or of some part of it).

The language of moving images does not, in fact, succeed in signifying in an autonomous way on the level of an elementary sign that may be compared with the moneme or the word, because its component signs cannot be generalized by extracting them from the reproduced reality. The elementary sign of the cinema is therefore the image (indeed, the immobile frame might spring to mind) with its specular mode of reproduction, but the linguistic unit of the cinema is another thing altogether. The elementary image, unlike the word, cannot be self-sufficient in an abstract and generalized dimension, because it is without a 'mental' content that is universally valid in differing situations.

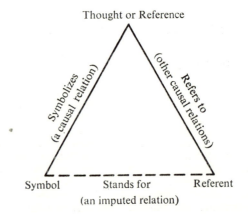

Thought or Reference

Symbolizes
(a causal relation)

Refers to
(other causal relations)

Symbol   Stands for   Referent
(an imputed relation)

When Ogden and Richards posed themselves the problem of the significant symbol, they resolved it brilliantly with the well-known triangular diagram, which is reproduced here with a brief summary of its authors' intentions and the results of their research. The thought or reference is the idea that the speaker has of the thing about which he must speak or that the receiver feels to be aroused in him by the symbol (= word) with which he comes into contact; the referent, on the other hand, is the thing signified. Symbol, thought, and referent stand at the vertices of the triangle, while at the sides are the relations between them.

Between the symbol and the referent there is no relevant relation other than the individual one, which consists in its being used by someone to stand for a referent. Symbol and Referent, that is to say, are not connected directly..., but only indirectly round the two sides of the triangle.[72]

But when the field of study is restricted to the cinema (or television), the side that will assume the most importance is in fact the third – the dotted line that joins the symbol to the referent, thus placing the symbol in direct contact with the object. Such, precisely, is the case with iconic signs – the symbol is

more or less directly like the referent for which it is used, as for instance, it may be when it is an onomatopoeic word, or an image, or a gesture, or a drawing. In this case the triangle is completed; its base is supplied, and a great simplification of the problem appears to result. For this reason, many attempts have been made to reduce the normal language situation to this possibly more primitive form.[73]

As we shall have occasion to make clearer later on, this does not mean that the iconic sign evades any type of codification – if it did, it could not even be qualified as a 'sign'. Which is to say that even the iconic sign refers to a mental content. Instead, the signified of the sign-image will apparently tend to coincide with the thing and is thus conditioned by the full contingency of the thing; the poetic idea (or at any rate the director's intention) is translated into the image and acquires a concrete and physical body in modifying reality and recreating it in the image. The image signifies the idea which, as has already been noted, was hypostatized in it, so that the tracing of the signified must overcome the limits of the elementary sign and achieve the dimensions proposed by the entire cinematographic narration. It is precisely the elementary sign of the cinema, which

[72]   Ogden and Richards (1923), 11-12 et seg.
[73]   Ogden and Richards (1923), 12, note 1.

does not permit its language to base itself upon an almost static foundation, that may be traditionally defined as a LANGUE.[74]

DOUBLE ARTICULATION

Martinet, referring to verbal language, individuates the possibility of two articulations – one on the level of words, and the other on that of separate sounds. More specifically, the primary articulation "is that whereby every fact of experience to be communicated, every need that one wants to make known to another, is analyzed into a succession of units each of which is endowed with a vocal form and a meaning".[75] The vocal form may in turn be analyzed into a "succession of units" – and this is the secondary articulation. In the case of the cinema and its signs, after all that has already been said, reference to the two articulations is impossible, unless one means by the primary articulation of the cinematographic language the analysis of the transmitted content into a series of units that have form and sense, and are therefore extended beyond the simple image to coincide with that minimal significant element which was described above; in the same way, the secondary articulation would have to coincide with the subdivision of these significant forms into a succession of component 'technical' units, such as the shot, the angulation, internal and external movement, etc. The two articulations of the verbal language, which respectively correspond to the subdivision between monemes (or morphemes) and phonemes, only acquire a sense in the cinematographic field if their definitions are subjected to a translation of referents onto an analogical level – that unit of language which can be defined as a 'cinematographic phrase' will come to be equated with the moneme, while with the phoneme one will equate a series of technical units that are (still analogically) nearer to the moneme or indeed to the word. It is only from this point of view that one can possibly talk about a double articulation of the cinematographic language,[76] and yet at the same time take into account the observations made by Barthes and Metz, who consider it

[74]   The same idea is put forward by Christian Metz in "Le cinéma langue ou langage?", *Communications* 4 (1964).

[75]   Martinet, *Elements of General Linguistics* (1960), 22-23.

[76]   It would seem that only in this sense can Gillo Dorfles conceive of a secondary articulation for cinematographic language. See his talk entitled "Soggettività Socialità Semanticità nell'inchiesta filmata" (official text, 17), for the conference "Cinema Reporting and Mass Culture" which took place on the occasion of the VII Premio dei Colli for cinema reporting at Este (1966).

practically impossible, granted the extreme proximity of signified and signifier when it is an image that must perform the signifying.[77]

The analogical translation of referents that has been singled out for the two articulations repeats itself throughout the linguistic corpus of the cinema, whenever this latter is considered in relation to a verbal language or to one of the many languages that may be easily generalized as regards their elementary components. Thus the parallel between verbal language and cinematographic language does make sense, if the correspondences between the respective relatable elements are established at different levels, all of these elements being uniformly shifted in the same direction when proceeding from the analysis of the first to that of the second.

The phonemes and morphemes of verbal language constitute the basic elements of two different articulations, yet they may be placed along a single axis of analytical orientation: the PARADIGMATIC one. But in the ambit of the cinema, on the other hand, a consideration of the elementary parts of a discourse also implies the individuation of the SYNTAGMATIC axis, that of the combination between selected elements, "...en vue de les enchaîner en un discours cohérent".[78]

This table, although excessively simple and summary, will perhaps give a somewhat clearer view of the problem:

Langue and Verbal Language		Cinematographic Language	
PHONETIC UNITS	PHONEMES (do not have an independent signified of their own)[79]		TECHNICAL UNITS
UNITS OF MEANING	MONEMES OR MORPHEMES (WORDS) (have an independent signified of their own)	TECHNICAL ELEMENTS THAT MAKE UP THE IMAGE (shot, angle, lighting, etc.) (do not have an independent signified of their own)	COMPOUND TECHNICAL UNITS
RELATIONAL UNITS	PHRASES (have a unitary sense and express an intention)	CINEMES (or ICONEMES) (have a unitary and almost independent signified of their own and express an intention)	UNITS OF MEANING AND OF RELATION

The first box in the column assigned to cinematographic language,

77   Metz (1965), 73.
78   Metz, "Un problème de sémiologie du cinéma", *Image et son* 201 (January 1967), 69. See also Greimas (1966a), 39-41.
79   Ullmann (1962), 24.

which has been left empty in the table, could in fact contain, by analogy, the smallest elementary units that in turn make up the technical parts of the image – a pan from left to right, for example, contributes to the formation of a shot and a movement (second box), but can in itself also be seen as the irreduceable element in a potential analytical subdivision. If phonemes are considered as the "minimum physical units of speech",[80] they can be made to correspond to the minimum physical units of cinematographic images, such as an elementary movement, the gesture of an actor (or better his image), a zone of lighting, and so forth.[81] However, this parallel does not seem to be of any great speculative interest. Situated in the second box, on the other hand, are those technically defined parts of the cinematographic image which are able to signify the director's intentions only if they are taken together with other components: for example, the lighting, the general movement of the image, or a whole shot that does not in itself suffice to express an autonomous and unitary signified. Finally, the third box holds the linguistic units of the cinema which, by virtue of the proximity between signifier and signified pointed out by Metz, must of necessity also take into account the relational aspects of a cinematic exposition – thus a unit of meaning and relation; a unit of communication or of expression. One may give it the name 'CINEME'; or else, bearing in mind the meaning that Pasolini has attributed to this term (a less specific one than that used here – for Pasolini, cinemes are the real objects that make up the shot), one can define it as an 'ICONEME'.

The iconeme is therefore a unitary fragment of the cinematographic discourse pursued by the author. Its unitary nature must be referred to its significative power which, in the case of the cinema, involves a relational evaluation of the differing parts that make up the unit. The word signifies by virtue of a process of abstraction from the object, but does not suffice to define an expressive intentionality; the iconeme (which could also be defined as a 'cinematographic sentence', granted that one bears in mind the analogical relation with the definition of 'sentence' proposed above) summarizes within itself, in a certain sense, the properties of word and sentence. The unit of the cinematographic language may never be abstracted from the context within which it exists, nor may it be reused in different contexts (unless it carries with it the sociological and cultural conditions that were set out hypothetically in the section on "A Certain Sociality"), if one wishes it to preserve a reliable constancy of meaning. The same holds for a sentence in verbal language (even though a certain

[80] Ullmann (1962), 23.
[81] These elements could be defined as the *figurae* of cinematographic language.

type of poetry tends to incorporate whole sentences from differing and unrelated contexts – advertising slogans, political declarations, newspaper headlines – conserving their original meaning, which does however undergo an appreciable translation of value).[82]

The relation between iconeme and sentence is so lively and spontaneous that the former may frequently be translated into the verbal means of the latter, perhaps undergoing a depreciation in poetic value, but losing very little of the 'idea' that the director meant to suggest by its use. Certainly, to propose that the unit of cinematographic language may be traced to the segment of a film that can be defined by a (single) sentence which translates its signified seems hazardous and lacking in scientific foundation – but it could be a first premise (on a hypothetical level, naturally) for a scientific definition of linguistic research in this sector. Seeing that the cinema will not let itself be bound by the traditionally assessed canons of language, it is necessary to discover scientific instruments that are adapted to the study of its own language. This relation of iconeme to sentence is undoubtedly useful for obtaining a general theoretical view of the problem and for direct application on the part of the author or the spectator. After all that has been asserted in order to arrive at a definition for it, one may attribute to it a considerable instrumental value as far as cinematographic 'writing' and 'reading' are concerned.

In his film *L'avventura* Michelangelo Antonioni concludes the action with a desolate scene of compassion, a desperate attempt at reconciliation: Claudia, the protagonist (Monica Vitti), has been bitterly disenchanted by her lover, Sandro (Gabrielle Ferzetti); disenchanted in a way that goes beyond the simple affective relationship to include overall problems of thought and feeling. She goes out onto the promenade at dawn in a state of almost complete psychological vacuity; here she is joined by Sandro, who realizes of his own accord the absurd emptiness of his behaviour (also, perhaps, that he is incapable of 'existing' in any other way), and slumps down on a bench.

The young man appears defeated, and he does not even have the courage to look at Claudia. His face is distorted and tired; he seems an old man. He slumps down exhausted on the bench. Both of them remain still, not looking at each other. The two figures separated one from the other, Claudia standing, Pietro sitting. In the background, the concrete framework. Beyond that, the sea. Claudia turns her head slowly toward Sandro. Her eyes are filled with tears. She looks at him as at something that causes her infinite pain. Then she takes a few

---

[82] See for example, *La ragazza Carla* by Elio Pagliarani, from *Il Menabo* 2 (Torino, Einaudi, 1960), 143. In the cinema, this type of expressive technique is used by Godard, while in the visual arts one merely has to think of Pop Art.

steps and comes nearer the bench. Sandro doesn't move. Claudia reaches out her hand. And slowly, with heart-breaking desperation, she caresses his hair.[83]

Antonioni has shot the scene at various distances and has used, among other things, close-ups of the two protagonists so as to single out her transformation from bewildered grief to desperate pity and his defeat and existential incapacity to be other than he is. One could not consider each close-up as a linguistic unit (even less as a unit of expression), because, taken as an element for analysis, it does not stand in relation to anything and its signified is, as a result, ambiguous – the close-up of Claudia shows a woman observing something in tears and, in the same way, the close-up of Sandro shows a man staring into the void, crying, but it is only with their connection, and their relation with other shots that one can arrive at the representation of a linguistically unitary action, signifying, for example, the simple phrase: "Claudia turns her head slowly toward Sandro."

Laying aside the definitive form that Antonioni's shots have assumed, it is easy to see how an action of this type could be cinematographically represented in other ways – at a limit, overlooking intermediate solutions, with one shot (a medium-long shot which included the two characters full-length, or a closer one, with both of them included) or with two shots (the two close-ups put together); in the first case the shot would coincide with the linguistic unit, which would, in the second case, be extended to two shots. But in each case, the action could be translated verbally by the phrase set out above (which is extracted from the scenario of the film) although the choice of a way of narrating the action cinematographically would be of no mean importance as far as the expressive ends of the work were concerned; it would involve considerations of a stylistic and cultural nature, not to speak of those of semantic syntax, so that the linguistic unit could indeed be confused with a unit of expression (which is what usually happens in the case of a verbal phrase).

In the film *Lasky Jedne Plavovlasky* (Loves of a Blonde) by Milos Forman,[84] the long penultimate scene takes place in the bedroom of the protagonist's parents, where the father, the mother, and the protagonist himself, the pianist Milda (Vladimir Pucholt), argue at length, shifting around continually in the bed, which is uncomfortably small for the three of them, since they have had to give Milda's cot to Andula (Hana Brejchova), a girl whom the young man slept with for a night and who has unexpectedly turned up at his house. Forman has envisaged, for this

---

[83] "*L'avventura*" *di Michelangelo Antonioni*, edited by Tommaso Chiaretti (*Dal soggetto al film*), general editor Renzo Renzi (Bologna, Cappelli), 140.
[84] Pr. Sebor-Bor, Ceskovensky Film, 1965.

scene, a continuous movement among the three speakers as they search for a more comfortable position, and shoots it with a fixed camera in one extremely long shot. About a hundred lines of the dialogue[85] are thus presented without a break, and without a change of angle – there are just three points where the image of Andula listening from the dining room or the kitchen is inserted. So this is an action that is set up with a view to forming an image which reproduces it mirror-fashion – and this choice on the author's part fits in perfectly with the style of the whole work, which sticks close to external reality, and to objects that are able to become cinematographic of their own accord.

Forman's approach is uninhibited and disenchanted, but aimed at making credible everything that occurs on the screen, by means of a realism that is without concessions and without symbolical superimpositions. However, the shot that we have examined cannot be reduced to a linguistic unit, let alone an expressive one; it is very complex, and may be analyzed into autonomous elements. So one can say that the various units may be traced within this lengthy shot, and may be identified with a movement on the part of one of the characters, a gesture, a phrase or line of their conversation. Here, too, one is concerned with a choice made by the director on a linguistic level which is preceded and justified by the original choices on an expressive, and consequently stylistic level.

Analogous considerations are at work, for example, in the lengthy shot from Godard's *Le petit soldat*,[86] in which the protagonist Forestier (Michel Subor) tries to explain to his girl-friend Veronica (Anna Karina) the strange, disengaged, and contorted reasons that lead him to political activity against the F.L.N., or in the very long shot from *Pierrot le fou*, also by Godard, in which the protagonist, played by J. P. Belmondo, meets a man sitting on the waterfront who is troubled by the fixation of an amorous memory that he cannot get rid of.[87] In Godard's case, the similar mode of cinematic narration is not brought into use by virtue of a faithful and psychologically objective adhesion to a certain prearranged reality, as it is with Forman, but is instead the result of a fragmentary and apparently senseless selection, within the body of reality itself, of elements that are diverse in nature and origin, and are mutually incommensurable, in order to compose them in a mosaic that acquires expressive unity thanks to an extremely subtle and refined stylistic approach. The two

[85] See the French edition of the scenario in *L'Avant-Scène-Cinéma* 60 (June 1966).
[86] *Le petit soldat* by Jean-Luc Godard, scenario and dialogue by Godard, photography by Raoul Coutard, prod. Georges de Beauregard, 1960.
[87] Godard's *Pierrot le fou* dates from 1965, and is taken from Lionel White's novel *Obsession*.

shots that we have considered are not, of course, linguistic units, but may be subdivided into linguistic and expressively elementary units.

Thus in the film *Persona*, the director Ingmar Bergman composes the narration of an orgy on the beach, which one protagonist recounts to the other (Bibi Andersson, the nurse, speaking to Liv Ullmann, the actress), with a long shot simply describing the woman who is speaking, interrupted by a very few shots of the woman who is listening. In this case it is evident that Bergman wishes to give the scene an epic quality; he does not want the content of the narration to exercise a suggestive influence on the public, and he therefore tries to stimulate a certain capacity for critical reaction on its part, in order to communicate to it what really interests him: the way in which the character confesses her erotic experience, and the ethical ambit within which her human dimension moves during this revelation.[88]

THE SYNTAX OF THE FILM

It should by now be evident that the analysis of a film, being obliged to refer back to linguistic units which always involve valuations of a relational and of an expressive nature, must always be undertaken adopting an approach of a SYNTACTIC and only partly GRAMMATICAL order. The subdivision of verbal language according to the physical aspect of words (phonetics and phonology) and their psychological aspect (lexicology, which may in turn be divided into morphology and semantics) does not make much sense for the cinematographic language. Since the iconeme may in some ways be compared to the phrase, SYNTAX and SYNTAGMATICS (see below) may well be the fundamental disciplines of a scientifically based linguistics of the film. Cinematographic syntax and syntagmatics will have to study the iconemes and the relations between them, structuring themselves each time according to the morphological paradigms (the composition of the elementary units of the narration, the way in which the various component shots are linked, the relations of cause and effect between one shot and the next, etc.), or according to semantic paradigms (analysis of the signifieds of all the morphological components and of the relations between them).[89] However, a morphological study of the film, even if conducted on a syntactic level, cannot leave out

[88]   *Persona*, direction, subject, and scenario by Ingmar Bergman; prod. Svensk Filmindustri, 1965-1966.
[89]   For syntax in verbal language, see Ullmann (1962), 31-35.

of account considerations of a technico-grammatical nature – it is perhaps hazardous to talk of a cinematographical grammar, when the grammar of a spoken language stems from a lexicological base (which the cinema does not have) and subsequently incorporates a number of implications of a syntactic nature.

Grammar, as Otto Jespersen wrote in *Mankind, Nation and Individual from a Linguistic Point of View*,[90] is concerned with "general facts of the language". The cinema does not possess the conditions for this type of study, because if one considers a few fragments that are capable of signifying in an autonomous way as if they were grammatical elements of the film, then they will also involve considerations of a relational nature, and will thus lead into the area of syntactic research; if, on the other hand, one leaves out of account the semantic evaluation of the elements that make up the image, they will not in any way lend themselves to inclusion within a linguistically analytical approach nor, above all, will they allow any procedure involving generalization. One can put forward hypotheses regarding the potential constancy of signified possessed by a few technical elements of the cinematographic image, but one cannot define a reliable grammar for it. The search for and study of the elements that make up the iconeme therefore consists in an analysis on the technical level, whose semantic values cannot be universalized, although it is now and then able to move within the ambit of those problems (movements, attacks, transitions) which are already of a syntactic nature, but which could by analogy be referred to the corresponding intersections between grammar and syntax in verbal language. It was in this sense that the expression TECHNICO-GRAMMATICAL was used a few lines above to define the level of morphological research that is involved in the interpretation of a film.

That it is impossible to invent a cinematographic grammar (and thus language) may also be deduced from considerations of another type. The film cannot be generalized in any of its dimensions; cinematographic space and cinematographic time do not exist, but the space and time of a particular film do. In the real physical and psychological universe in which we are normally immersed, it has been possible to conceive and select a unit of time and a unit of spatial measure, both of them valid for any macroscopic operation and, within certain limits, for research that goes beyond the visible and the so-called physically divisible as well. All actions that take place in the universe of reality may be objectively measured in terms of their spatial and temporal extension – and no matter what their nature may be, the system of measurement will always

90   Oslo, 1925, 32. See also Ullmann (1962), 35.

be the same, generic and conventionalized. In the same way that it is possible to establish a volume, an extension, a date, and a duration for any phenomenon of everyday life, so it is also possible to find in verbal language words that are suitable for spatially and temporally defining the description of the object itself.

Every language has had difficulties of an ethnological and sociological nature when attempting to include within its elementary formations symbols that are capable of quantitively defining the categories of space and time,[91] indispensable for the classification and comprehension of the objective world. Once the concept of number had been developed, and its linguistic implications derived, the problem tended to resolve itself in an outlook that was increasingly detached from the contingency of the object and inclined towards universalization. Thus the mathematical sciences were born, as were, in parallel fashion if somewhat later, the grammatical sciences – the latter as universal as the former, but limited to the expressive liberty of the speaker or writer. The successive abstractions that made possible the formation of this discipline of human knowledge were favoured and supported in their development by the relative uniformity of the measurable universe in its empirically verifiable manifestations. Man, that is, has, in the course of his researches, passed through a series of rational models that are slightly variable throughout the centuries on a macroscopic level, but which have allowed him to measure time and space by abstracting himself as observer from time and space. The laws of grammar, for example, fix the linguistic phenomenon in an objectual rigidity, which is able to prescind from its present temporal flux so as to allow a useful measure of its temporal coordinates – the same thing happens in the spatial definition of an analyzed object.

But all this is only possible in the face of a spontaneous reality, naturally present in the universe of the subject – a reality that can also be described by virtue of grammatical laws because it passes through the rationalizing and generalizing filter of its interpreter. Men are thus immersed in a universe that they measure, freeing themselves with adequate ease from the constrictions of the phenomenal. In the case of the cinematographic language, on the other hand, the photographic objectuality of the projection (which was discussed above) introduces the perceiver into a universe whose dimensions are unrepeatable, so that one could propose

---

[91]   See Ernst Cassirer's profound and thoroughly documented treatment of this subject in *Philosophie der Symbolischen Formen*, I. *Die Sprache* (Oxford). English translation: *The Philosophy of Symbolic Forms*, trans. Ralph Manheim (Yale University Press, 1953), 198-226.

that the spectator lives a new life every time that he is present at the showing of a film. The universe of the film has a spatial-temporal dimensionality of its own, which is unique to each film – and here one is not only concerned with psychological solicitations communicated to the spectator or with an 'interior' dimension of time and things (which is perceived by virtue of a personal integration and is already in itself of such considerable importance for the argument being developed here), but with actual, quantitive alterations, with references to systems that are original and autonomous for every film, so that every time one comes into contact with a new work this implies a process of self-adaptation to a complex of new and irrepeatable coordinates, in no way capable of generalization. Thus every film could have a grammar of its own, upon which one might base an analysis of the particular universe in which the film exists, and into which the spectator enters. There would thus be as many lives as there were films, and as many grammars too – but a single cinematographic grammar could never exist.

ANALYSIS OF THE FILM

The first analytical approach to a film implies, in the light of the preceding observations, a study on two different levels: a syntactic one, and a technico-grammatical one (in the sense defined above). Regarding the relational (syntactic) evaluation of linguistic units and of their combinations, it must once more be observed that, in undertaking such an evaluation, one cannot leave out of account considerations of a stylistic and therefore 'expressive' nature – the interpretation of a film may always be reduced to a personal encounter with the author, and with the language that he has formed in the matrix of his intentions. The cinematographic spectator interprets the film as a communicative totality, and is not faced with a series of signs that are more or less monosignificant in the various situations in which they are used. So the critic can never confuse his interpretation with that of the calculating grammarian, intent upon finding verifications and relations codified a priori; his work has, in itself, a specific technical component which cannot, however, leave out of account a basic cultural commitment that is capable of involving the whole of his interpretive personality. The risk of critical formalism is much less accentuated in the case of the cinema than it is in the case of literature. Here, in fact, language tends to become identified with things, without any possibility of generalization, and a critic's encounter with the work consists in looking for the ways in which it was formed and the inspiration behind it, not to speak of its autonomous laws, its forms, and its style. Analysis of a film can never be accomplished in icy detachment from the work itself, but instead must involve itself on the level of totally assimilating its mode of being. By contrast, the author realizes himself in the images of his film, constructing a world which is, however, always very similar to him.

At this point, the argument on the efficacy of applying semiological studies to the cinematographic language has need of an entirely autonomous base or, at any rate, of a demonstration of its reliability as a means of persuasion which, although still a long way from a scientific generalization in some respects, is at least available for rationally organized research. Contemporary studies on this subject are still limited to a phase of prudent supposition and hesitating induction – the more serious studies, naturally, because the violent derogations of those who see themselves as the champions of a stylistically impressionistic criticism or the facile praise of those who invent for themselves a structuralist culture may be reduced to apodictic and gratuitous assertions, valid within the ambit of the publicist's sterile polemics.

The hypothesis of a semiology of the film (or preferably of moving images) springs from establishing the existence of a process of codification, which ought to fundamentally condition every communicative exchange whose message is carried by moving images. After all, every interpersonal contact implies resorting to codes that are present and active in the universe of the sender and in that of the receiver, at times unconsciously – otherwise it would be impossible for the subjects situated at either end of the communication to comprehend one another. The codes are those of the society or group in which the intercommunicating persons live and, at a limit, derive their nature and formative power from the ideologies subtended by the cultural universe that nourishes society itself. In fact every communicative exchange, along with the denotative function of its signs and combinations of signs, implies a series of sign contents (or properties, as Greimas would say)[92] on a connotative level; and "...ce domaine commun des signifiés de connotation, c'est celui de L'IDÉOLOGIE, qui ne saurait être qu'unique pour une société et une histoire données, quels que soient les significants de connotation auxquels elle recourt".[93]

The analysis of a message may thus be traced to its structure, which in

---

[92]   Greimas (1966a), 22. Jakobson prefers to define them as "distinctive traits".
[93]   Barthes, "Rhétorique de l'image", *Communications* 4 (Paris, Seuil, 1964b), 49.

turn may be identified with the ultimate code of its interpretation and, finally, may be seen to lead the perceptor on to the ultimate ideological values that favoured its birth and formation. The group of connotative signifieds corresponding to the general ideology constitutes a RHETORIC (which, as Barthes notes, with the aid of one of Saussure's images, appears as the signifying face of ideology).[94] The existence of a codification that is immanent in every phenomenon that implies the exchange of a message (and therefore also in the universe of the television and the film) may indeed provide the starting-point for a study of all the combinations that are possible amongst the connotative signifieds involved in it, as well as their classification in such a way as to relate them to the canons of traditional rhetoric. So that even in the case of images one could risk the study and formation of a metalanguage of connotations, amenable to being structured according to paradigms of complex codification, that would all the same be extremely useful for a complete view of the senses transmitted behind the reality of the signs.

The authors that concern themselves with these problems are agreed as to the existence of a social, and therefore ideological, conditioning that is capable of interfering with all the communication by signs accomplished by a certain human group in a certain epoch of its history; it is thus evident that creative liberty within a certain linguistic situation (within the *langue* or the language) is much more restricted than a romantic aesthetic or a mystic conception of the creative act would have us believe. If we are spoken by the language,[95] if creative freedom is, in most cases, transformed into the laborious conquest of a certain recreative liberty at the margins of *moduli* and linguistic objects that owe their existence to tradition, then we cannot reasonably expect miraculous personal solutions from the ambit of audiovisual signs. We may suppose, that is, that man is equally conditioned by a series of expectations when faced by messages or structures which he receives by means of cinema and television screens – the systems into which these expectations are ordered could then constitute the necessary codification for deciphering the messages.[96] After all, the aesthetics of figurative art has for some time been seeking to define the problem of perceiving a work of art on different levels of meaning, and of the conditioning that the ideological components of the society in which the artist lived and worked have imposed

---

[94] Barthes (1964b).
[95] Umberto Eco, talk given at the 'Round Table' of the *III Mostra Internazionale di Pesaro del Cinema Libero* (1967b), p. 3 of the typescript.
[96] Eco (1967b), 4.

upon its structure (so that, for Panofsky, the level of iconological analysis, which is the most complex, also implies an awareness of all the historical and relational elements that may aid the interpretation of an astute critic).[97]

Ideology, considered as the "universe of knowledge"[98] belonging to the transmitter and the receiver of a certain message and to the social group to which they belong, thus constitutes a sort of formative premise or atmosphere conditioning a certain semantic space, within which it is perhaps possible to single out the parameters of a semiological universe, of a dynamic codification on the level of connotative signs. The opinions of the various authorities diverge notably and, even though their judgements are formed within an ambit of an inductive nature, that is frequently without the support of concrete research methods, they reveal, in fact, an all too evident subordination to the ideological components of their own thought.

SEMIOLOGY AND THE CINEMA

Jean Mitry does not even bring into *question* the possibility of attributing a sign-function to the image. He wrote recently in a short essay with a very significant title,[99]

non seulement l'image n'est pas comme le mot un signe 'en soi', mais elle n'est le signe d'aucune chose. Elle MONTRE, c'est tout. Elle n'est chargée d'un certaine sens, d'un 'pouvoir de signifier' que par relation avec un ensemble de FAITS dans lesquels elle se trouve impliquée... La signification en effet ne dépend pas d'elle seule, mais de sa relation avec une autre. Autrement dit, le SIGNIFIANT FILMIQUE (lorsqu'il s'agit d'une connotation) N'EST JAMAIS UNE IMAGE, UNE CHOSE CONCRÈTE, MAIS UN RAPPORT.

Thus Mitry thinks of the cinematographic image as the result of a process of auto-connotation on the part of the represented world, which would connote itself in the very process of denotation. The reality translated into images by the film-camera, and raised to a linguistic level by the formative intervention of the director, would make itself concrete in its sign,

---

[97] See note 24. See also Panofsky, *Studies in Iconology* (Oxford University Press, 1939). The introduction to this work is a sort of clarified and very valuable 'summa' of the author's thought. Also: G. C. Argan, *Salvezza e caduta nell'arte moderna* (Milano, Il Saggiatore, 1964); and G. Ballo, *Occhio critico* (Milano, Longanesi, 1966); English translation: *The Critical Eye*, trans. R. H. Boothroyd (London, Heinemann, 1969).

[98] Eco (1967a), 83.

[99] "D'un langage sans signes" (1967), 139-152.

which would thus reduce itself to a sort of *analogon*, to the "in itself of a provisory signification, of a characterized immanence".[100] With this essay, the author simply confirms what he had already written in the second volume of *Esthétique et psychologie du cinéma*,[101] where he had pointed out the strict correlation that exists, on a cinematographic level, between sign and symbol – referring, among other things, to the example of the window pane that reflects the knives in Fritz Lang's *M*, Mitry maintains that within the ambit of the cinema SIGN and SYMBOL are exact synonyms; the signification acquired by virtue of a thing gives to that thing the value of a sign and the thing becomes a symbol, but "...symbole momentané, contingent, et nullement symbole 'en soi' ".[102] As Christian Metz makes clear, Mitry uses the word 'symbol' in a particular way, which is of considerable interest concerning research on the film-symbol, that is, as an increase in sense "qui permet de dépasser la pure dénotation SANS JAMAIS L'OUBLIER NI LA CONTREDIRE".[103]

Every film ought therefore to display its own signs naturally, without indicating them as such by any special means; it ought, that is, to give the impression of recording its own symbology, its own connotative universe within the *corpus* of its own diegesis, within the immediate and apparent universe of the narration, that complete 'cosmos' in which all the elements (actors, sets, objects, actions, etc.) are brought to the same level of photographic reality.[104] We shall have occasion at several further points to return to the necessity of this anchorage between the thing represented and the signifier in the film, to the proximity of signifier and signified, and to the linguistic implications that this sign reality involves. But for the moment it is enough to observe how, starting from the premises outlined above, Mitry comes to deny the existence of a syntax of the film and to affirm the absolute creative liberty of the cinematographic author, and

---

[100] Mitry (1967), 145.
[101] Mitry (1965), Vol. II, 26, 381.
[102] Mitry (1965), 26.
[103] Metz (1967c), 216. "Symbol" is used here in a more open and less instrumentalized way than it is in Mitry's case. He is above all concerned with the cinematographic symbol's 'motivation', with its being anchored to a diegetic reality that is naturally credible and may in itself be accepted not as an instrument of communication, but as a reality that speaks by directly manifesting itself. Thus the cinematographic image can never communicate by virtue of an explicit convention, an *a priori* codification; each film would generate its own symbolism, and this could never be identified with a pre-established group of semiological relations in common use (see 218 of the same essay).
[104] Metz (1967c), 207. See also Metz, "La grande syntagamatique du film narratif", in *Communications* 8 (Paris, 1966b), 123. Diegesis "...est le SIGNIFIÉ LOINTAIN du film pris en bloc, alors que les éléments de diégèse sont les SIGNIFIÉS PROCHES de chaque segment filmique".

his absolute and spontaneous freedom from every codified restraint to his linguistic instrument. The film then becomes "revelation, deciphering, discovery", "a magic vision, the common and intuitive birth of the world and of things offered as an incessantly renewed testimony".[105] It is reality that, in a film, is organised into logos; cinematographic creation must not be at the service of meanings, but must become the very act of signifying.[106]

Mitry's lyrical enthusiasm is not shared by the detached and penetrating analysis of Christian Metz, who is nevertheless one of his sincerest admirers. On the existence of a syntax of the film Metz does not offer an opinion; but he introduces a critical model that is much better adapted to the dynamically evanescent characteristics of this language, the LARGE-SCALE SYNTAGMATICS OF THE NARRATIVE FILM. Metz does not conceal from himself the many difficulties of classifying a reality-as-image and, turning to Saussure's well known terminology, writes that the cinema is above all "*parole*" – the cinema provides rich messages from a poor code, rich texts from a poor system; "...le mot, unité de langue, fait défaut; la phrase, unité de parole, est souveraine".[107]

The fact that the cinema is a universal phenomenon derives from two characteristics of its language: the perception of the message is accomplished by virtue of a visual perception that is more or less the same the world over; on the other hand, we are concerned with a vehicle of communication in which an articulation analogous to the secondary one of verbal language is entirely lacking. And not only that – the cinema does not even conform to some type of primary articulation "...sinon par moments et en quelque sorte par hasard".[108] So that up to this point the results of Metz's research are the same as those of Mitry's, but the considerations that may be deduced from their respective analyses of the linguistic reality of the film differ notably. In fact Metz thinks that some constructions, some complexes of images, conserve a certain structural stability and a certain way of revealing themselves on what is in fact a semiological level, above and beyond all their possible, variable, and highly personal realizations in different films.[109] The film director (and also the television director) always ought to choose among a limited series of forms that make up his narration[110] – this syntagmatics could

---

[105] Mitry (1965), 455.
[106] Mitry (1965), 448.
[107] Metz (1964), 78.
[108] Metz (1964), 74-75.
[109] Metz (1967c), 220.
[110] Metz (1966b), 120-124; he then amended these suggestions in "Un problème de

indeed constitute a sort of paradigmatics, the proposition of a series of elementary units that are capable of entering into mutual combination while conserving their significative value.

These PARADIGMS OF SYNTAGMS[111] are the elements of a fragmentary CODE that function, for example, on the level of propositions in the ambit of the syntax of several languages – the choice of a "proposition consécutive", as Metz justly observes, does not of itself classify the act of the writer as banal or as original, because the problems involved in artistic activity are one thing, and those that emerge on a purely idiomatic level are another. Metz's work is at present limited to the visual aspect of the cinematographic image, and he states in all humility that he is not, for the moment, able to present a picture of the dialogue, music, and sounds that would equal the one that he has already put forward for visual images,[112] since semiology essentially proceeds by a slow and meticulous path. He does not propose to work miracles, but simply considers that semiological methods can help one to understand individual films better – they do not in any way allow one (but then, nor should any method, semiological or not) "...de répondre d'emblée au questionneur ingénu si tel film est bon ou mauvais, ni d'expliquer à l'enthousiaste inondé dans sa subjectivité pourquoi il a aimé le film".[113]

Criticism may therefore carry on with its work; semiological research will never attempt to take the place of its type of activity, because value judgements do not concern it and because, on the other hand, the formation of such judgements cannot absorb the entire attention of a student of the film. The semiology of the narrative film that Christian Metz has set out with such intelligence and finesse (he considers, among other things, that up to now the film has almost always served to tell stories, even in the ambit of documentary or didactic films) must in no way be confused with the structural analysis of the NARRATIVE in itself, where all the signifieds carried by the signs of the message are transformed into signifiers on the new level of semiological consideration. With regard to this, Roland Barthes does indeed propose the study of a language of the "récit", borrowing from linguistics the concept of LEVELS OF DESCRIPTION and applying it with operatively effective results to the development of his

---

sémiologie", *Image et son* 201 (January 1967b), 68-79, and in "Problemi di denotazione nel film di finizione: contributo a una semiologia del cinema", *Cinema e film* (Spring 1967a), 171-178; translated into Italian by Gianfranco Albano, with a preface and notes by Adriano Aprà.

[111]   Metz (1967b), 177.
[112]   Metz (1967a), 76.
[113]   Metz (1967a), 77.

hypothesis; his researches are backed up by those of Vladimir Propp,[114] Claude Bremond,[115] A. J. Greimas,[116] Tzvetan Todorov,[117] and others who study narrative communication on a structural level.

We shall have occasion to return to this topic a little further on, since it has a determining importance in regard to an overall analysis of the film – an analysis that takes into account all of its innumerable levels of signification. It should, however, be evident to what extent research like that of Christian Metz contributes to a more complex and totalizing study like the one Barthes refers to – at such levels, in fact, the vehicle of the communication loses the entire value of its presence and the student moves in an ambit of cultural presences and mental structures that are considered in a disembodied manner, and are not exemplified in any possible phenomenon; but in order to establish connections between the film, in its primitive and diegetic presentation, and the universe of its more complex connotations, the most trustworthy method of approach at present is perhaps that adopted by Metz.

In Italy, Pier Paolo Pasolini, after his first proposals for a cinema of poetry, has continued to develop the hypothesis of a semiology of reality, asserting that action may be considered the first and foremost of human languages and that, as a result, the objects that make up the various shorts are the minimal units of cinematographic language[118] – therefore a languages and that, as a result, the objects that make up the various shots on each occasion by the author of the cinematographic communication. The director, according to Pasolini, after having placed his camera in front of the multifarious aspects of reality (whether pre-arranged with dramatic intentions in mind or not), and after having allowed an almost absolute liberty to his visually curious subjectivity, would, in cutting, fix his personal experience in an expressively finalized objectivity, adapting all of the various subjective elements that had been shot to the ends of his poetic intentions.[119] The life that pulsates in the dynamic and disposable

[114] *Morfologija skazki* (Leningrad, Academia, 1918). English translation: *Morphology of the Folk-tale* (*Indiana Univ. Research Center in Anthrop., Folklore, and Ling. publ.* 10) (1958).

[115] "Le message narratif" and "La logique des possibles narratifs", in Nos. 4 and 8, respectively of *Communications*.

[116] *Cours de Sémantique* in *Cahiers Ronéotyés par l'Ecole Normale supérieure de Saint-Cloud* (Paris, 1964); "Eléments pour une théorie de l'interprétation du récit mythique", *Communications* 8 (Paris, 1966b); *Sémantique structurale* (1966a).

[117] "La description de la signification en littérature" and "Les catégories du récit litteraire", in Nos. 4 and 8, respectively of *Communications*.

[118] (1965).

[119] "Lingua scritta dell'azione", lecture given at the 'Round Table' of the Mostra di Pesaro in 1966, and published in *Nuovi Argomenti* (April-June 1966b).

reality caught by the camera and in the free and unordered complex of shots taken would thus be brought, in the process of cutting, to a definitive but necessary halt, chilling but useful.

A sense of death spreads out over the free universe of the cinematographically possible, over that LIFE that Pasolini considers to be an "indecipherable linguistic moment".[120] Its deciphering involves a synchronic stasis, even in the apparently diachronic nature of the film, and the interpretation of its signifieds ought to be accomplished by virtue of signs that are spontaneously offered by reality itself, by action as SIGNIFICANT GESTURE. Pasolini's assertions, which reflect the same cultural atmosphere as the researches of J. Mitry, are parried by Umberto Eco in the paper that he presented to the Round Table at Pesaro in 1967 and in a recent publication, edited by the Faculty of Architecture of the University of Florence.[121] Taking up Pasolini's concepts of cinema as semiology of reality and action as language, Eco maintains that man's significant gesturing is in itself not NATURE, but "convention and culture".[122] The language of action already has a semiology, KINESICS, which, along with PROXEMICS (which studies the meaning of the distances between people talking to one another), aims to attribute to every human gesture a semiologically paradigmatic value and to the complex of gestures the possibility of reciprocal compositive effects which may be regulated according to established codes on a syntagmatic level. Thus, for Eco, the universe of action that the cinema transcribes is already a "universe of signs"[123] and a semiology of the film cannot therefore be subordinated to the idea of transcribing a natural spontaneity which does not exist. One could thus make out the continuous presence of expectations conditioned by the personal and social history of the subject in any communicative phenomenon and, specifically, in that of the film; the images of objects that the film presents us with would not in any way be fragments of reality, with "immediately" and spontaneously "motivated" signifieds, but the final product of a series of successive conventionalizations, which permit us to attribute to these signifiers a certain signified by virtue of certain codes.

Eco, in his constructively critical work, does in fact go beyond the semiological zeal of Metz to hypothesize a tertiary articulation of the cinematographic language, which will be examined a few pages further

---

[120]   See Pasolini's talk at the 'Round Table' of the Mostra di Pesaro (1967), 4-5.
[121]   Eco (1967a).
[122]   Eco (1967a), 143.
[123]   Eco (1967a), 144.

on.[124] Along with the names cited above, one may also usefully mention the studies of Galvano della Volpe, who individuates in literary criticism the homogenous relation between instrument and object and in the cinematographic image the product of a composite technique of communication and expression;[125] and of Emilio Garroni, who particularizes the metalinguistic function present in every linguistic act, points out the lack of a codification at a more basic level than that of the film, affirms the indefinite and infinite number of EXAMPLES of structure (we move, he writes, in the realm of perceptive continuity) and, at the same time, puts forward the hypothesis of a finite – but dynamically finite – number of structures, or models, which would thus constitute "a sort of paradigm or linguistic-perceptive code".[126]

Having thus oriented ourselves, as is right and proper, and indeed necessary, we must now single out all the possible bases for a semiology of the film, deducing them from the cinema as it really is, considered from a historical standpoint and in its synchronic form as an instrument of communication. We shall try to avoid, from this point on, all analogical appeals to linguistics – indeed, in order to avoid any possibility of confusion, we shall not even use the terms 'language', 'phoneme', and 'morpheme' any longer, so as to avoid dangerous translations from the universe of words to that of moving images; instead we shall talk of codes, of processes of codification, of units of meaning, etc.

PREMISES FOR A SEMIOLOGY OF THE FILM

To begin, one may propose that a complex of *termes-objets*, adopted as the vehicles of communicative acts within a social group, must, in all cases, allow for a free choice of its elements on the part of the subject-author, and for the combinatorial and directional nature of the elements themselves, in order that it may aspire to systematic qualification. We are dealing with properties that have already been noted with regard to verbal language (and all 'indirect' languages), but that are here being built up on

---

[124] It should be remembered that Pasolini attributes the possibility of a double articulation to cinematic language.

[125] Della Volpe, remarks at the 'Round Table' at Pesaro (1967), pp. 4-5 of the typescript.

[126] Remarks at the 'Round Table' at Pesaro (1967b) and "Popolarità e comunicazione nel cinema", *Filmcritica illustrata* 175 (March 1967a), 79-100 (the quote is on p. 94). Another interesting essay, pointing out Metz's 'synchronic' imprudences, is the one published by Fernaldo di Giammatteo, in *Bianco e Nero* XXVII: 7-8 (July-August 1966): "Chi non conosce il basso bretone?", pp. 1-36.

a metalinguistic base which is more adapted to our present purpose. Any articulated message, any 'discourse', would manifest itself according to two easily distinguished semiological dimensions: the paradigmatic one, in which significant objects are opposed by virtue of conjunctive and disjunctive relations ("que nous aimerions désigner", writes A. J. Greimas, "si le terme n'était déjà pris, comme syntaxiques"),[127] and the syntagmatic one, in which the same elements are united among themselves by hierarchic relations, which Greimas defines as "hypotactic".[128] Any articulated message would structure itself according to two semiological dimensions, according to two AXES, which Metz defines respectively as that of selections and exclusions, and that of combinations.[129]

Yet in the world of the film, the *termes-objets* to which Greimas continually refers, breaking down their form and singling out their elementary significant structure, are almost infinite in number, imprecise, and as semantically indefinable as are the natural phenomena reflected in the film. Thus, as has already been made clear, we are not concerned with rationally codified elements, absorbed in a system that detaches itself culturally from reality in order to signify those of its aspects that will tend to be more useful as far as a communicative act is concerned; but with direct representations of this reality, whose codification may only come about on the level of perceptual habit, and of the more or less conscious expectations of the subject when perceiving a certain audio-visual message. Pasolini writes that these real objects that make up a shot are the minimal units of the cinematographic language; Eco corrects this assertion, introducing the suspicion of iconic codification – but in the one case as much as the other, we are still faced with the problem of a hypothetical cinematographic articulation on the level of these elementary units. Photography is brought into the argument and, by virtue of the complex codifications that regulate its formative processes, ascribes a significative value to all the elements that make up its dynamic '*tableau*'.

The study of cinematographic FIGURAE (the term 'FIGURA' was introduced by Hjelmslev and borrowed by Luis J. Prieto, in order to designate the unit of primary articulation in every linguistic system – in the case of spoken language, 'figura' substitutes for 'phoneme')[130] is extremely important and of great use, but even if the author of the communication is

---

[127] Greimas (1966a), 41.
[128] Greimas (1966a).
[129] Metz (1967a), 69.
[130] Prieto (1966). See also the exposition that he gives of the basic elements of his functional theory of meaning in *Principes de noologie* (1964). Eco has adopted Prieto's terminology in the two essays already referred to.

always conditioned in the range of his choice, and even if it is his society
that, even more than in the case of the spoken language, offers him the
forms and objects of his representation, and that incessantly suggests to
him the manner of their cinematographic composition, the concept of
articulation does not seem in any way extendable to the paradigmatic level
of the film. On the other hand Metz's syntagmatic approach seems much
more promising, and it is one with which I am much in sympathy. When
all is said and done, the *termes-objets* (Greimas's terminology is particularly apt at this point) included in the cinematographic image do not of
themselves involve signification, because the elementary significative units
must be sought at the level of the structures, and the consideration of this
approach implies an analysis of the semic relations between the various
terms, and of the semantic content of the relations themselves.[131]

The structures that human thought has re-elaborated and continues to
re-elaborate within the history of society and of the subject are qualitatively
and quantitatively limited, even though they are open to transformation
and integration. From this one could deduce that the ways of composing
the objects offered by reality are practically independent of the objects
themselves (or of their specular images) and that the attribution, for
narrative purposes, of a significant qualification to the material offered by
the film camera may be reduced to a discrete modal choice that may be
defined with a certain precision. The scheme presented by Metz is not
definitive and does not establish all the possible combinations of the
cinematographic paradigms. Metz himself declares the contingent limit of
his research and furthermore, as has already been noted, limits his studies
to a strictly narrative approach to the cinematographic work, whatever
genre it may belong to; in fact nowadays, the cinema, in its more significant aspects, is rapidly evolving towards forms of realization that are
far removed from the classic paradigms of 'story' and 'action', so that a
syntagmatic analysis might well have to base itself on other formulas than
those proposed by Metz, in order to find an effective area of development.[132]

But all this does not in any way mean that the cinema is unable to find
its paradigmatic structure at the level of syntagms or, to recall a more
specific term introduced a few pages back, of ICONEMES. The cinemato-

[131]   Greimas (1966a), 20.
[132]   An analysis of a number of Godard's films made by several students from the
'Cinema' section of the Scuola Superiore delle Comunicazioni Sociali and the Corso di
'Storia e Critica del Film' at the Università Cattolica del Sacro Cuore di Milano, under
the author's direction, often found itself hindered by a rather forced application of the
models proposed by Metz.

graphic image would thus conserve its powers of totalization and of re-productive synthesis in their entirety, but, at the same time, the aesthetic and communicative direction imposed upon it by the director-author would come to attribute a semantic power to the represented object of which this latter was quite innocent and which, furthermore, could be referred to a hypotactic co-ordination, to the co-ordinates of a semiolog-ical system. Moreover any semic analysis (or rather, the analysis of each particular 'semiosis')[133] cannot leave out of consideration the perceptual data which appear in every communicative relation. It is distinctly ab-surd to talk of reality, of its representation, of its signs, of all the symbolic processes implicit in operations that involve the realm of the imagination, while forgetting that the iconic nature of a sign (that which qualifies it as an 'image') depends above all on reproducing the conditions in which the object-referent is perceived. If one thinks of the sign as a mental schema, the tracing and singling out of a 'convenient' structure within the con-tinuous magma of reality,[134] and of the image as the most integral repro-duction of that reality possible, then the sign can indeed be thought of as an INTERMEDIARY between concept and image, and as a LINK between the two of them.[135]

Lévi-Strauss writes, referring back to Saussure:

Signs resemble images in being concrete entities but they resemble concepts in their powers of reference. Neither concepts nor signs relate exclusively to them-selves; either may be substituted for something else. Concepts, however, have an unlimited capacity in this respect, while signs have not.[136]

The fact that the sign takes its place as a mental reality interconnecting an exclusively rational and generalizing universe with another ruled by immediate sensation and inclining towards a continual reduction to the particular does not prevent its referential power – its significant presence – from translating itself to one of the other two extremes and, in particu-lar, to the image – that is, it does not prevent the image from having a predisposition towards acting as a sign immanent within itself. The matter appears even more evident if one considers that, at a more basic level than any image composed by man, there always exists a process of schematization, of choice, and, at any rate, of reduction to an abstract model.

In a study that displays considerable critical finesse, Cesare Brandi writes:

---

[133] Garroni (1967a), 91.
[134] In fact, to propose a metaphysical structuralism seems to me decidedly dangerous.
[135] Lévi-Strauss (1962), 18.
[136] Lévi-Strauss (1962).

The perception of a schema, in at any rate a rudimentary and primary fashion, must have its place within the perceptive act itself, as the abstraction from the datum offered by the retina, the hearing, or any other sense, of those particulars that generalize or summarize the object.[137]

The preconceptual schema is no more than a synthesis of the immediate impressions that reality makes upon the subject, who, by virtue of this reactive process and of certain of his expectations (formed by the society in which he lives and by his personal history), finds himself in possession of an image that is the fruit of a subjective interpretation of reality and, at the same time, a revelation of the way in which the '*mens*' of society is predisposed to integrate within itself things and ideas.[138]

Perception is the first level of consciousness, and from it develops the whole series of processes of conceptualization; and it is perception that conditions at any rate the formation of schemas, gnosiological models, and structures. The more man's thought is anchored to mental habits and a cultural atmosphere of a mythical nature, the more the so-called PERCEPT (or 'perceptual concept') will tend to satisfy the needs of his consciousness. But even the percept, however, reduces itself to a schema, to a way of looking at things which, however much it eludes generalization within the ambit of the absolute category, establishes itself as the subject's interior reality and as the primitive stage of the ascent towards reality. Children and primitive peoples do not draw their experiences, but synthesize them in signs which reproduce the schematizations that they have made of them; the type of image that they construct is very similar to certain graphic formulas that have typified the history of human civilization (see picture-writing and ideographic scripts), because within its form it encloses a number of interpretive possibilities that are clearly differentiated at a semantic level. If this image comes to be interpreted as the *sigla* of the preconceptual schema, "...and thus of that knowledge content that the schema individuates", it will only be of value for its semantic content; if, on the other hand, the consciousness of the subject "...takes up the image that lies at base of the preconceptual schema not for the nucleus of knowledge that is enclosed in that schema, but in its specularity...", then the whole cognitive act is reduced to the perception of this specularity and of its figurative values.[139] But this is not to say that the perception of the communicative vehicle at the level of an 'image' must necessarily leave out of account a partial consideration of its values as sign, and

[137]   *Segno e immagine* (Milano, Il Saggiatore, 1960), 15.
[138]   Bettetini (1964), 259-265, 313-323.
[139]   Brandi (1960), 15, 16, 17, 18, 19, 20.

vice versa – just as it is very difficult to separate out, in a clear-cut manner, all the various manifestations of man's consciousness, the cold and disembodied activity of reason from the incandescent fascination of the myth. Nor is one concerned with a cultural event that belongs to the realm of the child and the primitive savage alone – any man will tend to attribute semantic powers to an iconic reality, by means of convenient translations, and powers of reproductive magic to a sign reality (the example of Lévi-Strauss's *bricoleur* is very relevant in this instance); but if the iconic nature of any particular *terme-objet* is also subordinated to a schema of perceptive reception, one can easily envisage the subject transmitter and the subject receiver as individuals coming to grips with selected and to some degree codified signifiers, with a series of signs that are capable of making reference to a primitive structure of mutual understanding (and therefore of convention) even in cases where an iconic function prevails.

Any mimetic representation of reality, on a figurative level, is dependent upon the acceptance of certain perceptual codes that schematize at any rate its image. The entire history of painting, and of the figurative arts in general, continually re-proposes the theme of a gradual modification of modes of perception and of a consequent adaption of reproductive techniques to the schemata of new cultural 'visions' rather than to the dictates of new optical illusions that are necessary for the constitution of an 'idol' identical to reality. The theory concerning the technical ignorance of the artists of antiquity has had its day and, even if one must obviously admit to a gradual improvement in the instruments of art and the way they are used, one must not forget that the greatest revolutions in the ambit of the 'representable' were determined and favoured by ideological changes and by psychophysical insights, rather than by the perfecting of techniques or the improvement of instruments. Giotto would not otherwise have been understood by his contemporaries and the faults of perspective that are found in his paintings (faults relative to our sensibility, our optical predispositions) would have been transformed into dangerous 'noise' in the communication between artist and perceiver.

The mimetic parabola of the figurative arts was indeed concluded with the advent of photography, with the discovery of an instrument capable of forming images that possess a specular similarity to reality; Antoine Werz, the "painter of ideas" (as Walter Benjamin called him), hailed the new device as a sister art to that of antiquity, remarking that:

...this machine will be the brush, the palette, the colours, the ability, the experience, the patience, the nimbleness, the pregnancy, the tinting, the glazing, the model, the accomplishment, the extract of the picture.... Let it not be imagined that the daguerreotype kills art....

Baudelaire echoes his words when, in his *Salon de 1859*, he pessimistically wrote of the "commonplace stupidity" of those who consider that art can only be "a precise restitution of nature".

If photography is permitted to take over some of the functions of art, the latter will rapidly become superseded and ruined by it, thanks to its natural alliance with the crowd. It must therefore return to its real task, which consists in being the handmaid of the sciences and the arts.[140]

However photography may have been judged at its first appearance, it is clear that all the critical canons that had been experimented with up to that moment were in danger of being overthrown and surpassed. That pictorial mimesis represents conformity to a schema of personal and social classification rather than an exact and scientific direct reproduction may in fact be understood with reasonable ease, in view of the whole complex of psychological analyses and historical researches that have conditioned the most recent studies within this sector. Knowing 'what things are' does in fact condition one's vision and perception of reality (Jonathan Richardson had said as much at the beginning of the eighteenth century),[141] so that a mechanic and an ignorant farm worker will view the same automobile in decidedly different ways. Everyone views reality according to a personal schema, which is further conditioned by the expectations that the historical society in which he lives stimulate within him. The cultural exchanges that animated European life at the beginning of this century, for example, made artists aware of other expressive traditions, above and beyond the Greek, the Pompeian, and the Hellenistic; they thus came to know of:

... Cycladic traditions and Negro traditions, which do not follow the myth of beauty, but that of a more direct expression full of symbols and cadenced rhythms. Then there are other traditions: oriental, resulting in an art which has no resemblance to truth because the works are based on a different conception of space and time, pre-Colombian, Romanesque, Byzantine and numerous other traditions all speaking different languages.[142]

The combination of the various schematic angulations to which all these ideological positions could be reduced (for it is basically this that one is

---

[140]   All these quotations are taken from Walter Benjamin's essay "A Little History of Photography", in *Schriften* (Frankfurt, 1965a).
[141]   Ernst H. Gombrich, *Art and Illusion*, The A. W. Mellon Lectures in the Fine Arts 1956 (London, Phaidon Press Ltd., New York, Pantheon Books, 1960), 12.
[142]   Ballo (1969), 115.

concerned with) destroyed the centre of attention around which European figurative culture had revolved up to that time and vindicated the revolutionary appearance of, among others, the genius of Picasso. Any contact with reality implies the presence of a mode or system of classification which, although leaving the subject free to react according to a way of behaviour whose every act is apparently invented, favours the condensing of experiences according to clearly defined mental structures. Perhaps, after having read all that has been written on this subject, one may think that man regains a dimension of true liberty more in the critical selection and in the continual and dynamic correction of his schemata (many of which act on an unconscious level) than in direct contact with the objectual nature of things. Ernst H. Gombrich's analysis is undoubtedly one of the most pertinent and profound approaches to this subject; it is difficult to accept a theory of the absolute liberty and independence of the cinematographic artist, such as that proposed by Mitry, after having read the penetrating dissection of the traditional myths that surround the figurative arts put forward by the author of *Art and Illusion*.

"The artist could argue that it makes no sense to look at a motif unless one has learned how to classify and catch it within the network of a schematic form";[143] and, turning to the 'synchronic' observations of the psychologists, he adds a little further on that the schema to which, for example, a man copying a blot refers does not ensue from a process of ABSTRACTION, or from a tendency to SIMPLIFY – "...it represents the first approximate, loose category, which is gradually tightened to fit the form it is to reproduce".[144] When Gombrich writes that art is a study of nature and her laws, not on the level of the physical world, but on that of "our reactions to it",[145] he is simply proposing a useful and effective method of approach for the historians of all the figurative arts. He points out, that is, the possibility of discerning works from their own particular style by virtue of the 'conceptual' nature of all art, and of the fact that every representation starts life as the artist's reaction to the world, which is suggested and conditioned by an interior schematization. All this also comes about in abstract art, where the sense of natural mimesis and of interpreted reproduction of the tangible and the visible is programmatically lost – but it is an apparent loss, because while the author's point of view and his field of action are modified, his perceptive processes and the modality of his poetic activity do not change in the slightest. The artist

[143]   Gombrich (1960), 73.
[144]   Gombrich (1960), 74.
[145]   Gombrich (1960), 44.

dedicates himself to receiving and translating, sometimes by synesthesia,[146] the rhythms and forms that are hidden in his material, in the invisible nodes of its elementary structures, in the contacts and disjunctions that are intuited in all their liveliness beyond the threshold of perception and that physics and chemistry study in ever increasing depth, proposing for them a continually renewed succession of models.[147] Or otherwise he will seek to reproduce by means of informal chromatic groupings, or of signs that are apparently devoid of significative power, the birth of sensations and of forms of receptive perception that are not bound up with any material object in the mind of the perceptor. However, his representative activity is always structured around mental schemata which constitute the fundamental code for the interpretation of the work.

Nor does photography escape this type of categorization; the work of even the most modest and straightforward of photographers is always articulated around a complex of personal and social schemata, of subjection to tradition, and of more or less conscious and mature ideological assimilations, so that the complex of connotative significations in his work will always be greater than the immediate denotative designation. Yet the artist's personal view gives place to the impartial detachment of the lens, so how can the so-called 'schemata' of society and the individual find a place within this specular type of reproduction on sensitive film? The objects that make up the photographic image are singled out by the perceptor in virtue of the mimetic similarity that links them to the original reality – there is the possibility, that is, of interpreting the image in a way that is free from any apparent codification, and of spontaneously and immediately projecting oneself into the fictitious universe revealed by the photograph. But even within the limits proposed by this type of interpretation it may become necessary to know of or to intuit several 'schemata' that have guided the composition and formation of the reality caught within the visual angle of the lens. Even on the level of simple figurative denotation one must at times turn for help to a certain schematization, a certain CODE, in order to completely appreciate its representative value. So that when it is the photographer himself who operates upon reality (more or less validly – this depends upon the ends that he has in mind for his work), the modifications that he contributes assume a decidedly connotative value and the capacity to make out their signifieds

---

[146] SYNESTHESIA is the "production, from a sense-impression of one kind, of an associated mental image of a sense impression of another kind" (Shorter Oxford English Dictionary).
[147] Eco (1967a), 150-152.

already constitutes a part of the symbolical perception of the image.

There thus exists a sort of 'tautology' of the object within its photographic reproduction that exhausts the perceptive phase of the relationship between message and receiver – the latter, however, along with the denotative solicitation, receives all the semantic suggestions which the message offers him on the level that, along with R. Barthes, we may define as 'cultural'[148] and which are present in the image by virtue of the personal intervention of the photographer: illumination, filters, angulation, lenses, focal length, length of exposure, figurative composition. Here one is concerned with the more specific connotations of the sign, with the formation of an image that sublimates its reproductive function (without merely ignoring it), in order to acquire its own autonomous and objective presence as a significative element. The representative schemata, the cultural conditioning, the dominant influence of ideologies appear at this level with the same determining weight with which we have already seen them to act in the dimension of the figurative arts; side by side with a primitive language that cannot be codified, photography develops another which is based upon systems of codes that one cannot leave out of consideration if one wishes to fully understand the message.[149]

When photography becomes animated on the cinema screen, its ability to represent reality tautologically increases, because the movement, the sense of a third dimension that its perception involves, the sense of time 'lived' in durations that apparently correspond to those of the action portrayed, and the sound favour the reproduction of perceptive conditions very close to those of direct reception. But at the same time the linguistic instrument lends itself all the more to acts of ordered structuring, of schematization, and of codification.

One might in fact think that the cinema eludes every attempt to analyze its fundamental structures (the models that inspire its works) because its dynamic state, its unfolding within a space-time continuum analogous to that in which exist the objects that make up every-day reality, could invalidate the evolution of a synchronic model right from the start. In fact the contrast between diachrony and synchrony lies at the heart of every scientific discipline, and constitutes one of the most important points of conflict in the history of linguistic studies. For example Lévi-Strauss points out the independent nature of the two determinisms that originate respectively in synchrony and diachrony: system and demographic evolu-

[148] Barthes (1964b), 42-43. The reader is also referred to this essay with reference to photographic 'tautology'.
[149] Barthes (1964b).

tion; but at the same time he clearly distinguishes the modalities of relationship that exist between the two levels of study, in relation to the fact
that the cultural products of the social group under consideration are instruments of thought or of communication.

In the case of a language, there is a partial sensitivity to demographic
changes ("as long as its function is not compromised"); in the case of
mental structures, and modes of thought, the independence between
system and history is even more appreciable, because "...one either
succeeds or not in making oneself understood, but one can think more or
less well. Thinking admits of degrees, and a way of thinking can degener-
ate imperceptibly into a way of remembering."[150] Men tend, that is, to
offer a certain resistance to changes in their mental systems and, as a rule,
tend to eternalize every synchronic configuration of reality, whose
gnosiological efficacy instead lies in a full awareness of its instrumental
value, and of its contingent characteristics.

If man's cultural life presents these fundamental contrasts, the film will
tend to reproduce their articulations, with the apparent aggravation of
having to subordinate itself to a type of schematization that is even more
coercive than those that condition the reality of contemporary thought –
the film is, in fact, the result of a series of choices and intuitions, all of
which are guided by a conditioning and explicit mental model. Since it is
possible to conceive of the spectator at a film as projecting himself men-
tally within the object-image that the screen presents him with, we may say
that his experience is translated into the encounter with a world governed
by ideas, aims, and predispositions that may be apprehended and brought
into evidence in order to acquire certain results more easily than would be
the case in an analysis of every-day reality. The communicative object
with which the film is identified may thus be analyzed on the level of
carefully chosen synchronic schemata, even though it continuously extends its own forms in time and space.

The 'dynamicity' of its photographic nature must not be allowed to invalidate any attempts at semiological investigation; Umberto Eco has
deduced the possibility of a TERTIARY ARTICULATION of the cinematographic language from the very fact that the technical instrument reproduces a reality that is in movement. In the code that would lie behind
every film one could thus single out the FIGURAE (a restricted number of
units) which would combine to form SIGNS (without being a part of their
signified), the SIGNS which would combine to form SYNTAGMS, and finally
elements X which would arise from the combination of signs that would

[150] Lévi-Strauss (1966), 67.

not form a part of their signified.[151] Turning to studies in KINESICS (see above) Eco recalls how this discipline posed itself the problem of whether

the KINEMORPHS, significant gestural units (and thus, if you like, comparable to monemes, and at any rate definable as KINESIC SIGNS), may be broken down into KINESIC FIGURES, and thus into KINES, discrete portions of the cinemorphs that are not portions of their signified (in the sense that all these little units of movement, without any sense, can make up various units of gesture that have sense).

The cine-camera would then make it possible to accomplish, in the field of the gesture, what kinesics could not: the identification of discrete fragments within the continuum of gesture or action. Eco in fact writes that the camera "...ACCURATELY BREAKS DOWN THE CINEMORPHS INTO A LARGE NUMBER OF DISCRETE UNITS THAT CANNOT YET SIGNIFY ANYTHING BY THEMSELVES, and that have a differential value with respect to other discrete units". At the level of the frame it would, that is, be possible to individuate the kinesic figurae, devoid of meaning, which combining among themselves would give rise to the kinesic signs which, in turn, would produce, in combination, syntagms "that one might continue to add up ad infinitum".

In a study of the type of perception that marks out the phenomenon of the film, a hypothesis of this type could prove entirely useless; the spectator at the cinema is never in a position to make out kinesic figures on the screen. On the contrary, the dynamic illusion of the medium consists precisely in obliterating from the visual memory of the perceptor every sensation of the frame's static nature by recourse to the shutter. From the point of view of an analytic methodology, on the other hand, Eco's observations would seem just and worthy of speculative development; on the level of the search for a greater ambiguity for the cinematographic message (and thus of its poetic value) they could furthermore orient the theoretical foundations of new operative procedures: for example, in the field of animated cartoons, photographic animations, and, in general, all those operations that must and may be undertaken synchronically, frame by frame. In this instance (which has been considered a number of times in the course of the cinema's development) the cinematic work does not base its recreative fiction upon the illusion of a 'real' movement like that of the reality that surrounds the spectator in everyday life, but on the illusion of new kinematisms, that have been invented and semantically oriented. The entry of kinesics into the film's semiological ambit (and, at the same time, the help that the cinema could give to this scientific

---

[151] Eco (1967a), 145 et seg.

discipline) would finally involve the possibility of parallel studies between the universe of the film and that of the gesture, with a consequent
adaption of the art of gesture to photographic contingency – this would
be a matter of singling out the roots and the expressive modes of an indefinite series of acts, gestures, and types of behaviour which, on film,
would undergo a notable semantic differentiation with respect to their
primitive and direct orientation.

I have already attempted to define the types of gesture consistent with
the characteristics of projection onto a screen, in this case above all the
television screen, in a previous essay, to which I would refer the reader on
this point.[152] The spatial-temporal expression of an interior movement or
of the desire to stimulate the receiver into relationship acquires on the
cinema screen an autonomous form, which an analysis by means of
frames allows one to individuate in all its parts. The conditioning that an
actor in a film or on television undergoes on account of the lack of any
direct appreciation of his performance can then be studied, understood,
and overcome – in short, the actor himself can absorb it into the poetic
dimension of his character (and the process can be further aided by the
cutting, as we shall see further on).

In the opening scene of *Les enfants du paradis* by Marcel Carné, Jean-
Louis Barrault as Baptiste performs a gestural study of exceptional
brilliance when he reproduces, by means of gestures and attitudes alone,
the scene of a theft that he has unintentionally witnessed;[153] in this case it
is simply a matter of transposing onto film a gestural exhibition, so that
the cinematographic instrument is reduced to the level of a faithful and
passive transcriber and does not intervene to expressively modify the
original reality. But on the other hand, in the scenes of the protagonist's
erotic relations with her husband and her lover from Jean-Luc Godard's
Une femme mariée, the presence of the medium makes itself felt with considerable expressive relevance. In fact, the cutting of the various shots
creates autonomous relationships and a fictitious reality that is almost independent of the one that gave birth to the images; furthermore, the very
gestures of the actors conform to the expressive ends imposed upon them
by the director and, hieratically unreal, incredible in their fragmentariness,
lend themselves to the formation of a poetic universe that is real and

---

[152]   Bettetini (1965), 100 et seg.
[153]   The film, written by Jaques Prévert, was begun on 16 August, 1943, and, interrupted by the war in September and October, was resumed on 9 November. The public
first saw it on 15 March, 1945. Apart from Barrault, one should note other performers
such as Arletty, Pierre Brasseur, Maria Casares, Etienne Decroux, etc. (see *L'Avant-
Scène-Cinéma* 72-73 [July-September 1967]).

completely credible, but absolutely unrepeatable and not even remotely comparable to the objective one that gave life to them.[154]

So a semiology of the film cannot leave out of consideration the technical instruments that deform and recreate physical reality, nor less the cutting, whatever the expressive value that one wishes to attribute to it may be. The cinematographic 'figure', the portion of a gesture caught in its static fixity, will be capable of constituting the ultimate analytical level of cinematographic interpretation. But when problems of signification are involved, the work of investigation will always have to be oriented around the level of the large-scale narrative units. Their composition will also have to be analyzed down to the finest material detail (and in the following chapters we shall try to single out the direction that this research must take), but it does not for the moment seem apposite to postulate any serious possibility of semantic structuring at the level of the compositive elements. At some further point one will be able to move on from the individuation and study of large-scale units to a true structural analysis of cinematographic works, considered in their expressive entirety. One will, that is, be able to turn back to the type of study that postulates the search for the discourse's language and the narration's code – in short, for a Rhetoric of the film.[155] At this level, the points of contact between research on films and analysis of collateral phenomena in the ambit of verbal communication are in greater evidence than they are on the levels of elementary units or large-scale narrative units. Indeed, for Roland Barthes the discourse appears as a message belonging to another *langue*, on a higher level than the *langue* of the linguists: "...le discours a ses unités, ses règles, sa 'grammaire': au-delà de la phrase et quoique composé uniquement de phrases, le discours doit être naturellement l'objet d'une seconde linguistique".[156]

Since traditional linguistics halts at the sentence, which it considers as the last of its speculative interests (beyond the sentence, says Barthes, there are only other sentences), it may be that within the perspective of a higher-level linguistics, that carries through its scientific task upon the level of 'large-scale sentences', the possibility would come to light of a semiotics that is able to transcend the nature of the signs by which the message is represented, in order to trace out a systematization (and thus a codification) whose lines of signification are indifferent to the signifiers

[154] The film dates from 1964. The principle actors are Macha Méril, Phililpe Leroy, and Bernard Noël.
[155] Barthes "Introduction à l'analyse structurale des récits", *Communications* 8 (Paris, 1966b), 3.
[156] Barthes (1966b), 3.

used. This is an argument that brings us back to the work of A. J. Greimas, when, in order to maintain the utilitarian and intellectual predominance of linguistic description over other types, such as the symbolical-
mythological for example, he asserts that it does not matter whether the
signifier is composed of NATURAL objects or combinations of phonemes or
graphemes, as far as analysing the signification is concerned.

La grande supériorité du plan linguistique provient du fait que tout autre
langage – et, par conséquent, celui des OBJETS SYMBOLIQUES – peut être traduit
dans une langue naturelle quelconque, mais que l'invers n'est pas toujours vrai:
on ne voit pas comment un poème de Mallarmé pourrait être traduit dans un
LANGUE DES CHOSES.[157]

I cannot pretend to entirely agree with Greimas's formulation, much as I
admire the scientific character of his attempt to rationalize any communicative phenomenon – is it really true, in fact, that every language may be
translated into any natural *langue*? Any attempt at translation involves an
analysis in depth, and runs the risk of considerable semic losses, or of
limiting the work to a single level of signification. An analysis of the
contents of a work for cinema or television could perhaps be considered
as a translation into the forms of verbal language, but it would be a
partial and incomplete means as far as a full grasp of the work were
concerned.

But above and beyond any agreement with what Greimas and Barthes
propose, there remains the possibility of making use of forms of research
that are common to both the verbal and the audio-visual languages within
the ambit of narrative structures. It is a working hypothesis that ought to
give rise to highly articulated research on an experimental level.

A consideration of the large-scale units of cinematographic analysis
will always imply that the verbal commentary has a metalinguistic function, aimed as it is at the deciphering and naming of the senses attributable
to the work. Returning once more to Greimas, we shall thus be able to
define this approach on the part of language as "condensation" (the
corollary of the discourse's other mode of metalinguistic functioning –
expansion; one may develop both of them in the course of studying a
film); it is a matter of "...une sorte de décodage compressif des messages
en expansion" which in most instances arrives at a DENOMINATION (while
expansion frequently arrives at a DEFINITION – a typical example of condensation is the crossword puzzle, while that of expansion might be the
ideation and composition of such a puzzle).[158] Now, in the case of verbal

[157] Greimas (1966a), 59.
[158] Greimas (1966a), 72-77.

language the metalinguistic function of the discourse is homogeneous and autonomous; in the case of the cinematographic language it is indirect and mediated. Which is to say that the basic problem of the relationship between language and cinema, that difference in semantic values that we have seen to place a notable distance between the two universes of communication, will always turn up again. However, on the level of the fundamental codifications and on the level of narrative structures it is perhaps possible to risk establishing analogical relationships (with all the dangers that this involves) which are more effective and useful than they would be in the ambit of elementary signs. But the path that leads to those problems is as yet a long and difficult one. For the moment we shall begin with an analysis of the technico-grammatical elements of the film, considering them within a perspective that is adapted, as far as possible, to their heterogeneous and contingent nature.

2

FOR A THEORY OF FILM MAKING

SUBJECTIVE INTERVENTION IN THE REPRODUCTIVE PROCESS

In his essay "Cinema and Reality", published in a collection of essays with the significant title *Film as Art*, Rudolph Arnheim writes that

...people who contemptuously refer to the camera as an automatic recording machine must be made to realize that even in the simplest photographic repro-duction of a perfectly simple object, a feeling for its nature is required which is quite beyond any mechanical operation.[1]

In a later essay, "How a Film is Made", the same author writes that

... as distinguished from the tools of the sculptor and the painter, which by themselves produce nothing resembling nature, the camera starts to turn and a likeness of the real world results mechanically.... In order that the film artist may create a work of art, it is important that he consciously stress the peculiarities of his medium. This, however, should be done in such a manner that the charac-ter of the objects represented should not thereby be destroyed, but rather strengthened, concentrated, and interpreted.[2]

If the cinema offered no possibility of transcending an automatic repro-duction of reality, the communicative effectiveness of the medium would be reduced to the praxis of a passive reproductivity and its function on the level of signs could be easily contained within the limits of a straightfor-ward list of possible cases, halfway between the theory of a new mode of expression and the conception of a new method of investigation.[3] The

[1]   Rudolph Arnheim, *Film as Art* (London, Faber and Faber, 1958), 19.
[2]   Arnheim (1958), 38.
[3]   It would seem somewhat difficult to realize the hypothesis put forward by Antonio Pagliaro as to the rational perfectability of cinematographic language. "Naturally by way of hypothesis – indeed utopian dream – one may imagine that, granted the tend-ency of the human mind to abstraction and symbol, even the language of images could one day become formal, and elevate itself to the level of an instrument combining the advantages of abstract rationality with those of intuition. A process analogous to the one that opened up with ideographic writing could come about here, but on a far vaster

cinema is all this, and a great deal more; it is capable of expressing itself in documentary language, but may at the same time be adapted to the approach of any interpreter or author, offering to every type of poetic intention the widest possibilities for visual formation.

Even in cases of the strictest objectivization, where the film transmits historical, environmental, or sociological analyses of the most impersonal type, the cinematographic language is at the mercy of those who use it; if the director tries to make his approach to the work impersonal, so as to disappear behind the objective image of reality that he is trying to form, his choice and the way in which it is expressed, even when this assumes the detached qualities of a piece of evidence, are the paths by which his directive intentionality, his creative sensibility, and his cultural relations with men and with the world – in other words, his whole personality – are brought into evidence.

Cinematographic narration cannot hide the narrator and, although being a work dedicated to a certain topic, developing a certain theme in a certain manner, it is fundamentally the work of a man (or of a group of men) who expresses himself in its images.

This paradox is the fundamental aesthetic principle ruling the life of the cinema – the cinematographic narrative stems from the figurative contribution of an instrument that photographs nature; the signs of the cinema have at their roots a deep-seated *raison d'être*, that places them among the phenomena of a reproductive and generally mimetic order; and yet the man directing the film consciously intervenes so as to mould it according to his poetical ideation, by means of a continuous process of choice.

The document offered by an edited film is not so much the impartial description of an event or a phenomenon as the expression of an interpretive act on the part of the subject who directed the film – even when televising events directly, so that the image is perceived by the spectator at the moment in which the reality that it reproduces is taking place, the personality of the producer intervenes, imposing his own viewpoint (the

---

scale in relation to the incalculable possibilities of the technical medium. By such a means, the creation of a universal language, which was the dream of many great intellectuals, foremost among them Leibniz, would at last find the possibility of a complete and grandiose realization. Anyone can see the decidedly utopian element in such a hypothesis, which presupposes the possibility of even the abstract becoming visible; in other words, the possiblity of the image becoming an emblem, of it almost reestablishing the form of language that Giambattista Vico postulated as 'the second speech, which corresponds to the age of the heroes'" (Pagliaro, *La parola e l'immagine* [Napoli, Ediz. Scientifiche Italiane, 1957], 132).

positioning of the various television cameras), a certain, variable distance from objects (the choosing of lenses), and, above all, a particular selection of images and a rhythmic succession that are solely conditioned by his sensibility and by the way in which his interpretive personality approaches what he is narrating, in synchrony with the actual occurrence of the event.

The television producer concerned with a direct transmission may indeed give a personal interpretation to the reality that he is investigating, distorting its development and its basic elements; he need only insist upon certain negligible particulars and fail to make evident other more fundamental elements, for example, in order to entirely reverse the values objectively present, and to create an artifice in the illusory play of images.[4]

The essential aspect of the cinema and television is represented by the fact that the sign elements making up their communicative acts are IMAGES, which exist in a reality entirely different from that of the world they represent. One can never find oneself confronted by a part of the object, or by the object itself; instead, one is always faced with one of its signs, which the sensibility of the author will know how to realize in the form best suited to the expression that he is aiming for.

The act of interpretation comes up against an image-reality, whose reproductive nature will, in most cases, escape the analysis of the spectator; the universe of the film may appear to hold together of itself, but it will always be the result of a spatio-temporal fiction. The cinema and the television find both their vitality and their justification in the fact that their expressive structure consists of an organization of images which, irrespective of their relation to reality, always remain images, spectres of the external world, appearances, impalpable entities whose nature is entirely different from that of the object that they reproduce or represent.

The effectiveness of these media as spectacle lies in the illusion that their activity creates in the mind of the spectator – an illusion of similarity and an illusion of movement, both of them controlled by the skill of the author.

THE ILLUSION OF SIMILARITY

On the screen everything is fictitious: the figures that move there are the result of the reflection of a cone of light, whose rays are weakened or coloured in various gradations while passing through a film, or, in the case of television, the photonic stimulation caused by the monotonous to-and-fro of an electron beam.

[4] Bettetini (1965), 27 et seg.

THE PRIMARY ILLUSION CREATED BY THE CINEMA IS THAT OF SIMILARITY TO THE REALITY THAT IT REPRESENTS, a similarity that comes about in spite of all the differences between viewing reality and viewing a cinematic phantasm, and in spite of the fictitious character of the image. Arnheim says:

Many people who are accustomed to clear thinking will feel that... [the] theory of 'partial illusion' is vague.... Is not the very essence of illusion that it should be complete? ...According to an outdated psychology that is still deeply rooted in popular thought, an illusion can be strong only if it is complete in every detail. But everyone knows that a clumsy childish scribble of a human face consisting of two dots, a comma, and a dash may be full of expression and depict anger, amusement, or fear. The impression is strong, though the representation is far from complete. The reason it suffices is that in real life we by no means grasp every detail.... Hence if these essentials are reproduced we are content and obtain a complete impression that is all the stronger for being artificially – artistically concentrated.[5]

The author of a film makes use of the technical means available to him to create moving images, and thus creates the most extraordinary illusion ever arrived at by man's activity in the field of signs and, generally, of representation by means of images. Paradoxically, the man of the cinematographic civilization makes use of precisely those elements that in themselves constitute a dividing-line between the world of phenomena and the world of appearances as his vehicles of expression; he is capable of elevating such limitations to the level of an instrument and of creating for himself an expressive formula capable of giving birth to the most suggestive illusions of similarity, despite the fact that they stem from the very material that stands barring the fundamental path between the object represented and its representation on the screen.

If the cinematographic author were not able to have recourse, in his work, to an image chosen from a particular angle, using a particular style of shot, a certain tone of lighting, an appropriate sound commentary, in fact all those elements which, considered by themselves, reduce the relation between reality and image to a phenomenon of incomplete reproduction, he would not in any way be able to intervene in the composition of the film and his action would be reduced to a chilling and useless exercise in repetition. In the first place, the film director finds himself in the presence of a certain reality that is destined to be reduced to a visual image, granted the aid of a film camera. This point of departure involves, above all, the choice of a certain portion of reality to film, since the human eye may unlimitedly explore a variety of details or may take in the most ex-

[5] Arnheim (1958), 33.

tended of groupings, while the camera lens must perforce limit itself to
the width of angle that its optical apparatus allows it. So that before
pressing the shutter of the film camera, the director must choose that part
of reality that he is concerned to translate into images and foresee the
actual limits of the framework within which the projection will take its
place. In short he must, by virtue of his imaginative capacity, succeed in
grasping those aspects of the objects around him that are best adapted to
the formation on a two-dimensional surface of the poetic phantasma that
has been maturing within him.

In this strange transposition of reality and its elements onto celluloid
the director must bear in mind all the distortions to which the objects
will be subjected during the process of projection; he must bear in mind,
that is, all those optico-geometric limitations that constitute some of the
film's most important instruments of expression.

The first thing with which the director must concern himself, after
establishing the projective area within which the shot will be taken, is the
position in relation to one another and to the camera of the plastic
elements, objects, and actors that make up the reality to be filmed. The
arrangement of all these potential components of the image is a particularly delicate operation, because it must always be undertaken with projection onto a flat surface in mind, and therefore be guided by a criterion
that has nothing to do with a hypothetical three-dimensional arrangement.

For example, one object that appears beyond another, observing its
position on a table, may completely disappear when projected on film, or
may equally appear in a completely different form.

Another element that clearly distinguishes reality from its projected
image is to be found, as Arnheim points out, in the fact that once the action has been reduced to a two-dimensional extension, the two fundamental properties that govern the direct relation between the human eye
and objective reality – constancy of dimension and constancy of form –
lose their *raison d'etre*.

Physically, the image thrown onto the retina of the eye by any object in the field
of vision diminishes in proportion to the square of the distance.... Hence in a
photograph of someone sitting with his feet stretched out far in front of him the
subject comes out with enormous feet and much too small a head. Curiously
enough, however, we do not in real life get impressions to accord with the
images on the retina.... It is the same with constancy of shape. The retinal image
of a table top is like the photograph of it; the front edge, being nearer to the
spectator, appears much wider than the back; the rectangular surface becomes
trapezoid in the image. As far as the average person is concerned, however, this

again does not hold good in practice: he SEES the suface as rectangular and draws it that way too.... That is what is meant by constancy of form.[6]

Bringing the object nearer to the camera involves a considerable increase in the dimensions of its projected image, at whatever distance the virtual plane on which this image is formed may be; the virtual plane, which is determined in the optical relation by the focal length of the lens, will then coincide, during the projection of the film, with the plane of the screen.[7]

THE LIGHTING

To these technical elements which condition all phases of projection one must add another, of decisive importance as concerns the expressive power of the image – the distribution of light in the surroundings. One could say that the technical ability and the expressive effectiveness of a director's or of a camera-man's work is revealed above all in the lighting. Even those theoreticians who are most strongly inclined to recognize in the cutting the structural substance of the film must, to some extent, agree as to the primary importance, regarding meaning, of providing the amount of light best suited to the expressive act that one wishes to accomplish.

In a black and white film, the tonality of the various greys that make up the image may always be reduced to a choice on the director's part as to the distribution of light. The placing of the various light sources, their individual intensity, the possible combinations of their effects, the direction of reflecting surfaces, the corrections that may be made with shields or masks, are all extremely effective instruments in the hands of someone who knows how to use them properly.

One cannot establish norms that have a universal validity with regard to lighting; but, this being a problem of taste and of aesthetic conception, they will be brought into being in each individual case according to the personality of whoever is responsible for the film. The director and the cameraman may make use of various instruments, which are intended to

---

[6]   Arnheim (1958), 20-21.
[7]   According to Kurt Koffka, it is quite mistaken to suppose that visual space is two-dimensional. "Since the retina is two-dimensional (on its surface), it would seem that visual space must also be two-dimensional. It is quite wrong to suppose this, since the retina is only the outer edge of the entire optical sector of the brain, which is three-dimensional, and the forces excited within this linear surface determine a process which is extended along the whole three-dimensional sector" (Koffka, *Die psychische Entwicklung des Kindes*, 1921).

produce their relative results on the level of projection – corrective and generally formative intervention may in fact go well beyond adjusting the light source and may indeed be directed towards the objects to be illuminated, the elements whose images are intended as components of the shot. Their position relative to one another, and to the lighting plant, their colour, or rather the type of average chromatic density displayed by their surfaces, do in fact make possible a free play of combinations, which should prove particularly stimulating to whomever is responsible for making the film.

In a black and white film, a red colour may appear much darker in relation to its environment than it would in reality, while a yellow colour may appear a lot lighter – which means that the colours of the objects and of all the elements that make up the shot have a fundamental value even in films of this type. Thus the function of colour does not possess an absolute expressive aim, but is linked bi-uniquely to the relation between the various colours that appear in the fraction of reality that is intended for filming – this chromatic relation is then translated, in projection, into a relation between tonalities of grey. The combined results of the distribution of light sources and their respective intensities, the relative position of all the objects that are to appear in the frame and their colours produce the luminous quality of the scene intended for filming; the tonalities and the luminous effects of the image on film are however subject to other technical factors: the optical characteristics of the lens and of the saline solution that covers the sensitive strip of the celluloid band inside the film-camera.

Thus the director, when he has fully mastered the expressive techniques available to him, may obtain an average tonality of luminosity and a complex of effects that should be entirely adequate for his creative needs; he will arrive at this by means of an intelligent mixing of different elements, whose relative proportions are only subject to the general form of realization.

Some of the operative details that we have briefly reviewed allow one to arrive at apparently identical results, if they are used in a certain way: for example, a shading off of outlines may be obtained with equal ease by opening the diaphragm or by placing the correct quantity of light behind the person or objects that occupy the camera's field; in the same way, a sudden increase in luminous intensity on a surface or, in general, on an object could be achieved by concentrating on it a greater quantity of light (and thus by moving the light source or adding another one) or by moving the surface itself until it is in a position to receive more light.

As may be deduced from these two trivial examples, the equality of the results is only apparent, and may at best be put into effect on a theoretical level; in the reality of a 'reproduced' image one will always note some differences, maybe imperceptible to the rough glance of quantitative analysis, but very important from the aesthetic point of view and decisive in regard to the expressive utility of the image. In this case as well, the rules of selection are established by the taste of those realizing the work.

A further limiting condition, as restrictive as all the others that may be placed within expressive limits, is constituted by the fundamental nature of the cinematic spectacle, which is always structured on the basis of two-dimensional images. Even taking into account the presence of an optical system differing from that of the human eye, and the reproductive quality of a photographic film, one could all the same liken the techniques of cinematographic lighting to those of theatrical lighting, were one able to situate the images of a film in a three-dimensional space. Since in reality this is not the case, stage-lighting conforms to norms that are entirely independent of those that concern the film director; he, in fact, being forced to imagine the section of reality in front of him as squashed up and with all its depth compressed onto one plane, has to anticipate a distribution of light which, once it has been projected onto that plane, will enjoy the characteristics of a *sfumato* or a juxtaposition of pictorial masses, rather than those of spatial diffusion over objects in depth.

Light has, among its physical effects, the basic characteristic of three-dimensional continuity; this continuity is interrupted by the presence of opaque bodies, which reflect the light striking them, and are thus made visible to the observer. Transposing a corporal reality onto the screen involves the projection onto a two-dimensional surface of the entire space related to the phenomenon, of all the three-dimensional forms within it, and thus the virtual form constituted by the interrupted continuum of the light as well – the result of the work of lighting on the screen or frame is simply the result of the geometric projection of a luminous projection. The latter, real one is flattened according to the rules of the former and assumes an aspect that is the fictitious image of the three-dimensional one, but which can in turn take on a sign value entirely detached from any relation with the reality represented, precisely by virtue of its being projected onto a plane.

One could indeed assert that the form of the image in the frame and on the screen is entirely made up of masses of light that co-exist in a relationship ruled by the director's intentions. The hypothesis is exceedingly stimulating, above all because it would confer upon that fictitious sign, the cinematographic image, a nature very close to that of light, which generates it, and which is only apparently corporeal. To an element that is impalpable in its form and in its dimensions would thus come to correspond, in one of its realizations as sign, an element that is equally immaterial, and may be perceived in visual form alone. From a technical point of view, the hypothesis is fully confirmed by the fact that the image projected onto the screen is simply the result of a series of optical operations, in which light is always the protagonist, either actively, as in the impression left on the film, or passively, as in the final operation that carries the sign from the film onto the surface of the screen.

The cinema may therefore be considered as a vehicle for signs of considerable expressive effectiveness, which draws its strength from its own illusion of similarity and thus of representation, not to speak of its free recreation, its combination of luminous masses, and its appropriately directed and selected play of light. Light is thus the fundamental constitutive element of the cinematographic image.

THE ACTOR

The presence of actors in the film has caused some of the biggest misunderstandings in the history of the cinema and has, at the same time, made possible some of its most remarkable aesthetic and linguistic advances. When the cinema had not yet discovered its own individuality, and limited its reproductive activity to a meager and rigid documentation of reality (but within limits that notably reduce the faithfulness of the cinematographic image to the phenomena and the objects fixed on film), the first attempts to involve the new medium in some form of communal entertainment were reduced to a simple transposition onto the screen of pre-existing types of spectacle, particularly those of the theatre.

The cinema's part in this hybrid and useless match was negligible and, above all, did not succeed in imposing a rhythm of its own upon the communicative formula that was being established with the public. The theatre was shifted onto film without any attempt at reduction or adaption; since the camera was fixed, without any possibility of movement, in the middle of the hypothetical audience that would have been seated in front of the proscenium had the action been taking place on stage instead of in a studio, the spectator seated in the cinema had the impression of being in front of a stage – no more, no less.

The limits of the frame coincided with the rigid and constrictive limit of its visual potential; the action always took place at the same distance, at the same angulation, and with the environment always retaining the same dimensional proportions in relation to the cinematographic frame. Since it was a matter of reproducing photographically a theatrical spectacle, the actors who first came to grips with the problems of the cinema came directly from the theatre, where they had already played the parts that they were now playing in front of the film camera. The subjection of cinema to theatre was fatal as far as the production of those years was concerned, and is useful only as a witness to the inefficiency of so empirical and unjustified a method. The failure of that attempt did not, however, stop people from falling into the same, and perhaps a worse trap when the appearance of sound put into question all the aesthetic and technical results of the previous period.

When the theatrical actor was performing in front of the camera, he made no attempt to adjust his expressive techniques to the needs of the cinema; nor indeed was it thinkable that he should have done so, seeing that no-one had yet ventured to clarify the fundamental aspects of the new language. The actor performed Hamlet in the studio as he would do so that evening on stage, perhaps reducing his interpretative enthusiasm on account of the lack of direct relations with the public, and of the consequent break in the interior and unpredictable dialogue that establishes itself between stage and auditorium, that mysterious dialogue which the theatrical actor knows so well, fearing it and hoping for it at the same time.

But even if the basic characteristics of the cinematographic medium had been reduced to a flat and impersonal reproduction of a real event, and therefore of a theatrical spectacle as was then the case, the techniques of theatrical acting ought never to have intefered with the behaviour of cinematographic actors, if only because of the lack of a third dimension that stands at the heart of the process of film-making. In an essay on figurative form in the film, the Russian director M. Ciaureli justly writes that

... in the theatre, despite the conventional nature of the scenery, real live people – the actors – move and act in a real three-dimensional environment. The final result of a cinematographic realization is, instead, the film on which are imprinted the reproductions of men and of objects; these, although arranged in perspective, are in the last analysis fixed on a flat surface. They are photographed in such a succession that, reproduced on screen, they seem to move, but always within the limits of a flat surface.[8]

[8] M. Ciaureli, "Della forma figurativa del film", in *Il mestiere di regista*, which presents essays by Gherassimov, Ciaureli, Pudovkin, Raisman, Roscial, Borissov: trans. P. Zvetermich (Milano-Roma, Bocca, 1954), 94.

Ciaureli's words refer to the chromatic composition of the shot rather than to the task of the actor; but their value remains the same in both cases. Indeed, one might claim that the adaption of any means that contributes to the composition of a cinematographic image, according to the synthetic canons of this new language, cannot be done without considering the two-dimensional element that the Russian director considers to be so important. In itself, the screen already involves a deformation of objects and movements so evident as to discourage any attempt at a straightforward and gratuitous transposition of theatrical modes of acting into the field of cinematic realization. (If the area of projection grows bigger, so do the figures – since the durations of the film maintain themselves constant with and identical to those of reality; being determined by the film's speed of rotation which is constant, the internal movement of the images will undergo an acceleration proportional to the expansion in the screen's dimensions.)

The myth of applying theatrical acting to the cinema was rapidly destroyed when a few true artists of the language of images discovered how to confer upon the film its own very personal aspect, and with the introduction of cutting, camera movements, and the use of differing lenses, they were able to create the forms of a new means of narration, disconcerting in its very modern powers of suggestion.

When the works of David Wark Griffith, Sergei Eisenstein, and Charlie Chaplin appeared, indicating the possibilities and the values of a new visual syntax, the work of the actor in the cinema was brought within the limits of providing an integral contribution to the cinematographic discourse. On the screen stands not an actor, but his image, which is a great deal freer from the somatic and psychological characteristics of the character represented than would be the most perfect interpretation on stage, no matter how accurately it realized Stanislavsky's ideology of total identification with the character or the paradigm of the actor as critic of the character established by Diderot and popularized by Brecht.

Whatever happens in the film, it is always the shadow of the actor moving in a world of appearances. If the presence of the actor on the screen is reduced to a two-dimensional representation, then his physical presence will conform to the same limiting rules to which we have seen the reproduction of inanimate objects to be subject; his image, that is, will come to make up a part of a composition organized with a view to projection.

The succession of sudden moves nearer to and further away from the observed reality that constitute the basis of cutting necessitate that breaking up of the acting, so typical of the process of filming, which constitutes the basic division between the world of the theatre and that of the film. The film actor is at the mercy of a highly complicated routine, entirely alien to him, within which he can find a place by humbly accepting the rules imposed upon him; in the cinema, an actor must only work in relation to the image that his action leaves imprinted on the film. This image will be endowed with an expressive value that complements that of the entire film, with respect to which the actor must employ all his interpretive capacities. The actor ends up by being an instrument in the hands of the director, and the more flexible he is, the more useful he will be. An exceptional instrument, naturally, because he is capable of a life of his own, and of seeking to adapt himself to circumstances, capable of transferring to the cinematographic image of his action those personal gifts best adapted to conferring an effective form upon the ideas that have inspired the work.

Even in the case of a director concerning himself more with the truthfulness of his actors' behaviour than with their interpretive effectiveness (in the case, that is, of an actor finding himself completely free in regard to his interpretation), the actor's image would be subordinate to the choices in cutting made by the director. At a limit, even when the director reduces the scene to one continuous shot (see below), appreciation of the actor's interpretation will always be mediated by the image, which selects it, characterizes it, and finalizes it. No element of technical recreation or free cinematographic distortion is inserted into the dialogue in the train between the protagonist, Anna Wiazemsky, and Francis Jeanson in Jean-Luc Godard's *La Chinoise*. Yet the meaning of the scene may none the less be traced to the predisposition of the two speakers and their environment to the action of the film-camera, and to the positioning of the scene itself within the diegesis of the work (to the relations established with what precedes and follows it by the process of cutting).[9]

The flattening of the actor's figure, projected onto a plane, and the breaking up of his performance caused by the demands of scenario and cutting are the principal elements of a technical type that mark out the work of the film actor, isolating him and personalizing him in the most concrete of forms; but there exist fundamental motives that are perhaps even more valid than those given above, and are capable of conditioning a whole new orientation within the search for an effective principle of

[9] Regarding this dialogue, see also Godard's remarks in "Lutter sur deux fronts", propos recueillis par Jacques Bontemps, Jean-Louis Comolli, Michel Delahaye et Jean Narboni: *Cahiers du cinéma* 194 (Octobre 1967).

interpretation. The theatre is basically structured upon the function of the word within the drama; the principal sign that reaches the spectator from the stage is a verbal one, supplemented by visual elements that can even disturb the effectiveness and clarity of the communication, if used inopportunely or in excess. When the drama derives its existence from the juxtaposition of forces and characteristics engaged in an action that constitutes its back-bone, the action itself is developed in conformity with the fundamental outlines assigned to it by the word, drawing its life from the dialectical play of the parts. Dramatic action demands a suitable verbal language, capable of conditioning its rhythm or of adapting itself to it, and derived from the same cultural sources that inspire the poetic and social atmosphere within which the work is created. Greek tragedy, in which the conflict that determines the course of the action finds effective symbolic concentration in the men and the gods and blends into the immense struggle of the earth against the dark forces of the universe, demands an aulic and poetically cadenced language, capable of revealing the elevated level of the values at stake.

On the other hand the baroque tragedy, which came into existence to celebrate the triumph of reason in an epoch of illuministic culture, found the verbal means best adapted to its expressive forms in conceptual language; it defined, as Francis Fergusson notes in a penetrating study on the evolution of conceptions of the theatre throughout the ages,

... a dramatic medium natural to reason: that of word and concept. For this reason, the classic French style of acting, capable of great subtlety within its narrow range, tends to identify acting with recitation. The action Racine is conveying generates, as it were automatically, the Alexandrines in which the tragedy is audible and understandable to us; and through his logical and musical verse Racine controls the actor's performance as completely as Wagner does through the musical score.[10]

Shakespeare's theatrical works, so varied and incoherent in their aesthetic and, more generally, cultural concerns, derive their vitality from the forms of a verbal language that is able, when necessary, to orient itself towards the most spontaneous of common expressions, or the most delicate inventions of poetical metaphor. But the Elizabethan and Shakespearean theatre already brings us to the consideration of works that, unlike the Aristotelian imitation of action, develop by virtue of an analogical relation with it. The verbal language of the characters, which constitutes the heart and soul of this relation, has a more common, simple, and familiar basis because the dramatic action is more human, more normal, and

[10]   Francis Fergusson, *The Idea of a Theater* (Princeton Univ. Press, 1949), 53.

above all is constructed upon a less direct symbolic basis; the elements of
the imitation are not, in this case, those of a likeness, but depend upon a
reciprocal inequality, at the heart of which they take on the atmosphere
created by "...une certaine unité".[11]

The theatrical spectacle has always been constructed around the word
and has always developed the terms of its action in the form of a verbal
dialectic, so much so that, as a direct result, variations of a linguistic
order within the form of the work have come to correspond to the
ideological and cultural variations in the concept of the drama throughout
the ages. The theatrical actor is thus made to give the utmost attention to
his technical preparation on the level of speech and diction, and to subordinate to a verbal phenomenology all of his gestural behaviour and all
of the mimic elements that make up his interpretive action on stage.

Rudolph Arnheim writes:

The theatre depends on the spoken word.... Perhaps the point has never been
made explicitly how unnatural, how stylized all stage art is because the actors
never stop talking. Every action is overlaid and clothed with words. Even in the
first outline, every scene is so planned that the plot shall be unfolded by un-
ceasing conversation. Indeed, every preponderance of mere action over the
spoken word is regarded as a defect. The spoken word, the most important
distinguishing trait of the drama, has developed into a medium of radical
purity during the evolution of the art through thousands of years. That this
method of presenting an event is not a matter of course will be clearly realized
only after seeing from a good silent film how the action proceeds quite easily
without any use of words at all.[12]

The theatrical spectacle is, furthermore, autonomous, unrepeatable, and
absolutely valid in itself; even in cases of strict fidelity to the canons of a
universally binding production, it would be distinctly difficult to make
out automatic repetitions within the execution of different performances
of the same work. The theatrical spectacle is an act of communion between a dramatic proposition, put into effect in a space and time common
to actors and spectators, and a direct reception – an act of public communion which involves the total attention of each transmitter and each
receiver, an interplay of receptive exchanges that takes place in a precisely
determined place, in the presence of people who are aware of its rules and

[11] This is from the second part of a general definition of Analogy given by Padre
Penido in his *De l'Analogie*. Fergusson quotes it as follows, when discussing the analogical relation between drama and action: "D'une manière très général, toute analogie
suppose deux conditions ontologiques: 1° une pluralité réelle d'être, et donc entre ces
êtres une diversité essentielle. Le Monisme est l'ennemi né de l'Analogie; 2° au sein de
cette multiplicité, de cette inégalité, une certaine unité" (Fergusson [1949], 234).
[12] Arnheim (1958), 76.

in basic agreement as to the laws governing its development. It is precisely this implicit and indispensable agreement (which may be analogically related to the act of faith that induces in the believer a complete acceptance of the liturgical act) that allows the actors and the producer to embody, in a physically determined environment adjacent to that of the auditorium, in a temporal dimension coincident with the spectators', a theatrical fiction whose universe may go far beyond the real conditions that give birth to it. The theatrical spectator, well aware of the dramatic character of the manifestation at which he is present, voluntarily disposes himself to an attitude of imaginative integration with regard to the magical propositions that come to him from the stage and thus initiates, along with the actors, a series of mysterious and lively communicative exchanges which occur in both directions, between stage and auditorium, during the course of a performance.

The theatrical public is collective and implies a local presence among those attending a theatrical event. The reaction of the public to the drama is choral and, even in the discrepancies of its heterogeneous formation, it is induced by a field of accumulative forces that are susceptible to definition in their reciprocal encounter. For Jean Vilar, the perfect theatrical game requires a public that believes in something to a man;[13] and although the expression may appear exaggerated these days, it is all the same useful to emphasize the necessary presence of a common link between the spectators in order that the performance may have a sense. This mutual understanding will perhaps be nothing more than the simple acceptance of a socially conventional act or admiration for a certain author or, in extreme cases, a desire for entertainment and relaxation, but in every case the buying of a ticket and the occupying of a seat imply entering into a clearly defined choral situation that is ready to establish a dialogue with the stage. When instead one is concerned with a cinema audience, the absolute, unique, and unrepeatable qualities of the realization disappear, as does the physical presence of the public at the scene of the dramatic action, and the spectator's integration of what he perceives, the potentially collective appreciation, and hence the necessary agreement on fundamentals among the audience are all structured in a very different way.

The film actor cannot use words and dialogue as the principal points of reference for his interpretive action, which will come to make up a part of a complex image that, of whatever type the complementary elements that define it may be, tends not to prescind from its visual character, even when the sonic element has greater weight. The image of the action that appears

[13]   Pierre-Henri Simon, *Théâtre et Destin* (Paris, Librairie Armand Collet, 1959),17.

within the complex of the finished work is the result of a synthesis on the director's part, joining to the images of objects those of the actor – the image of his face, his movements, his voice, or a dubbed voice. Even in the exceptional case of an actor shooting all the scenes in which his character is involved without the aid of any stand-in in the reverse shots and long shots, and using his own voice, recorded at the same time as the take, without recourse to dubbing, the human figure that appeared on the screen would only be a detached ghost of his personality, a shadow animated by the imagination of the author, who had been able to exploit the expressive gifts of the actor in a compositorial game structurally alien to the interpreter.

This external action, which in theatrical texts is left to the re-elaborative imagination of the actor-manager or producer, is often pre-established in a film down to the last detail, because its reproduction constitutes one of the most crucial elements of the work. Theatrical texts have always left it to the stage directions to suggest the movements and attitudes of the actors, and in this respect have always proceeded with great delicacy, in a spirit far removed from any hypothetical attempt at coercion. Perhaps it is simply chance, but the golden ages of theatrical production coincided with the appearance of texts almost entirely without stage-directions – one need merely consider the sixteenth century Spanish theatre or the Elizabethan theatre. Stage-directions have begun to assume a certain quantitative importance in contemporary theatrical texts; but in this unexpected flowering of parentheses before, after, or during the actor's speech, one senses the distinct influence of cinematographic techniques upon the composition and preparation of the theatrical spectacle.

The scenario of a film, unlike the theatrical script, is a text in which the exterior actions of the actors are described in their entirety. If some directors work in an elastic relation to the written text, it is nevertheless true that the movements within each shot are always foreseen or intuited by him well in advance of realizing the scene.

The written text that, in its final realization, precedes the work of filming – the scenario, that is – is so detailed and complex that it has given rise to speculation, among students of cinematographic aesthetics, as to its possible literary value. To ask oneself if a scenario can already be considered in itself as a finished work, irrespective of its potential transposition into cinematographic images, is the equivalent of wondering whether a sign, or rather one complex of signs destined to produce another that acts in an entirely different sphere of communication, may also be semantically and (since we are talking about artistic signs) aesthetically effective in the communicative sphere in which it naturally operates. For the Russian director Gherassimov, the answer is affirmative. The scenario of a sound-film, in the literary version that it assumes before taking on the form of a technical instrument, may indeed enjoy, according to him, a greater autonomy than that of the theatrical text.

Because of its possibilities for embodying reality, the contemporary sound scenario is nearer to a realistic story or novel,[14] free from any exterior convention and able to make ample use of the most detailed descriptions.... A completely valid scenario must be able to be read like a story or a novel, although it has some differences that derive from the particular nature of cinematographic art.[15]

Sergei Mikhailovic Eisenstein, on the other hand, denies that the scenario, and indeed precisely the type that aims at a literary description of the forming of images capable of translating onto the screen the author's thoughts, has an autonomous artistic nature. He emphasizes its instrumental value when he writes that:

... the cinematographic subject-matter... is only a shorthand version of an emotive explosion that is put into effect through a series of plastic visions. It is the wooden last that serves as a model for the boot until such time as a real foot comes to substitute for it.... It is a cipher that is transmitted from one temperament to another.[16]

The debated but well defined nature of the film scenario is another element in favour of the thesis that proposes an absolute incommensurability between the working conditions of the theatrical actor and those of the film actor. The latter finds himself confined by the author's intentions within the forms of a pre-established set of actions, which leave very little room for extemporization. The film actor appears within the communicative relation between author and spectator as a component sign element who confers, with the images of his body and his actions, the value of credibility upon the universe evoked by the film. Contrary to what frequently happens in the theatre, the film actor cannot interpret characters that are very different from each other, and almost always remains bound to a limited range of types; in the theatre, technical ability and the distance between actor and public allow him to take on an almost unlimited number of characters, irrespective of his somatic characteristics, his tone

---

[14]   Than it is to playwriting.
[15]   S. Gherassimov, "Il mestiere di regista cinematografico", *Il mestiere di regista* (1954), 26.
[16]   Eisenstein, "Soggetto e sceneggiatura". The quote is taken from *Essenza del film,* ed. Fernaldo di Giammatteo (Torino, Il Drama SET, 1947), 50.

of voice, and at times even his age. In the cinema the actor cannot cheat. Since the action of the character is observed in its every detail and followed throughout its entire development, since the actor's face is often close to the lens and recorded on film in close-up, since the spectator is inserted directly into the action of the characters, projectively moves with them, and curiously shifts his glance to their hands, or face, or eyes, the actor's physique and gestural behaviour must conform to the type of character that he is playing. Even if the cinematographic spectacle is the fruit of illusory images and illusory movement, the elements that make up this illusion must, in themselves, evoke so clear a relation to concrete reality, that they stifle every doubt as to their 'unreal authenticity'.

The actor's image may be identified with that of the character in all the acts of meticulous examination to which the spectator's analysis should reduce itself. It thus comes about that, under a good director, an actor of little weight in the theatre or, indeed, somebody taking on the interpretation of a character for the first time will end up by representing it a great deal better than an expert actor would have done. H. H. Wollenburg, referring back to a course given at the University of Cambridge, states

...since the artistic purpose of the stage is to individualize, acting becomes all the higher the more the actor individualizes. Think of a Hamlet performed by John Gielgud; a Hamlet performed by Donald Wolfit or Alec Clunes. Each of these Hamlets is an original and individual interpretation. The stage actor interprets. The film actor should not 'interpret'. His individuality should submerge in his part. He should become one with his character on the screen. His performance is the greater, the more the spectator is made to forget that there is an actor at all. The greatest achievement of screencraft is to give the perfect illusion of real life accidently caught by the camera. Hence the unique effect of children on the screen. They are the best of all film actors.[17]

When the cinema was as yet without sound, and the substance of its evocative effectiveness was reduced to a rhythmic interplay of visual images, the actor rightly tended to differentiate his interpretive action from what he might have done in the theatre, emphasizing the gestural aspect. One might suggest that the gestures of the film actor, reduced to a silent succession of movements, aimed to create a new mime, entirely different from the theatrical type; it was in this direction that the greatest actors, above all Charlie Chaplin, directed their interpretative research. They had, first of all, tended to exaggerate the basic elements of theatrical gesture, in an attempt to substitute for the word with an over-elaborate version of the

[17]   H. H. Wollenberg, *Anatomy of the Film, an illustrated guide to film appreciation* (London, Marsland Publications Limited, 1947), 41.

visual physical sign that usually accompanies it – rather as if the cinema were an inferior and incomplete means of communication and did not in itself possess the possibility of an autonomous linguistic existence which, being structured on the basis of the image, did not have to concern itself with any exaggeratedly rationalized exposition. Little by little, the inventive gifts of a few actors, above all comic ones, convinced the critics and public of the extraordinary aptness and linguistic independence of an action-image developed by means of a new technique of gesture and mime, a technique dictated by the expressive needs of the image (projected onto a two-dimensional screen) and the cutting themselves. Even in the epoch of silent films, bringing the actor near to the audience by means of close-ups had made the absurd transpositions of theatrical acting techniques typical of the early years of film production ridiculous. Nothing could be done about it – the time, the space, the atmosphere, the units of measurement, all of them were different.

The advent of sound presented the original problems once again, and caused a repetition of the dangerous possibility of adopting an absurd and denigratory concept of the cinema, which risked being considered as an evocative means of reproduction without any expressive life of its own. The possibility of giving a voice to the characters of the film and sounds to the environment in which they moved, brought back into the limelight the problem of the function of words in the ambit of cinematographic expression. The biggest crisis in the history of the cinema perhaps coincided with the discovery of recording techniques and of synchronization; the entire industry then oriented itself towards the production of spectacles rich in dialogue that did not in any way distinguish themselves, as far as the director's intentions were concerned, from the formulas of the theatre.

The language of the cinema was dead, and all the theoretical and experimental research that had been lavished upon the new medium seemed to be reduced to the faint memory of a transitional epoch. The dialogue had returned to its old, essential role in the development of the dramatic action, and the devices thought out by the actors and directors of the silent epoch in an attempt to achieve cinematographic expressiveness were abandoned, without any attempt to discriminate between those linguistic elements suggested by the necessity of overcoming the lack of sound, and those spontaneously generated by the needs of the film medium. While it is true that many mimetic aspects of the interpretation demanded by silent films were seen to be exaggerated and redundant once the introduction of sound had been achieved, it is equally true that some of the types of interpretation and, generally, of action conceived in those films had within them a validity above and beyond the limits within which they were engendered.

Some critics, amongst them Arnheim, do not hesitate to concede to the silent film an authentic quality, considering the autonomous expressive possibilities of the film, once sound had arrived, as concluded, or at any rate barren. All this seems somewhat exaggerated because, despite the saddening example of the first sound films and of most of the production derived from it, and even admitting that the sound film has not yet found an expressive dimension that is essentially its own, it is difficult to disregard the positive example of many films that are committed to the search for linguistic autonomy. The arrival of sound accentuated the precarious nature of some of the gestural instruments of the silent film, but did not destroy all of the most effective conquests of those ingenious men who had worked for so long in the studios of Pathé, or Cines, or United Artists. The most important directors of the silent era were also the first to realize sound films that were valid on an expressively autonomous level: Eisenstein, Chaplin, Dreyer, and Clair gave with their works the most meaningful reply to the prophets of doom, who ostentatiously clung to an absurd purism.

The actor's technique thus ended up by becoming crystallized, little by little, within the forms of a behaviouristic realism, prompted by the screen-phantasm's need for credibility. In fact, the cinematographic image, despite all the distortions of reality that it represents, and that constitute a good part of its expressive effectiveness, is nevertheless always a photographic reproduction of the object and, above all, aims to create in the spectator an accentuated illusion of truth. The cinema lives by creating in the spectator a poetic illusion of reality, and the actor's performance must be thought of in the same way.

Amongst all the men of the theatre, the one who perhaps came closest to interpretive models similar to the corresponding cinematic ones was Constantin Stanislavskij, who, happening to be present at a performance of the drama *The Shipwreck of the Nadiesda* in a hall "...so small that the spectator found himself in close proximity to the actors, and thus received the impression of being in the same room as them...", realized the extraordinary change that this physical situation involved within the valuation of normal expressive means. Pudovkin writes:

All the details and the most subtle nuances of the actor's interpretation acquired, as a result, a decisive importance. The outward accentuation of the theatrical gesture and of the voice lost all meaning as a result of this extreme proximity between actors and public. This intimate communion, unusual for the theatre, between actor and spectator gave birth to a new and singular sensation of profound sincerity and of extreme simplicity. The actors seemed to have had the possibility of behaving as men do within the real environment of living reality.[18]

Reality, truth, and simplicity, or rather the illusion of reality, truth, and simplicity – these are, generally speaking, the fundamental characteristics of film acting. The actors are committed to adapting their entire expressive capacity to the *unum necessarium* demanded by the form of the character-phantasm on the screen. Unlike the theatre, the transposition of actor into character does not come about by a process of gradual and continuous mastery, but by means of a broken-up insertion into a pre-established mosaic of interpretive acts that are frequently alien to the actor himself. His interpretation must contribute to the composition of every shot and every scene in which he is involved, adapting itself to the partial laws of both, and to the general criteria to which the director and the actor refer the construction of their character.

The movement, gestures, and action of the actor must not only be referred to a generally realistic technique that simplifies the interpreter's every act and gesture, but must also be organized according to the weight of their appearance within the spatio-temporal interval of a certain fragment of the cutting, whose vitality stems from rhythmic and expressive needs of its own.

In this sense, the personality of the director is decisive regarding the unity which the actor's interpretation, which was originally broken up into various takes, will have to possess within the finished work. The definitive action, as it appears after cutting, may include within it shots of the actor's stand-in or, in any case, of figurative elements extraneous to his image, with the choice of which he has absolutely nothing to do; and yet the life of his phantasm on the screen may also be traced to these insertions, which contribute to the creation of that general rhythm of the images and that figurative structure which derive a great deal of their effectiveness from the actor. The movement of the actor within the shot (relative to the border of the image, that is) thus acquires a considerable importance regarding the language of the work, and conditions the actor himself to submit entirely to the demands of the scenario. Pudovkin writes:

Every time that I have begun work with an actor on a given image, I have had to

---

[18]   V. Pudovkin, "Il lavoro dell'attore nel cinema e il sistema di Stanslavskij", *Il mestiere di regista* (1954), 127.

draw the conclusion that, if one has not sounded out the characteristic moments of physical behaviour within this image that is as yet only thought of and in the process of formation – moments such as his way of walking, of sitting down, or of standing, everything that goes under the general heading of 'his way of behaviour' – one will never succeed in getting from the actor a life-like behaviour within the image itself.[19]

Everything artificial that exists within the body of the most 'authentic' and 'realistic' theatrical interpretation must therefore efface itself when the actor finds himself in front of a cine-camera, and must make room for the simple and delicate nuances of an interpretation that is conditioned even more by the characteristics of the medium than it is by the historical, aesthetic, and generally cultural considerations suggested by an analysis of the character.

The communicative subject thus has recourse, within his film, to the figurative elements offered to him by images of other men, which can be useful to him in order to make up his sign-structures; man's image and the phantasm of his actions become part of a sign vehicle, whose effectiveness is conditioned by the adequacy of their reproductive and expressive function.

This also happens in other forms of communication, as in the simple gesture of the actor on stage that commonly accompanies or substitutes for verbal discourse; but in the case of the cinema everything is so autonomous and original, that it has not seemed out of place to dwell upon the difference between the two different forms.

THE DYNAMICS OF THE FILM-CAMERA

The analysis of internal movements within a shot, mentioned while studying the film actor's interpretation, favours the consideration of a relativity of movement between the object (in this particular case, the actor) and the film-camera. Along with the actor's movement, one must in fact take into account, while shooting, the possibility of moving the lens, and thus the spectator's eye, relative to the object during the scene, without any break or any other technical tricks. The film camera is in fact capable of rotating around its vertical axis, or a horizontal one, or an oblique one, thus reproducing the rotating movement which the eyes can achieve either on their own or with a movement of the entire head.

This movement, commonly known as a 'pan', is narratively effective for description, because it favours the spectator's cognitive contact with

[19] Pudovkin (1954), 182.

the environment reproduced and with the people that inhabit it. The continuity inherent in the pan allows the spectator to insert himself concretely within the action represented on the screen and to refer with certainty to the physical dimensions and cultural components of the scene presented in front of him.

However, the value of the pan is not exhausted by a series of descriptive acts, since it can achieve an expressive effectiveness unknown to other means of cinematographic narration. A quick pan from one actor's face to another's, for example, or from an object to an actor, has a capacity for communicating the reaction of the second image to the action described by the first in a much more tense and dramatic way than would be the case with a cut. The spectator in fact feels himself to be taking an integral part in the action and, being a prey to emotive suggestion, easily identifies the movement of the camera with that of his own eyes, placed right in the midst of the event, between the two extremes of the pan.

Another narratively effective element is the 'tracking shot'; this consists of moving the whole cine-camera on a mechanical device known as a 'dolly'. The moving camera-support can be reduced to a normal vehicle, either free or on wheels, or indeed to a cable.

By means of the tracking shot, the spectator can move towards or away from the object of his attention in a continuous movement, without sudden breaks; the angle of vision does not change, because the camera lens is always the same, but the position of the viewpoint does change continuously, so that it is possible to pass from the image of an environment in its entirety to some detail among the various elements that make it up or live within it or, vice versa, to insert a detail within a certain environment, employing the tracking shot in a reverse direction. In most cases, this movement of the camera does not aim at description, as in the case of the pan, but rather at dramatic expression. It is also possible to make use of it in order to indicate the surroundings within which a person or object is placed, above all in cases where the cine-camera recedes, but usually one makes use of the tracking shot in order to bring into evidence the most visually effective element among the many that make up the scene. The tracking shot may assume complex descriptive meanings when it is combined with the pan, in a movement that puts the camera-man's skill to the test, and that allows a brilliant solution to several complicated problems of visual linguistics.

Nor must one forget that it is technically possible to arrive at an 'optical' tracking shot with an immobile camera. By making use of a complicated system of lenses, called 'pancinor' or 'zoomar', it is in fact possible to vary in a continuous progression the focal length of the shot and, therefore, to move the lens with apparent continuity towards or away from an object or person.

The resultant image is by no means identical to the one arrived at by moving the camera on a dolly, because the unchanging focal length of this latter type of shot implies an unchanging angle, and thus an unchanging mode of distortion when the reality involved is projected two-dimensionally, all of which is a far cry from the results of the zoom shot. This basically consists of a continuous changing of lenses, whose focal length is varied in the passage from one to another. But changing the focal length also implies moving the imaginary plane on which projection will take place further away from or nearer to the object – since the reality being shot is three-dimensional, the changing of the plane of projection implies changing the type of image and the type of distortion undergone by the represented objects; the image corresponding to a plane of projection, and thus to a certain focal length, is not geometrically similar to the one corresponding to another different plane and focal length. The zoom shot does however enjoy the considerable advantage, with respect to the tracking shot, of not obliging the film-camera to move. It is, furthermore, possible to realize with the 'pancinor' an extremely rapid and violent movement towards or away from the object, this being beyond the limitations of the normal tracking shot.

The zoom shot is used above all by virtue of this particular characteristic, which can turn out to be extremely effective from a narrative point of view. The scenes of the bombing of the prison from Rossellini's *Il Generale della Rovere* spring to mind immediately. Here, the vertical and anguished movement of the lens, searching out the most dramatic details, creates as a result a more tense and violent atmosphere than any elaboration at the cutting stage could.

Frequent use is also made of the zoom shot when one wants to follow a person or object moving continuously away from or towards the lens, and thus varying the dimensions of his image with respect to the frame of the shot. The 'pancinor' makes it possible to preserve this dimensional relation unchanged, to some degree, and in an almost unnoticeable form if the object's or person's movements in relation to the lens are not very fast. The use of the 'pancinor' is widespread for the filming of newsreels, both for television and the cinema; since in such a case one must translate into images an event whose spatial extension and temporal development (from the point of view of the speed with which a certain space is filled) may be entirely unpredictable, a lens with a variable focal length allows an immediate and continuous adaption of the filming to any turn of events.

All the movements that have been examined in order to clarify their narrative effectiveness, and thus their function as signs, take place within a real spatial dimensionality, during the process of filming; the actor moves, the film-camera moves in a pan or a tracking shot, and even the lens with an adjustable focus moves, positioned by the operator's hand.

THE ILLUSION OF MOVEMENT

By combining the movements of the actors and objects with those of the film-camera, one can obtain shots of a complex of relative movements that are very effective expressively, and whose signified is conditioned, as far as cinematographic narration is concerned, by the director's intentions alone. The same things happen from the kinetic point of view as have already been clarified with respect to the formal aspect of reality: the public finds itself confronted by an image of the movement that in fact took place during the shooting, an image that distorts its original structure according to the well-known laws of optics. Cinematographic movement is one of the illusory aspects from which this type of spectacle draws its life – the images appear to be animated, in fact, not because the phantasms within them are moving, but because the human eye is imperfect, and forgets a visual impression with a certain difficulty.

This is the basic factor in the second part of the 'great illusion' which governs the relation between public and screen.[20] The frame in itself, the

[20] According to Wertheimer, one of the principal exponents of Gestalttheorie, the perception of movement demands a subjective integration as much in the case of real movements as in that of apparent movements. On this subject, Cornelio Fabro writes that "what is seen (of the movement of an object) is that movement – not only does one see that the object is now in different conditions from those that is was in before, and know that it has moved, but one perceives the movement itself. What is phsyically given? One could say, by analogy to physical reality, that seeing the movement consists in the fact that the visual object has shifted itself in a continuous manner from a position p^1 through intermediary placings to p^n; given such a sequence of intermediary placings, one has also established the perception of movement.

"If this SEEING the movement is now considered as an illusion, that is, as something that from the physical point of view is only given as, first, a simple point of repose, and then as a certain distance from the first point, at another point of repose, one ought to be able to get a subjective integration to intervene in coincidence with it. The act of passing through the intermediate positions, and taking them as a whole (*das Eingenommen haben*) would in some way be subjectively integrated.

"The supposition, which is already probable for 'real' movements, becomes necessary for 'apparent' movements" (Fabro, *La fenomenologia della percezione* [Brescia, Morcelliana, 1961], 274-275).

two-dimensional image of reality, is inanimate, dead, and has no value as a sign from a kinetic point of view in the linguistic region in which it is born with a function entirely alien to the substantial possibilities conferred upon it by the physical lacunae of human awareness.

The image of the movement may be speeded up or slowed down relative to the real temporal sequence; it may be distorted by particular angulations or by virtue of the camera's distance from the object. Arnheim states:

The particular angle at which the camera captures the object will influence movement, not only because speed depends on distance but also because perspective foreshortening will diminish the path of the movement, that is, increase visual speed. Oblique shots, therefore, will often intensify movement, thus adding the dynamics of velocity to that of slanted position.[21]

If to the illusory variations of movement permitted by regulating the rate at which the film runs during the take or by the position of the camera in relation to the event that one wants to film, one adds the possible variations and distortions of reality permitted by the complex of relative motions at which one may arrive by combining movements of the film-camera with those of the objects or actors being filmed, then it may be imagined what great possibilities for directly intervening in the manipulation of reality are also offered to the author by the kinetic element, which constitutes the *raison d'etre* of the film.

The figurative distortion that filming necessarily involves also leaves its traces in the illusory movement that one thinks that one is seeing when watching the screen; and this is an evident consequence of the fact that the spectator is deceived by the rapid succession of images each slightly different from the next. The apparent movement that results from this is marked by the characteristics of the component images, and in turn assumes its own individual aspect, which frequently has no direct relation with the reality from which it is derived. Concluding the remark quoted above, Arnheim states:

Any displacement of the camera produces and modifies the movement. Traveling shots show objects in illusory movement, even though the reason tries to remind us that they actually are immobile. Objects that are at different distances from the camera appear displaced with regard to each other when their picture is taken, for instance, from a moving train; and the objects will appear to go faster, more slowly, or stand still, depending on the direction and the speed of the moving camera.[22]

The extraordinary possibilities that cinematographic techniques offer to

[21] Arnheim (1958), 153-154.
[22] Arnheim (1958), 154.

those who know how to adapt them to their particular expressive needs appear with the utmost clarity in this ability to directly intervene in the definition of the movement and, indeed, of the time that delimits the illusory world created by the images on film. The cinema dislocates the normal laws of temporal evaluation, even without resorting to cutting and other similar devices; the figurative illusion of reality inherent in the image does not disappear even when its movements and, generally, the time governing the succession of events is altered. The credibility of the forms is so valid and effective as to even confer an element of truth on the movements that animate them; the spectator is brought to regard the fictitious universe unfolding before him on the screen with trust, and thus becomes used to the notion of a distinctly relative unity of time that is geared more to the aesthetic or psychological value of phenomenon than to its actual physical occurrence, and conditioned more by the reaction of an interpreter to the sign function of the event than by the event itself.

In a penetrating study on physical time in the cinema, which appears within a spirited analysis of more general problems, Jean R. Debrix writes that

...le mouvement, au cinéma, n'est donc qu'une illusion. Mais c'est une illusion féconde puisqu'elle a permis d'en dissiper une autre, sans doute beaucoup plus dangereuse: celle qui consistait pour le commun des mortels qui ne se fiait jusqu'ici qu'aux données sensorielles, à croire que le temps est une mesure invariable des choses. Aujourd'hui, grâce a toutes les altérations du réel qu'autorise le cinéma, n'importe quel spectateur est à même de prendre conscience de la relativité foncière de la notion de temps et de se convaincre de l'illusion de réalité qui lui procurent ses sens.[23]

The images filmed by the camera remained firmly fixed to a celluloid band which constitutes the vehicle for translating reality into a projection onto a screen. The film is now in the hands of the director, and of all those collaborating with him in the composition of the spectacle, and is open to a large number of formative interventions.

THE CUTTING

The work of cutting may theoretically be reduced to a form of external intervention upon the cinematographic material that is so profound as to dissolve the original links between one scene and the next, between one

---

[23] Jean R. Debrix, *Les fondements de l'art cinématographique* (Paris, Cerf, 1960), 70-71. This is the first of three volumes. Its subtitle is *Art et réalité au cinéma*.

shot and the next, and to favour the composition of spatial and temporal relations that are heterogeneous to the reproduced reality, and are governed by the rules of a grammar and syntax subordinated to the narrative and aesthetic principles that guide the nascent work. By virtue of the possibilities offered to him by this extraordinary means of synthesis, the cinematographic author can overcome the morphological aspect of the image presented to him by the film-camera and arrive at the formulation of a free and syntactically coherent narration.

If the cinema were not able to make use of cutting, understood as the free re-elaboration and integration of the data that appear fixed on film, then its function could easily be reduced to that of a passively reproductive medium, despite all that has been said about the free and open aspect of the illusion of image and the illusion of movement. The impossibility of freeing oneself from a spatio-temporal convention corresponding to the one used as an instrument of measure in the phenomenal vicissitudes of reality (even taking into account the possibilities for distortion inherent in filming) would in fact prevent a coherent and imaginatively re-elaborative intervention on the part of the author. The cinema would be reduced to a series of documentary acts, capable at most of achieving a trace of auto-sufficiency and of hinting at the first elements of wider linguistic horizons in the shooting of actions naturally adapted to the cinema, and destined to create an effective play of images on the two-dimensional screen.

The first attempts at cinema existed in a condition of complete subjection to the concrete object that they translated into a luminous phantasm, now and then winning the applause of the spectators by virtue of the suggestive spatio-temporal distortions that their cameras allowed them, or of rhythmic play within the image, carefully pre-arranged and coordinated by the director. Perhaps it was the possibility of simultaneously shooting a scene from various points of view, and using lenses with differing focal lengths, that persuaded the men of the cinema to search along a considerably more complex path than that of continuous shooting for the structural essence of film narration: the necessity of making up the cinematographic action with portions of different takes, so that the spatial and the temporal illusions were in perfect synchrony with the real physical data of the filmed phenomenon, aided the search for an aspect of the cinematic image as sign which went far beyond its figurative capacity, its kinetic data, and the interior rhythm that animated it.[24] The new sign

---

[24] Arnheim states that "montage of an event coherent in time and space must be distinguished from the cross-cutting of events that are dissociated from each other. It was with the latter that montage began historically, because it is the less revolutionary

function of the shot sprang from the consideration of its figurative and kinetic relation with the other visual images, deftly juxtaposed by virtue of an external and synthetic intervention.

H. H. Wollenberg writes:

There is no limit to dramatic force in this pictorial method [referring, naturally, to cutting: author's note]. You can oppose social contrasts: show the dining table of a rich glutton and give as your next shot the emaciated bodies from Belsen concentration camp. You can create the drama of human situations: show a miner, buried alive deep down in the colliery, desperately trying to get out, and show in the next shot sweet little children innocently playing in the sun. Both psychological elements of the film combine. The EMOTIONAL power of pictorial rhythm is integrated with the suggestive force of ILLUSION immanent in SCREENCRAFT.[25]

The cutting confers new life upon the images of reality imprinted on film, attributing to the narration spatio-temporal co-ordinates that are entirely independent of the filmed phenomenon. The figurative juxtapositions that may be achieved with the Movieola are able to make up the appearance of an environment that does not exist in reality or is, at any rate, entirely different from each of the physical and scenographic conditions recorded in the various shots that together go to make up the film;[26] the rhythmic succession of the various elements and the relative duration of the different shots may in turn create a temporal illusion governed by norms that are entirely alien to those of the phenomena which have taken

---

process; the different shots were joined to each other, just as different scenes were acted in sequence on the stage" (Arnheim [1958], 116). Georges Sadoul attributes the first attempts at juxtaposing shots of the same object taken from different positions to G. A. Smith of Brighton, who "...drew his inspiration from illustrations in books and magic lantern slides when dividing a single scene into various shots" (Sadoul, *Les merveilles du cinéma* [Paris, Les Editeurs Français Réunis]).

[25]   Wollenberg (1947), 35.

[26]   According to Gestalttheorie, the psychology of perceptual space reduces itself to a relationship between an element of the environment and the environment itself, between object and background. "It is because of this", as Guillaume puts it, "that Gestalttheorie maintains that the psychology of perceptual space can be no more than a theory of the relations that exist between a given fragment of experience and the 'whole' that it is a part of. Except that instead of looking for this 'whole' in previous experience, as do traditional schools, the theory of form finds it within the entirety of present experience, considered not as the sum of juxtaposed elements, but as a 'form' organized according to its own laws" (Fabro [1961], 278). The idea informing a film would condition the cutting so as to bring the elements serving expressive ends to the foreground in a suitable atmosphere. The impression that the composition of moving images left upon the spectator would thus be the result of a combination of visual elements, whose relationship is governed more by their integration within the form of the work than by any logical localization, in correspondence with reality, that they may possess.

place in front of the lens. The film always lives out its actions in the present – the spectator, while watching the cinematographic narration, feels himself immersed in a temporal condition coincident with the phantasy event projected onto the screen.

Cinematographic shots are not conjugable according to Béla Balàzs, and Alain Resnais's experiments bear this out. Because of this characteristic, the cinema is, by very nature, closely related to one of the fundamental aspects of contemporary fiction and drama, as represented by Joyce and Beckett, Duras and Robbe-Grillet, which tends to overcome the barriers of time by conferring a personal and auto-symbolic presence upon the objects, and moving the people around them in a confused and suggestive unison between past and present, reality and dream, truth and subjective distortion – always, however, in an action conjugated in the present by those taking part and those looking on.

Referring to Resnais's film *L'année dernière à Marienbad*, Guido Aristarco writes that the image is

...entirely in the present. There is no real looking back, no moving towards the past or remembering by means of blurring or other technical devices. The 'past' and 'future' that 'A' sees are purely imaginary. 'A' is not reliving the past, but sees a present that 'X' narrates to him in the present....

As Hauser notes, one becomes aware relatively quickly of the fact that the contemporaneity of two series of events is an essentially cinematographic theme, and that discontinuity of plot and of representation within the individual scenes, the unexpected arising of thoughts and frames of mind, relativity and incoherence in the measurement of time are precisely what remind us, in Proust and Joyce, Dos Passos and Virginia Woolf, of the cuts, dissolves and interpolations of the film.[27]

Jean-Jacques Mujoux demonstrates how Samuel Beckett has decomposed and restructured the temporal dimension in his theatrical works, so as to make out of it a dimension of the absurd, a continuous haemorrhage of existence.

Il ne reste, il n'y a jamais qu'un présent vague et perdue dans une double brume de non-être: un présent dans lequel tout (ou plutôt RIEN) se déroule, marqué par une langue autant que possible accompagnante, inchoative, tâtonnante.... Ce présent en effet se dilate, se gonfle comme une bulle, on en rapprochera ou on en éloignera indéfiniment les limites: un instant semble contenir une vie....[28]

The influence of cutting upon the temporal characteristics of the narra-

[27] "Senza passato né prospettiva l'oro' di Marienbad", *Cinema Nuovo* X: 153 (September-October 1961), 399-400.
[28] Jean-Jacques Majoux, *Vivant piliers – Le roman anglo-saxon et les symboles* (Paris, Juilliard, Les Lettres nouvelles, 1960), 273.

tion is not limited to the chronological aspect of the event and to the potential breaking up of the continuity of action, but gets to the point of also making an impression on the spatio-temporal synthesis that constitutes the physical nucleus of the film and gives an illusion of movement to the phantasms projected onto the screen. The cutting may directly interfere with the physical elements of the visual action, creating an apparent acceleration or deceleration in the movements, this being one of the means whereby the action may be made to conform to the rhythm demanded by the poetic idea in the process of realization.

Arnheim writes:

After a scene has been taken, the motions it records undergo further modifications in the cutting-room. A section of a movement, cut from its original context, is likely to change its quality, and the combination of movements in montage causes a good deal of mutual interference. Movements that oppose and thus balance each other are often shown together: in the first scene a train travels from the left to the right, in the second a door closes from the right to the left.... Again, an action seems slowed down when it is flanked by faster ones; and vice versa.... Montage influences speed in that motion looks the faster, the shorter the time of its exposure. When short pieces follow each other in rapid succession, intense dynamics result, which may suit a dramatic episode....[29]

Putting together the constitutive parts of a single scene, or a single movement, which correspond to shots of the same action from different angles and with different lenses, the cutting process is frequently obliged to build up the spatio-temporal structure of the film in conformity with that of the filmed reality: at times, it is unthinkable to make a visual jump from one part of an actor's gesture or from other movements; the evident but illogical gain in space and time would favour the immediate eclipse of the cinematographic illusion that has been slowly maturing in the spectator.[30]

[29]   Arnheim (1958), 154.
[30]   According to Benussi, and Gestalt theorists in general, the reason for illusion lies "in the tendency that we have to seize upon the object as if it were a 'whole', and so true is this that when, by means of special artifices, one succeeds in perceiving the parts of the object in isolation, the illusion disappears" (Fabro [1961], 225). An evident jump in time within the development of the cinematographic action will make it easy for the public to perceive the single elements that make up the action itself as separate parts; according to Gestalttheorie, the loss of a sensation of 'form', the detachment from the totality of the object, would thus bring about the end of the kinetic illusion and reveal the mechanisms lying behind the spectacle. This is all perfectly valid as long as one expects the cinematographic action to conform to a hypothetical real and 'external' action which the one on film represents, and which could in fact take place within the world of objects. But when the director wants to make use of cinematographic language in order to overcome the barriers of time and space to which exterior action and man's phenomenal existence are linked, the cutting may also be freed from the shackles of spatio-temporal continuity, and may allow itself all the imaginative leaps that the author can conceive of.

Cutting frees itself from the yoke of an objective slavery that is unable to sustain any form of free re-creativity when it is transformed from a means of simple dynamic connection into an essential narrative instrument. The juxtaposition of movements, gestures, the actors' faces, the alternation of objects and human figures, become little by little the basic modes of its operative intervention: the cinematographic action thus assumes a dimension of its own and is to be referred to in a complex of coordinates that are only valid within the spatio-temporal ambit in which the author has placed the development of the narration.

The real three-dimensional action that has been translated into images on celluloid no longer makes sense in the universe of the film and every one of its values finds itself reduced to an instrumental intervention, necessary in order to form the sign that the author wishes to present to the public.

Dynamic-figurative matching and juxtaposition have frequently allowed a brilliant solution to many problems of cinematographic expression. The second sequence of Federico Fellini's *La dolce vita* is linked to the first by the ascending movement of a dancer's head juxtaposed with the descending movement of the statue of Christ suspended from a helicopter, the shot which closes the first sequence. The figurative matching has, in this instance, a double value, because along with the visual and formal element of the inverse movement there is an exceptional symbolical value, conferred upon the passage by the content of the two juxtaposed images.[31]

Il ferroviere, by Pietro Germi, begins with a succession of alternating images which show a train about to arrive at a station and a boy running through the streets of a city. The rapid and essential cutting allows one to connect the two movements (which are shot in opposing directions) and to intuit a psychological relation between the boy and the train. The train seems to be going to meet the boy, and vice versa: in fact, the engine-driver is the boy's father, and his son is running to the station to meet him. In this case, the cutting of the scene is very effective from the rhythmic and narrative point of view.[32]

The possibility of liberating the cinematographic author from the constraints of time comes clearly into evidence in a number of films structured on the basis of memory and, generally, on the narrative superimposition of past, present, and future. *Hiroshima mon amour, L'année*

[31] *La dolce vita*, by Federico Fellini, produced by Riana Film and the Pathé Consortium Cinema (1959).
[32] *Il Ferroviere*, by Pietro Germi, produced by C. Ponti-Excelsa Film.

dernière à Marienbad, and *Muriel* by Alain Resnais offer a convincing example of the results that may be arrived at by means of an intelligent and inspired subversion of the kinetic and logical laws to which man's every-day experience is linked.

But cutting perhaps reaches its highest expressive function, providing the work with a symbolic aspect that is, in most cases, simple and meaningful, when it succeeds in linking the images together by virtue of their relative analogical effectiveness.

Cutting by analogy is a method of cinematographic narration that was studied and applied above all by the most important Russian directors, and it consists of inserting visual material that has no logically necessary relation with the action taking place on the screen. "Some times, two shots are associated", writes Arnheim, "whose connection is not realistic, but conceptual and poetic."[33]

To emphasize the moral emptiness of a person, one could juxtapose his image with that of a peacock, as did Eisenstein in *October*; or one can follow up the image of the doctor drowning in the port of Odessa with that of the worms writhing in the rotten meat set aside for the sailors, which the ship's doctor did not wish to point out, as Eisenstein, once more, did in *Battleship Potemkin*.[34] The images inserted by virtue of analogical cutting amongst those that describe the action projected on the screen may therefore be entirely independent from the others in regard to formal content – their function is purely poetic, and has no need of a realistic justification.

An analysis of symbolist poetry is a very effective way of coming to grips with the aesthetic validity of this type of narrative procedure: the works of T. S. Eliot, C. Péguy, Yeats, Paul Valéry, Paul Éluard, Allen Tate, and A. Blok often use unexpected images, skillfully inserted into the poetic narration and completely detached from its potential logical core. They do not even make an effective comparison or a valid metaphor because they are far removed from any relationship or similarity to the object of the content. Their sign function has its origin in that mysterious source of junctions and disjunctions that is the subject's unconscious, no doubt conditioned by cultural and sociological predispositions, but, at the same time, ready to compose into a single linguistic fact (or to accept, by suggestion, as a unity) sign elements with completely alien references

[33]   Arnheim (1958), 80.
[34]   Eisenstein, *Battleship Potemkin*. See also the scenario derived from the cutting process by Pier Luigi Lanza (Milano-Roma, Bocca Editori), 80. "N. 586 – detail – looking down on the sea from above (18). The spray as the doctor plunges into the water. N. 587 – detail (42) greatly enlarged – worms on a piece of rotting meat."

in reality that are capable of engraving themselves with coherent expressive power upon his receptive awareness.

Pierre Marois writes that the Renaissance and the Baroque periods were content with the allegory, understood as a "...façon d'expliquer une pensée pour la rendre compréhensible"; but symbolism is a very different matter or, at any rate, enjoys distinctly superior properties: "...le signe ou le symbole", Marois continues, "s'identifient au contraire avec ce qu'ils veulent représenter, ils peuvent le suggérer, ils ne l'expliquent pas".[35]

The symbol does not limit itself to a representative or substitutive action; it may condition the acceptance of the poetic work by virtue of the fascinating appeal that its presence has for the subject, even before he has engaged his own rational faculties in the work of clarification and analysis.

The mode of poetic production that draws its inspiration from the laws of symbolism leaves entirely out of consideration the explicatory and rationally clarifying image and, overcoming the bonds of necessity and of origin that link the forms of reality, aims at constructing a logic of signs.

The methods of cinematographic cutting by means of analogy are very similar to those of symbolist poetry, and were in an even closer aesthetic relation to them when, in the era of silent films, the cinema possessed an essentially visual nature and, precisely because of this, removed itself from every possibility of a complete relationship with reality. The greatest authors of the silent film had come, little by little and with perfect expressive coherence, to attribute a fundamental function to the visual rhythm in which the images succeeded each other on the screen, even leaving out of account the logical relations between their contents – cutting had become the very heart of the spectacle, and all the linguistic and aesthetic studies had been directed towards the search for absolute visual pleasure, suggested by the dance of images cleverly distributed by the cutter.

The lack of sound removed the film from the realistic situation that had given form to the phantasms of its images, and shifted it to an unreal and phantastic dimension. The silent film, in its action upon the public, gave rise to sensations related to those provoked by a mime or a ballet: the content of the single images lost its importance as an independent linguistic element and reduced its function to that of the passive element within a rhythmic interplay which, although making use of the forms re-

---

[35] Pierre Marois, "Art religieus, art sacré", *La vie intellectuelle* (March 1950), 318. These observations were taken from *Le Signe*, by E. Masure (Paris, Blond et Gay, 1954), 321-322.

gistered on the film, imposed upon them a form of cutting that was alien, and at times antithetical to them. S. Gherassimov writes:

It was asserted... that the content of the film is not expressed by those pictures of reality that are given by the shots, but by the cutting, that is by the way in which these shots have been combined. It was asserted that the shot is a mere sign which does not have, or at any rate ought not to have, a real content, and that this content only derives from the combination of shots obtained through cutting.

It was further asserted that the aesthetic value of a film is contained within its rhythmic form alone, that is, once more in the construction of the cutting.... However much these conceptions may have diverged, one common characteristic linked them: the conviction that cutting was the alpha and omega of the cinema, that cutting introduced into the content of the film something new that was lacking in the shot. And instead, the cutting... still remains simply a means of enucleating the content of the shot, a means of organizing the pictures of reality fixed in the individual shots, so as to compose an artistic, harmonious, and complete image of this reality.[36]

The typically rhythmic structure of cutting was turned to excellent account in the best of the silent films, so much so that people thought of the rules of cinematographic syntax as being close to those of musical harmonization and composition – they conceived of magical forms of melodic visualization and of contrapuntal juxtaposition of different actions, mutually linked by their relative rhythmic effectiveness. After this triumph of the relationship of the various shots' duration and succession over their content value, analogical cutting was all the more easily able to establish itself, and helped to augment that separation from every direct relation with the represented reality towards which the cinema seemed to be heading during the last years of the silent film.

One should, for the sake of information, observe that many contemporary cinematographic authors once more possess a fundamentally musical idea of the structure of the film. Despite the use of sound and the development of all the techniques relating to it, some directors have frequent recourse to cutting as their most important narrative instrument, attributing to its rhythmic values a good part of their film's expressive effectiveness.

Ingmar Bergman writes:

The succession of images operates directly upon our emotions, without touching the intellect. Music works in the same way; I would say that no other form of art has as much in common with the cinema as has music. Each of them influences our emotions directly, and not through the intellect. And the film is above all rhythm; it is a continuous inhalation and exhalation. From childhood on,

[36]   Gherassimov (1954), 60-61.

music has been my great source of recreation and stimulation and I frequently experience a film or a theatrical work musically.[37]

To Bergman, who in his latest films (and above all in *The Silence* and *Persona*) has been developing a concept of cutting in which less is entrusted to rhythmic values and there is a greater concern for the audio-visual content of the single shots,[38] one may add René Clair, whose work is often deliberately oriented towards the search for rhythmic expression and towards bringing the pulse of the narration into line with the rules of a musical temporality. These exceptions apart, however, the advent of sound brought the cinema back to a state of greater credibility, and of greater adherence to reality's normal courses of development. The insertion of images cut off from any concrete relation with the represented object, even when they could be related to it in terms of metaphor or poetic necessity, was shown to be perilous and, at times, downright negative.

The succession of images, integrated through the contribution of the dialogue, the sounds, and the noises, must naturally conform to a criterion of logical credibility that may only be separated from that of reality by virtue of elevating the whole work, or at least part of it, to the poetic climate of an explicitly imaginary or paradoxically absurd universe. It is very difficult to create visual links (even if they are symbolically effective) between images that differ in nature and origin, when the characters talk with every-day voices and words, when they open a door which makes the noise that doors really make, when they walk and their steps resonate in the room, reproducing the sonic situation of reality.

The cutting of a sound film has a concrete rhythmic value, but more as an element contributing to the general composition than as the one and only depository of the work's total expressive force.

It is not only the coordinated succession of visual elements that comes within the rhythmic structuring of the film, for all the elements contributed by the sound-track also find a place there, with the realistic consequences that this implies. Along with a time and a space of a visual order are born a time and a space linked to sonic coordinates; the two together ought to compose themselves into a synthesis which should, in theory, always avoid every form of redundancy and every informative defect.

The technical enrichment of the expressive means has thus apparently constricted and reduced the freedom to intervene enjoyed by the author's

---

[37] The introduction to *4 film di Bergman*, trans. Bruno Fonzi and Giacomo Oreglia (Torino, Einaudi, 1961), p. XV.

[38] *Tystnaden* [The Silence] by I. Bergman, prod. Svensk Filmindustri (1963). For *Persona*, see part I, note 88.

creative faculties, since it has placed at his disposal far more effective instruments for reproducing reality. The director's imaginative powers, which found in cutting their most fruitful field of expression, thus found themselves bound to the rules of an apparently realistic development of the action (even from the visual point of view), from all of which they had previously been able to free themselves, slowly but surely. Once the addition of a sound-track had been accomplished, the process by which the cinematographic image was increasingly made to conform to reality became accelerated, and a complex of technical factors was introduced into the process of shooting that was capable of completely bridling the public's critical reactions, and immersing their sense organs in a pool of docile credibility. The use of colour; the continuous search for an instrument capable of overcoming the limits of two-dimensionality and of giving the spectator the impression of being in a real space that has depth in all directions;[39] stereophonic sound; attempts to involve the spectators' olfactory faculties as well, by letting free perfumes and smells in the cinema that correspond realistically to the events on the screen – with each of these technical innovations, a further attempt was made to tear the cinema away from the linguistic terrain within which it had developed by reducing the obstacles and reproductive limitations in which all the expressive potential of the new medium had been concentrated. In making the mechanical apparatus ever larger and more complicated, and in perfecting its reproductive capacities, one ends up by reducing its function as

[39] According to Musatti, the many efforts to resolve the problem of film stereoscopy are useless, because the spectator already feels the scene projected on screen to be three-dimensional. "The objective situation that is brought about on the screen is made up of a series of immobile images; with the phenomenon of apparent movement ...a constant image is grasped that contains elements of movement. The situation's objective conditions ought to determine the impressions that the moving complexes give of distortion and movement; the image of a man coming nearer or drawing away in fact corresponds, ON SCREEN, to making that image larger or smaller.... Normally, ...and in those viewing conditions that would be considered the best, this deformation of things is not noticed – the man who gets nearer and draws away is seen to preserve his dimensions. But the self-deforming image can only transform itself into the image of an 'object' that has constant dimensions, and is therefore inflexible (or almost so), in so far as that object 'is placed' in a three-dimensional environment, and is thus really seen to get nearer and to draw away. Nor is this a matter of simply interpreting the perceived image: the environment itself, within which the movements take place, is intuitively seen as three-dimensional.... So that when one starts talking about the attempts made to resolve the problem of film stereoscopy, as Musatti observes, one never considers that the problem is, at any rate for the most part, already solved, since one is concerned with scenes that contain large numbers of moving elements; consequently the problem is without any foundation, and has emerged artificially, based upon the two-dimensional nature of the screen without taking into account formal factors" (Fabro, [1961], 284-285).

spectacle to an extraordinary exercise in reproduction and, in certain cases, documentation. In the best cinemas of any city, one may go to see films that lack all narrative construction and all expressive validity; films conceived with the precise scope of showing off the reproductive capacities of the latest cinematographic inventions.

This is simply a matter of high-class display, of a series of sensations concentrated into a short time, and at a low price – a view of Paris from the top of the Eiffel tower, opera at the Teatro alla Scala, a helicopter flight over the Andes; all of it just as if the spectator were 'really there'. Perhaps the cinema is returning little by little to its original state as a magical distributor of illusions and, even if the former make-shift booth has been replaced by an auditorium with indirect lighting and air conditioning, the public flock there with the same hunger for sensations with which it queued up for tickets in front of Italo Pacchioni's *Padiglione Cinematographico* at the Fiera di Porta Genova in Milan.[40]

In this expressive regression one may discover a particularly significant element regarding the function of cutting within the linguistic economy of the film. Just as the arrival of sound at first notably diminished the author's liberty when making up the figurative elements of the various scenes, so the reproductive orientation that technical progress increasingly attributes to the cinema takes away from the cutting any expressive possibilities, and reduces it to a simple instrument of connection, capable of discovering the rules of its operative intervention more in the straightforward composition of a logical succession than in taking upon itself an expressive coherence with respect to the ideas lying behind the film. The harmonic composition of the elements within an individual section gives way to the adding together of the parts themselves so as to form a chain of phantasms monstrously close to the world that generated them. The parabola that the cutting process thus describes should not cause any great surprise, since it is the first and necessary consequence of the distortion that cinematic production has undergone with the advent of more elaborate reproductive techniques.

The cinema aims to recreate in the spectator the sensation of reality, and this applies to all the subject's sensitive organs. The image no longer has any symbolical value and, if it is still a sign, its function is so inexact as to prevent any exact semantic classification. The image is reality, and

---

[40] *La Piazza*, popular Italian entertainments described and illustrated by A. G. Bragaglia, A. Cervellati, R. Leydi, A. Mezzanotte, E. F. Palmieri, V. Pandolfi, S. Piantanida. Edited and introduced by Roberto Leydo, Collana del "Gallo Grande" (Milano, ed. Avanti, 1959). This work contains an interesting essay by E. F. Palmieri on the subject in question: "Cinema, dalla baracca alle sale".

must at all costs be so; but in every-day life the subject sitting in front of a screen, intent upon enjoying a three-dimensional, stereophonic, colour film that broadcasts scents in harmony with the olfactory content of the scene represented, observes objects and phenomena from a single point of view which is his and his alone. If he wants to see a particular element closer, he cannot change the system of lenses in his eyes, but must instead move physically closer to the object of his attention. Cutting doesn't exist in reality, and it thus has to disappear almost entirely in the meticulously exact reproduction that the cinematographic instruments are making of it.

After the arrival of sound, the cinematographic authors who wanted to express themselves in the forms of a symbolic language, making use of the analogical coupling of images which take on a meaning beyond that of their content by virtue of their reciprocal relationship, brought the figurative and rhythmic exigencies of their narration into conformity with a continuous and valid link with the possibilities of the real.

The films of Dreyer, Bergman, and Fellini are particularly significant from this point of view, because their authors are fascinated by a set of spiritual and metaphysical problems that condition their entire mode of narration. The key to the narrative in their most important works is often to be found in the symbolism of the situations, the characters, and the images that exists within an apparent action whose elements occur in complete accord with the laws of reality. The author makes use of the material offered to him by the world around him in order to make it up into an audio-visual construction which, without doing violence to the conditions of its origin, is able to communicate to the spectator the expression of a language of symbols. Dreyer, Bergman, Fellini, and other directors with them, are also able to detach themselves from the operative moduli of reality, and to penetrate into the realm of dreams and of the absurd. In this instance, the figurative elements can be juxtaposed without any logical justification, and without any apparent credibility, since the narration is explicitly alien to any realistic praxis and convention. The basic orientation of these authors' creative personalities encourages them to look for those narrative situations in which the figurative aspects of reality can be altered in their form or their mutual relations, without violating the credibility of the action.

So one cannot say that with the advent of sound analogical cutting has entirely lost its effectiveness. The methods of application and the rules (if they may be thus defined) of the visual joint have altered; they have had to adapt themselves to the linguistic demands of an expressive form which has drawn the characteristic elements defining its originality and its essence (both of them, perhaps, entirely alien to the epoch of the silent film) from the presence of a sound-track. The problem of cutting remains, just as it has been set out by those of the latest generation of directors who have been most committed to a sincere and effective linguistic research; but there will be occasion to examine this stylistic aspect of the contemporary cinema further in the final part of this study, which once more takes up all the problems connected with the phenomenon of cutting.

THE SOUND-TRACK AND ITS INFLUENCE AS A SIGN ELEMENT

At this point, after pausing to consider the influence of sound films on cutting techniques, it would be a good idea to single out some of the linguistic aspects of the cinematographic spectacle that arise when dialogue, sounds, and noises are added to the movement of images on the screen. The essence of the cinema is basically visual, and every sonic intervention ought to limit itself to a justified and necessary act of expressive integration.

It is extremely difficult, as has already been observed, to express an idea or a concept by means of images, since the language that uses them is far more adapted to arousing affections and emotions than it is to laying out in a clear synthesis the basic elements of an act of rational speculation – often a whole film is needed in order to make clear a single concept. The cinematographic author, faced with the necessity of expressing an abstract idea, often lets himself be persuaded by the simplified solution of dialogue or a voice off-screen.

After the film had been able to free itself from the theatrical limits that had so heavy an influence upon its first attempts, the advent of sound unexpectedly revealed itself as threatening a return to the ignominious conditions that had characterized the first days of the cinema. To this risk, which was furthermore confirmed by the results of the first sound films, was added the danger of letting the expressive cinematographic forms become fossilized within a rigidly bounded system, far removed from those possibilities for linguistic and aesthetic independence that the absence of sound had spontaneously, even if slowly, conferred upon the silent film. The Russian director M. Ciaureli writes:

Those working in the cinema who had come there from other artistic fields continued for some time in their stubborn refusal to apply to the sound film the figurative forms that they had previously discovered. Words imposed upon the first sound films the necessity of giving up brief, expressive forms of cutting, and sharp, intense figurative forms; in their place were used lengthy shots, extensive dialogues, a decidedly theatrical *mise-en-scène*, and, if one may put it like this, frontal solutions when showing men and events. The man on the screen acquired the possibility of expressing his emotions in words; but at the same time he seemed to be tied down by the meager portrayal of the environment in which he moved.... So that to start off with, the word was not considered as an expression of the essence of the character's thought, or a manifestation of his interior world, but instead, and more simply, as one of the means that the artist had at his disposition in order to create an image, express the development of the subject, or reveal the idea lying behind the work.

Further on, Ciaureli, talking about the film *Ciapaiev*, remarks that within it

...the word and the sound have a value in as far as they are not noticeable, and do not stand out amongst the other components that make up the film. They are in perfect harmony with the content, or more exactly, they appear as the only elements that can justly express a given ideological content, which is revealed by the artistic form adapted to it.[41]

Word and sound, introduced by technical progress in making up the cinematographic work, completely overthrew the linguistic nature and aesthetic laws of the silent film – the sound film is an entirely different means of expression from the silent film, and no sign relationship may be established with complete coherence between the two types of spectacle. The withering of the image's symbolic power, which was noted when talking of analogical cutting, coincided with a real revolution in techniques of expression. The silent film

...had created a union of silent man and silent things, as well as of the (audible) person close-by and the (inaudible) one at a far distance. In the universal silence of the image, the fragments of a broken vase could 'talk' exactly the way a character 'talked' to his neighbour.... This homogeneity, which is completely foreign to the theatre but familiar in painting, is destroyed by the talking film: it endows the actor with speech, and since only he can have it, all other things are pushed into the background.[42]

The author found himself forced to abandon the forms of the language of symbols that the silent film had been able, little by little, to take on as a characteristic, and at times fundamental element of its essence. This renunciation, and the search for new modes of expression that followed from it, helped to produce new linguistic forms that were almost alien to the previous ones. While in the silent film the characters' actions sought to

[41]   Ciaureli (1954), 79, 80, 82.
[42]   Arnheim (1958), 186.

prescind from their verbal expression, and were channeled into those attitudes and forms of gestural behaviour that could most easily suggest to the public the meaning of the narration, the advent of sound brought back into evidence the necessity of seeing the person in the act of vocal emission, of showing his mouth accomplishing those gestural movements corresponding to the words heard in the auditorium. The initial enthusiasm engendered by the possibility of recording on film the actors' dialogue, the sounds of the environment, and the background music coincided with the production of a series of shapeless and confused films, compared to which the films of Georges Méliès, Alberto Capellani, and Ferdinand Zecca at least enjoy the privilege of a spontaneously attractive ingenuity, and of a respectful unpretentiousness in attempting to master the laws of movement. Words and sounds were for several years the undoubted masters of cinematographic production, which, inspired by American industrial successes, believed that it had solved all its economic and aesthetic problems by resorting to a transposition of successful theatre pieces, or commissioning from the most important authors of scenarios subjects rich in jokes and sound effects, hardly differing from the texts intended for theatrical performance.

With considerable efforts, some of which are not yet exhausted, the sound film began to look for its linguistic forms, locating them in precisely that zone of inter-reaction between visual and auditory elements which, although leaving to the former the basic task of defining the expressive heart of the work, recognizes the potential that the latter possess for an indispensable and irreplaceable integration, ingrained in the ideas that lie behind the whole work.

A sound film must be conceived and thought out as a sound film – it can never be the result of an adaption or a transposition; it can never effectively satisfy the needs of a communicative act, if the nature of the act itself is alien to it. The sound-track does not, therefore, attach itself to the silent film as a simple addition, nor does it increase its communicative capacity by simply conferring upon it new means of expression. A silent film, conceived as being structured without any sonic support, gains absolutely nothing from the possibility of adding a sound-track; on the contrary, it risks losing the genuine and unified nature of the form that it has acquired in harmony with the idea lying behind it.

The sign effected by an audio-visual image is essentially different from the one corresponding to a silent image, even though man's greater responsiveness to visual stimuli (the perception of which undoubtedly preceded that of every other type of sensorial signal in the individual's biological evolution towards a balanced perceptive activity) means that even a sound film can, fundamentally, be reduced to a communicative act made up of moving images. The necessity of a sound-track cannot be subordinated to some fortuitous requirement of the narration, but must make itself implicitly felt from the earliest stages of the imaginative elaboration that is destined to give birth to the cinematographic work.

The sound-track may be made up realistically, recording the words spoken by the actors, and the sounds of the environment; or else it may be thought of as an element of expression to be subsequently integrated with the image. Directors use one method as much as the other; background music thus acquires a decisive importance, in regard to the expressive power of the film, and may be of the greatest help in the general composition of the cinematographic image.

Even the authors of the silent film felt the need to link their works to specific musical commentaries, which played upon the spectator's sensibility, suggesting to him those psychological states best adapted to an appreciation of what was projected on the screen. Many directors suggested the titles of pieces of music that they would have preferred to listen to during the projection of their film; but generally the orchestras in the little cinemas "...round the period 1912 ...were quite happy to play selections of light café music quite unrelated to the film on the screen and ...after a given period of the *William Tell Overture*, Tchaikovsky, and Rubenstein, get up and leave the film and its audience to the deathly hush of silence".[43]

Later on, it was attempted to remedy this awkward situation by enclosing musical scores with the copies of the film, containing indications as to which visual actions were intended to be accompanied by what music. Most of these scores were written for piano – for that old, out of tune, upright piano which made our grandfathers' flesh creep, indissolubly linking its sound to the capers of Ridolini, the antics of Charlie Chaplin, and the statuesque and sensual attitudes of Bernhardt. Basically, even though the purists turned up their noses at such musical contaminations, the silent film was doing no more than repeating an experiment that had already been tried out in the theatre with great success. The insertion of an artistic means of expression that was by nature alien to the one which bore the fundamental weight of the communication, and was in itself already complete throughout the vast range of its possibilities, did indeed bring with it a grave danger of confusion and linguistic ambiguity.

[43] Roger Manvell and John Huntley, *The Technique of Film Music* (London, Focal Press, 1957), 18-19.

The cinematographic author found himself able to influence the public with greater suggestive power by taking advantage of a musician's work and of the spectator's receptiveness to a type of sign stimulus that ought not to have been in play within the ambit of film communication.

The cinema was, with difficulty, searching out the path towards aesthetic independence; and yet the introduction of music seemed to slow this spontaneous development down, leaving almost all the directors to settle into a placid conformism. Basically, the polemics on the nature of the cinema that had sprung up with predictable violence when sound first appeared already had historical precedents in the disparate judgements that were engendered by the application of musical commentaries to silent films. When it became possible to attribute a voice to the actors and the environment, the problem of musical accompaniment returned – but this time its appearance was justified by far more valid motives, if not indeed by an expressive necessity that was directly connected to the nature of the new technical sorcery. Music became an almost indispensable element of film-making.

Some of the greatest artists of the cinema have personally supervised the musical commentary of their works, such as Charlie Chaplin, who is entirely without musical training, or Ingmar Bergman, who works with a composer friend, suggesting to him motifs and tempi; other directors have instead collaborated with great musicians who possessed a sensibility close to their own, and a creative flair for translating into musical images the director's integrative intentions. For example, the collaboration between S. M. Eisenstein and S. Prokofiev has produced excellent results: the musical commentary to the two episodes of *Ivan the Terrible* and *Alexander Nevsky* not only reveals the essential and strictly functional nature of the orchestral contribution, but also offers clear evidence of the identity of inspiration that marked the work of the two artists. Referring to his very able collaborator, Eisenstein writes that one could undoubtedly consider as one of his most important qualities the

...ability to build up sound equivalents for the representations that come within his field of vision. Any composer setting out to write music for the screen, as well as any director with an ambition to work in the sound film, to say nothing of the chromophon film (that is, a colour musical), must possess this ability, although not so highly developed as in the case of Prokofiev.

A little earlier in the same essay, S. M. Eisenstein had given clear indication of the importance that he and Prokofiev attached to the music within a cinematographic spectacle, alluding to the heated discussions that they had as to the choice of a work method.

As a rule, Prokofiev and I bargain long and earnestly over 'which is to be the first': whether he should write music for unedited pieces of representation which would then be edited accordingly, or I should complete the montage of a scene first, and have music afterwards.... I am pretty well familiar with the 'inner mechanics' of the process [evidently referring to the first].... To cope with it successfully one must remember very distinctly all the plastic material to be dealt with. Then one must have the recorded phonogram 'run' an infinite number of times, patiently waiting for the moment when certain elements of one order suddenly start corresponding to certain elements of the other. For instance, the texture of an object or a landscape and the timbre of a musical passage; the possibility of coordinating rhythmically a number of long shots with another musical passage, the rationally inexpressible 'inner harmony' of a piece of music and a piece of representation, etc.[44]

Another director who meticulously supervises the sound-track and musical commentary of his films, Alfred Hitchcock, considers that the music may indeed condition the cutting of a scene or sequence, imposing an exterior rhythm to which the internal one of narration by images must adapt itself. Hitchcock states that in one of his films, *Waltzes from Vienna*, "...naturally every cut in the film was worked out on script before shooting began. But more than that, the musical cuts were worked out too."[45] Hitchcock firmly advocates that the director should have a thorough knowledge, or at any rate some prevision, of the whole musical score before he begins shooting; R. Manvell and John Huntley, referring to his work methods, write that

...music is part and parcel of the film, and its use in the development of the action and the establishing of atmosphere should be determined while the film is planned. This has never been the normal practice in the studios, but Hitchcock's observations [about making the director get to know the score before using the cine-camera] show real appreciation of the need for a close integration between the music and the other elements in film-making, both in picture and sound.[46]

This audio-visual integration must, of necessity, be subject to the laws of the dialogue and, in general, of the addition of sound themselves, as far as its distribution within the economy of the whole work is concerned.

The music must thus constitute an indissoluble whole with the other sound elements and, above all, with the film's visual action. It must not be allowed to go beyond its limits, and should not be appreciated in itself; on the contrary, it ought to contribute to the formation of the general impression that the film makes upon the spectator, without ever becoming

---

[44] Eisenstein, *Notes of a Film Director* (London, Lawrence & Wishart, 1959), 156-158.
[45] Manvell and Huntley (1957), 46.
[46] Manvell and Huntley (1957), 45.

noticeable as an isolated element. The public ought to become aware of the musical commentary after reflecting upon the spectacle that they are or have been watching – only an expert critic, who is used to analyzing the various expressive elements that make up the image on film, should be capable of separating the visual component from the auditory one at the same time as the action is taking place on the screen, weighing up their relative effectiveness and the potential success of their cinematographic synthesis.

The sound-track reaches the peak of its own expressive value with an efficient musical commentary. The sign constituted by the visual image is in fact autonomous and sufficient for the needs of a complete communicative act when it is inserted into a linguistic structure that takes into account its limitations and possibilities. It may indeed be absorbed into a universe of aesthetic appreciation, when the language of the film comes into contact with the expressive requirements of a poet, who is able to transform into its forms the internal stimuli to which his imaginative powers are subject.

The insertion of a notably different sign component, such as the sound commentary, into the ambit of the primitive image and the composition deriving from it ought to involve an enrichment of the medium's expressive potential. But from the artistic point of view, expressive phenomena generally organize themselves along lines of force differing from the norms of communication, and an increase in the means of expression almost always leads to a depreciation of the aesthetic nature of the sign complex. The loss of instrumental simplicity almost always coincides, in the various artistic disciplines, with a loss of expressive coherence and with coarsened regressions in the development of the work. This has happened several times, for example, in the field of the melodrama, which only succeeded in finding a genuine expressive structure of its own by synthesizing voice and orchestra into the forms of a single musical language,[47] and in the field of the theatre, which only succeeds in conserving

---

[47] "Undoubtedly the work's fortunes stem from the exigencies of spectacle rather than those of music. The need to place a musical creation within the ambit of one's own experience, and to attribute to it a value relative to the world of everyday emotions finds satisfaction in the possibility of linking it to a given new objective. Neither the intervention of rationality, nor indeed an intellectualistic rhetoric of passion, as Nietzsche put it, can give an account of the work and its success on a phenomenological level, but rather the need for a formal determination of experiences and sensations, according to a disposition that has deep roots within human nature, and within its way of operating as a cognitively active force. Thus when one cannot base it upon emotive situations that are concretely defined by word and 'image', musical experience remains suspended in the void" (Pagliaro [1957], 122-123).

the function and freshness of an original artistic communication by situating the dialogue at the centre of the action. Rudolph Arnheim writes that

...the compounding of different media – for example, moving picture and speech – cannot be justified simply by the fact that in the experience of everyday life visual and auditory elements are intimately connected and, in fact, inseparably fused. There must be artistic reasons for such a combination: it must serve to express something that could not be said by one of the media alone.... A composite work of art is possible only if complete structures, produced by the media, are integrated in the form of parallelism. Naturally such a 'double track' will make sense only if the components do not simply convey the same thing. They must complete each other in the sense of dealing differently with the same subject. Every medium must treat the subject in its own way, and the resulting differences must be in accordance with those that exist between the media.[48]

In a combination of expressive factors, every component should preserve all its characteristics intact, and should act within the communicative threshold corresponding to its nature: but this purity, this individuality of the medium that contributes to the general form, must by no means reveal itself in the action of an isolated sign, separated in some way from the context, if the work is to aspire to a poetic validity. In order that a judgment of aesthetic value be possible, the enrichment of the expressive means must coincide with their relative and synthetic integration into an expressive unity, whose nature differs from that of the elements making up the composition. The unity is more easily achieved when a certain similarity already exists between the instruments used for expressive ends; everything may help to achieve this similarity, from the inner nature of the sign to the subject's mode of sensitive receptiveness, or to the differing sign groups' innate subjection to similar harmonic or rhythmic laws. Song and music are brought together by virtue of their common nature as sound; a composition in colours may find a match and the possibility of integration, leading to a new expressive form that would surpass it without alienating it from its true nature, in musical elements harmonized according to rules similar to those that govern the distribution of colours.

One cannot establish universal laws of similarity in a field so open to personal perception and the contingencies of inspiration. However, one can state that the rhythmic laws inherent in a montage of moving images may be matched with those used in the composition of a piece of music.[49]

---

[48] Arnheim (1958), 177.
[49] Commenting upon Alain Resnais' film *Hiroshima mon amour*, André Hodeir speaks

This relation may avoid the canons of identity and, for expressive reasons, may enter those of contrast or of parallel simultaneity of differing affective states. The language of music and that of cinematographic images do not, in origin, enjoy any apparent similarities; yet the innermost and irrational structure of their expressive development favours the meeting and synthesis of the two media into a third communicative instrument, which is different from either of its components, even though generated by their union.

Music, apart from one or two compositions bound by a specific relationship to a real object, is a fundamentally asemantic art, an art whose signs do not exist by virtue of a two-way, rational connection with an idea or a phenomenon or a concrete aspect of the apparent world. Music does not 'represent', and does not 'substitute' for facts and objects, but rather evokes the sentiments and atmospheres that the author means to link with those facts and objects. The language of visual images is, as has already been observed, far from any form of rationalization or abstraction in its communicative development; even if, in reproducing its image, it draws far nearer to the object than does music, it is only with difficulty that it arrives at the formulation of a thought or a judgment about the object itself. Generalization belongs no more to the film than it does to music: both of them make their imprint upon the emotional sensibility of the subject, providing him with a complex of stimuli that could hardly be related to a sign in a rational way, or hardly be valid in spite of the succession of perceptive acts and of the qualitative differentiation of the perceptors.

One can therefore understand what the path towards integration be-

---

of a concept of cutting that makes its first appearance there: Resnais "introduces a notion of specifically musical discontinuity and thereby creates a complex relationship of time organizations. In the non-realistic sequences – and frequently even in the realistic ones – the text is used in a contrapuntal spirit. There would be no novelty in this if it were a linear counterpoint à la Hindemith that was employed, but what is used instead is a kind of discontinuous, virtually SERIAL counterpoint." Referring to the scene in which the protagonist's German lover is killed, Hodeir sees "... a correspondence ...between structure and poetic effect for which we would be hard put to find an equivalent outside the art of music. And if we were to point to some precursor, the dramatic innovations of Alban Berg (particularly in *Wozzeck*) come to mind rather than Orson Welles' hesitant attempts to explore time in *Citizen Kane*.

"Another analogy with musical form is the division of the work into a certain number of parts. I make out ten: some, extremely brief, function as interludes, like the third movement of Beethoven's Fourteenth Quartet. Each is subject to its own *tempo*. Oddly enough, the tempo grows slower after the lyrical sequence of the parade: we proceed from *andante* to *adagio* to *largo*." ("An Analysis of Alain Resnais' Film *Hiroshima Mon Amour*", trans. R. Howard, *Evergreen Review* 12 [March-April 1960], 102-113.)

tween visual image and sound could be, and what expressive effects could be derived from it; although they differ in their physical structure and in the physiological act necessary to receive them, film and music find a meeting point in their common inadequacy with respect to logical speculation and abstract information.

We have already noted Ingmar Bergman's ideas regarding the relation between cinema and music, but it would be as well to repeat their fundamental terms.

The written word is read and assimilated by a conscious act of the will united with the intellect; little by little, the imagination and the emotions become influenced by it. For the cinema, the process is different; when we go to see a film, we are consciously prepared for an illusion.... The succession of images operates directly upon our emotions, without touching the intellect. MUSIC WORKS IN THE SAME WAY; I WOULD SAY THAT NO OTHER FORM OF ART HAS SO MUCH IN COMMON WITH THE CINEMA AS HAS MUSIC. Both of them influence our emotions directly, not by means of the intellect.[50]

The analysis of the relation between word, sounds, and visual image is worth pursuing further, above all taking into account the expressive orientation that increasingly conditions the more carefully planned aspects of contemporary production, and that tends to revalue the contribution of the sound-track, often allowing it a greater importance than the visual aspect. We shall return to this subject after pursuing one or two basic arguments that are necessary for an exact formulation of the problem.

COLOUR

Another important aspect of cinematographic expression is the use of colour, with respect to which all film directors have always behaved with great humility, more often than not giving up chromatic integration in order to turn back to 'black and white', which is susceptible to greater technical control and is supported by an almost complete experience with regard to shooting and developing.

Colour stands in relation to the film as does any other of the many possible means of integration. The cinema can exist in an entirely inde-

---

[50]   Ingmar Bergman (1961), p. xv. Also Pagliaro (1957), 121. "Without any doubt at all music is, in a certain sense, the freest of the arts, because the process that is carried out between the moment of poetic creation and its formal determination is homogenous and, as it were, synergic.... The form constitutes the mediation between the poetic moment and the work; the accoustical image, which in music constitutes the form, generates itself from within, as it were – it has no external references and it obeys no other law then that of its interior congruency."

pendent expressive form, even if it lacks colour, just as the silent film had found an artistic originality of its own that was far removed from any potential sonic integration.

But when one wishes to achieve the kinetic composition of coloured images, one cannot limit oneself to a simple additive intervention, an expressive enrichment carried out on the basis of an ancient iconic form; instead, one gives rise to a new means of audio-visual communication, governed by its own linguistic laws which are, at times, in contrast with those that may be deduced from the other forms of expression. The greatest difficulty that the director comes up against when investigating the possibilities of colour is the impossibility of a thorough and secure control of chromatic combinations. It is, in fact, difficult to foresee the tonality and intensity that a certain colour will assume when printed on film, despite the fact that the latest technical advances have made it possible to notably reduce the difference between the colours of the filmed reality and those of the projected image, and to dominate within a certain limit the tonal rendering of the various shades. But even supposing that the cinematographic response is perfectly adapted to the chromatic stimuli of reality, or that it is distorted in a completely controlled manner, the author of the film will find himself compelled to create a dynamic equilibrium amongst the colours, an interplay of relations between tints and tones which is always valid, both in static scenes and in moving ones. All the infinitesimal temporal acts from which the cinematographic action is made up must in fact enjoy a chromatic equilibrium that is valid in itself and is, at the same time, able to establish an adequate point of reference for the action itself, in its expressive development.

The attainment of this admirable result is almost beyond realization, since it involves a real respect for the laws of chromatic integration in every figurative variation within the shot and, even more complicated, in every cut. The relations between different shots are indeed revolutionized, at times, by the use of colour, which can become the element that conditions the entire narrative procedure. In order that two coloured shots may link harmoniously together, there must be an effective chromatic relation between them such as to justify joining them. The expressive coherence of the communicative medium does in fact demand that none of the integrative elements, and even less colour, should detach themselves from the others in their narrative or expressive function and assume a differentiated aspect that is notably isolated from the unified development of the work.

The search for a dynamic equilibrium in combining colours is further conditioned by having to adapt the moving image's chromatic function to the expressive needs of a certain part of the entire work's narrative procedure. Colour, an integrative element of the image's sign function, cannot reduce its task to that of a simple decorative presence, or to the exact photographic reproduction of a real colouration. At the cinema, one hardly ever looks for a gratuitous playing with, or exact repetition of, the object's concrete condition. Despite the fact that the cinematographic spectacle's *raison d'etre* lies in the photographic nature of its elementary images, one cannot overlook the author's recreative interventions, to which Jean R. Debrix refers, when he states that

...l'erreur constante de la plupart des cinéastes ...a été la recherche d'un réalisme *physique*, d'une imitation impersonelle, inésthetique de la réalité tangible. Encore une fois, l'important, en cinématographie, n'est pas de créer une illusion sensorielle... Le réalisme au cinéma est aux antipodes d'une reproduction vulgaire de la vie réelle; il est tout entier dans la suggestion d'une réalité cinématographique valable.[51]

Colour simply cannot lead a life of its own when it is involved in the composition of a cinematographic sign. On the contrary, it must subordinate its entire expressive effect to the demands of the narration, so as to form an aesthetically valid reality. The author must sacrifice any effect or gratuitous play to the coherence and simplicity of his iconic exposition.

The film is a two-dimensional spectacle and its colours exist within a two-dimensional rectangle, by virtue of an illusory projection, within which the figures 'appear' to be moving. The cinematographic phantasm's incorporeal nature is also shared by the colour which, despite all appearances, only extends over one plane. To some degree, this characteristic brings together colour in the cinema and colour in painting, film techniques and painting techniques. The Russian director M. Ciaureli writes that

...as ...in painting, in which the compositional laws of perspective are also widely used, so too in the cinema we have, essentially, the huge canvas of the screen.... This is why ...the use of the gamut of colours in the cinema ought to follow the path of a total assimilation ...of the development of the principles of painting....[52]

However, it is also Ciaureli who rejects the gratuitous transposition of a chromatic solution using blobs of flat colour from pictorial procedures to cinematographic ones. "Colour painting is a chromatic symphony made up of blobs of colour limited by the outlines of the depicted object."[53] This

[51] Debrix (1960), 127.
[52] Ciaureli (1954), 94.
[53] Ciaureli (1954), 97.

technique of manipulating colours is not neglected *a priori* by the author of a film, who must, in so complex an operation, lay himself open at all costs to the influence of every expressive form that has ever been tried out. But he will turn to it in those limited cases in which the formal resources offered to him by the pictorial instrument coincide to perfection with the demands of his narrative inspiration, as does no other chromatic technique. Distributing the colour in blobs can, for example, be of use to the director when the cinematographic narration makes him describe a certain episode in documentary form, or accentuate the simple and ingenuous aspect that typifies the ambience of a certain narrative passage (and sometimes a whole film), or intentionally bring into relief the decorative and formal aspects of a certain situation.

In the history of painting, artists have turned to 'flat colours' above all when faced by the necessity of reproducing in images aspects of a religious world or of a legendary and mythical universe: this is the case, respectively, in Byzantine iconography (which also reveals, on the level of content, the necessity of composing with the image a 'rational' sign of divinity) and in oriental miniatures. Colour is almost always applied in blobs by 'primitive' painters, by the naïfs of every era. Naturally, the cinema does not refer to this pictorial technique alone, despite the fact that the action of its phantasms takes place on a two-dimensional surface; on the contrary, the figurative movement that is fundamental to the film implies a chromatic research that is almost always oriented towards those periods of the history of painting that had as their fundamental goals plasticity, perspective, and kinetic suggestion. Ciaureli writes

Nearer, by nature, to the art cinema is easel painting, with its complex interplay of coloured surfaces, its tendency to portray the great variety of chromatic shades created by the light, and by the reflections of various objects, the mobility of colour, of light, and, consequently, of the material as well, just as it is naturally.[54]

So that by attributing to colour a simple integrative function and avoiding every exaggerated evaluation or servile submission to the fascination of a harmonic but unjustified composition of spots of colour, the author of the film may find among the results of the latest psychotechnical researches stimuli well adapted to the preliminary formation of a receptive disposition in the spectator. Colour may, in fact, act as an integrative sign vehicle of an aesthetic order, but it does not exhaust its communicative possibilities in this function. For it is also an excellent vehicle for psychological conditioning, and may favour an unconscious predisposi-

[54] Ciaureli (1954), 98.

tion on the part of the receiving subject to the acceptance of a certain type of sign relation.[55]

Colour possesses no absolute expressive efficacy, linked in a bi-unique relation to its chromatic nature. One cannot, for example, state that yellow expresses a state of jealousy, envy, or distrust, without taking into account the degree of intensity with which the colour appears, the type of light that brings it into evidence, and above all its spatial relation and mutual interference with the other colours that may accompany its appearance. The subject's psychological reaction when faced with a coloured image is not governed by the presence of various colours, as such – it does not develop on the basis of defined chromatic units. On the contrary, it is determined by that harmonious composition of tonalities, surfaces, and luminosities from which the form of the entire phantasm derives its existence. The aesthetic experience is thus joined by a simultaneous experience of a psychological nature, which should be regarded by the director as one of the elements that go to make up the public's response to his film.

Within the combination of the various chromatic parts of the image, the colour may take on a symbolic validity of its own that is, at times, quite independent of the one to be attributed to the figures that appear on screen. Colour may, by acting directly upon the spectator's unconscious, solicit a condition of psychological reactivity which is necessary for the reception of the message, and which other means of cinematographic expression could only arrive at with less immediacy and simplicity.

A director wishing to concern himself with colour cannot afford to ignore any aspect of colour symbology, nor can he leave out of account any of the research that has been carried out in this field by psychologists and

[55] W. Ehrenstein is of the opinion that the perception of colour has much in common with that of movement. He has noted that "...the merging of movement corresponds to the merging of colours; the simultaneous contrast of movement corresponds to the simultaneous contrast of colours; the successive contrast of movement corresponds to the successive contrast of colours.... (The) perception of movement, which springs from the presentation of an object's successive positions in space, presents an evident analogy with the impression of 'depth' that one gets from the 'fusion' of the two retinal images: in one case we are concerned with simultaneous and static spatial disparity, in the other with successive and dynamic spatial disparity. That the analogy is a real one may be demonstrated by the fact that the sense of movement, united to the sense of space, can give rise to new perceptive qualities; just as depth united to colours generates the perception of corporeal colours (Oberflächenfarben), so movement exercises an influence upon the structuration of space" (Fabro [1961], 305-306). From these considerations about the affinity between the two perceptive acts one may deduce the possibility of an effective encounter, within the film, between the laws of cutting and movement, and those of colour distribution.

painters. Without adapting himself in an impersonal manner to any experimental result, thus behaving in a way that would finally lead him to
sterile laboratory entertainments, he ought to reduce the interplaying
forms within the dynamics of his inspiration to the indicative schematism
suggested to him by statistical observations and by checking upon normal
reactions. Guido Ballo writes:

The dynamics of expression – for the sign is always linked to a more or less
latent expressiveness – springs from the relations between: colour and sign;
colour and other colours; colour, sign, and environment.... Concerning symbology within the language and dynamics of colour, one cannot neglect the
contribution of avant-garde painters; from pointillism to the abstractionism of
Kandinsky and Mondrian, they have made felt the need for concreteness:
colour may not be understood as an abstraction, because it acquires a particular
expressiveness – and thus a differing symbolical effectiveness – from the gradations, the light, the spaces, the relations with other colours, and with the whole
environment.... There are no colours that should be considered abstractly:
they always acquire a shade of their own and fit into their surroundings in different ways, nor can their emotional resonances be easily reduced to fixed schemes:
these schemes are always bases, above which, in the concreteness of history and
of life, variety moves continually.[56]

Using colour involves a risk of creative impotence that has often made
the most sensitive authors draw back and that has seen many of the
most committed attempts to avoid it fail. Colour may, furthermore,
accelerate and indeed bring to a head the rush towards the magical reproduction of the laboratory, bringing the images into a perfect and impersonal conformity with the forms of nature, a tendency which is to
some degree latent in the entire history of the cinema and which the film
industry still presses for.

THE SIGN FUNCTIONS OF THE 'PHOTOGRAPHIC' FILM

If the cinematographic sign loses its expressive efficacy and transforms itself into a simple instrument of information, its semantic value will be
reduced to a denotative relation with the represented object – a relation in
which every consideration of an aesthetic order must be left out of account. This is so to an even greater extent when the sign link with the object is reduced to a passive imitation of the represented object, which
works all the better on the communicative level the more slavishly it

[56] "Linguaggio e dinamica del colore", *Cornigliano* 4:4 (July-August 1960) (a ma-
gazine for the distribution of administrative information).

succeeds. The specular coincidence between object and image in itself becomes transformed, in all its expressive nullity, into a cause for 'amusement', a form of 'spectacle'.

The emotion that the cinema offers and the public demands in such cases exists within the limits of the indirect experience of a certain sensation or a certain environmental condition which the film is able to offer at a low price – an epidermic experience which gives the impression of a certain satisfaction and which initiates psycho-physical activities that are doomed to dispersion because they are disappointed by the inanity of their stimulus.

The magic rites which, in primitive societies, aim to attribute to the object a nature and a substance that are not its own so as to establish it at one end of a binary relationship, at the other end of which stands the subject involved in an empty and false experience, do not greatly differ from the sign situations created by the majority of cinematographic spectacles, which are unable to resist the attractions of identity and photographic reproduction. Every element that comes into the composition of a film may be driven, in its expressive function, to the frigid limits of perfect copying, and colour perhaps tends to be the victim of this attitude more than any other element, because the technical operation that underlies colour printing is one of the most complicated and least easily controlled, and because it is very hard to give up the colour distribution offered by the object's spontaneous self-manifestation.

Rudolph Arnheim asserts that "the complete film", the film in which the imitation of reality is at its most perfect and suggestive, is none other than "...the fulfillment of the age-old striving for the complete illusion. The attempt to make the two-dimensional picture as nearly as possible like its solid model succeeds: original and copy become practically indistinguishable"; regarding colour, the same author refers back to what H. Baer wrote "...in a remarkable little essay in the *Kunstblatt*",

Graphic art, of which photography is one branch, has always striven after colour.... Uncivilised man is not as a rule satisfied with black-and-white. Children, peasants, and primitive peoples demand the highest degree of bright colouring. It is the primitives of the great cities who congregate before the film screen. Therefore film calls in the aid of bright colours. It is a fresh stimulus.[57]

The cinema has large amounts of money at stake and initiates economic movements that are particularly complex and delicate; its works find their place within a phenomenology of an industrial order, which is linked to the law of supply and demand. The producers are concerned

[57] Arnheim (1958), 133.

with conforming to the requirements of the public and, in most cases, only take linguistic or aesthetic problems into account when the public demands a really well-made film with a solid narrative structure, or in the few cases in which authors succeed in imposing a style of their own.

One will only be able to resolve the problem of colour by means of thorough-going and free research when, for example, the public show signs of wanting a functional and linguistically effective form of chromatic expression – when the mass becomes tired of admiring spiritless postcards and oleographs destined for display (the experiments conducted by M. Antonioni in *Il deserto rosso* and *Blow-up* are, in this respect, significant both in themselves, and in the type of response they drew from the audience), when it no longer finds any enjoyment in a "voyage across the world on a cinema seat" or in a "ride on the switchback at the Prater", when it feels the need for artistic emotions or truthful narrative experiences, rather than three-dimensional images or stereophonic sound.[58] Perhaps this will never happen, and the 'complete cinema' will always represent the finishing point for the productive development of all those industries that are in some way concerned with the phenomenon; perhaps the public will always need a drug available to all pockets, a big box full of colours and sounds in which they can immerse themselves so as to escape into another world for an hour.

Perhaps we shall always be forced to search laboriously in the great sea of anodyne and stupid productions for those few films whose nature may be related with greater ease to the imaginative presence of a man than to the reproductive presence of an optical machine.

[58] In 1921, during the era of the silent film, Hugo von Hofmannsthal published an essay in the Viennese *Neue Freie Presse* called "Der Ersatz für Träume" (The Substitute for Dreams), "...in which he identified the crowd of cinema-goers with the masses living in the big cities and industrial centres, factory workers, white-collar workers, etc. Their heads are empty, because this is the type of life that society imposes upon them.... So they escape into the cinema, and silent films owe their primary attraction to the very fact of being silent. In them the spectator finds that fullness of life that society denies him. He has dreamt of it from childhood on, and the cinema is a substitute for such dreams" (in Siegfried Kracauer, "Lo spettatore", *Film* [1961], 201).

3

FILM CUTTING AND TELEVISION CUTTING. THE INVASION OF REALITY AND THE PERMANENCE OF THE IMAGE'S SEMANTIC VALUE

FILM CUTTING AND TELEVISION CUTTING

In ideographic forms of writing, and in the civilizations that condition their formation, the graphic formulation of an abstract element, and more specifically of a concept, almost always coincides with laborious attempts to make up a sign, thus inducing an atmosphere of spontaneous and stimulating creativity.

Although the graphic sign can easily achieve the representation of an object or a concrete reality by means of a relationship of formal similarity and of relative generalization on a conventional level that will be valid within the communal limits of a certain social group, the iconic process becomes complex when the reality to be translated into a graphic image evades every form of dimensional verification and natural concretion.[1] Chinese and Japanese ideograms resort to the formation of conjunctive hieroglyphs which, by placing together the elements representing two or more concrete realities, incite in the reader a perceptive reaction with very similar connotations to those generated by the results of the latest literary syntheses. The compound ideogram, which tends to represent conceptual and abstract elements, obtains by means of combining two elements that can be represented a result that in itself cannot be. The direct relation between a simple ideographic sign and an object, a designative relation in which the linguistic convention also derives from the perception of natural forms, gives way to indirect representation, to a graphic idea derived from the product of a number of simple signs brought together to form a single signifier, the process of perceiving which coincides in a certain sense with the discovery of its signified. Thus bringing together the sign representing man and the one representing fire gives the meaning "table-companion", the sun above the horizon signifies "dawn", the sign for a rice-field above the one for labour gives the result "mas-

[1] Eisenstein, *Film Form*, trans. Jay Leyda (London, Dobson, 1951), 28.

culine", man beside word signifies "truth, sincere, steadfast", a flame within a lamp extends its reproductive effect, meaning "gentleman, master, to control", the sign of the mouth with two words and a flame coming out of it takes as its meaning "words" and "to speak", the sign for ten above the one for a mouth means "ancient, that which has come down to us from ten generations".[2]

A script of this type is very concrete, very close to things and to their existential relations, but, at the same time, it is distinctly indifferent, if not hostile, to all problems of generalization. The figurative nature of its functioning as a sign leads to the choice of an ideogram for every situation that must be graphically signified, adapting its form to the specific qualities and particular features of the case in question.

"Like nature, Chinese words are alive and plastic", writes Fenellosa,[3] "because THING and ACTION are not formally separated." Attempts at abstraction when using an ideographic script almost always end up by elaborating a metaphor which, borrowing from natural experience several processes or phenomena, unites their images in a single graphic synthesis, implying from the formal relations thus established a meaning that may be traced by means of an integrative intervention on the reader's part. But in this metaphorical construction, the ideogram acquires no powers of abstraction and, on the contrary, conserves the same applicability to the particular situation that characterizes its reproductive action in a more concrete phenomenal field.

There are, for example, five different forms corresponding to the pronoun 'I':

there is the sign of a 'spear in the hand' = a very emphatic *I*; 'five and a mouth' = a weak and defensive *I* who tries to keep the chattering crowd at a distance; 'to conceal' = a selfish and private *I*; 'self (the cocoon sign) and a mouth' = an egoistic *I*, one who takes pleasure in his own speaking; the '*self*' presented is only used when one is speaking to one's self.[4]

A script conceived in this way exists within clearly defined cultural limits and its efficiency is always qualified by the ambiguity that it incurs as a result of the semantically compound nature of the ideographic sign. It is, in fact, a matter of a representative instrument that is valid for the formation of poetic compositions, the elaboration of myth, and the graphic reproduction of phenomena, facts or thoughts that are expressed in (or

[2] E. Fenellosa, *The Chinese Written Character as a Medium for Poetry*, ed. Ezra Pound (London, Nott, 1936).
[3] Fenellosa (1936), 21.
[4] Fenellosa (1936), 25.

may be related to) forms whose perception through a representative image is complete or, at any rate, satisfactory. When the discourse to be translated into graphic signs moves into the area of rational speculation and becomes based, in its linguistic development, upon abstract categories, when it becomes transformed into a scientific discourse or a technical statement, ideographic writing still continues to accomplish feats of synthetic virtuosity, but at the same time reveals itself as a clumsy and, above all, ill-adapted instrument.

The ideographic sign, although it belongs to a complex of characters making up a script, is basically an ICONIC sign, and is thus linked to the thing that it has to represent by a solid bond of formal similarity, and by an almost identical perceptive scheme. The ambiguity of ideographic writing stems, in fact, from using for the purposes of abstract signification signs that were created to function as images. One man may transmit to another a complex of informative data, and he may also enrich it with a formulation that tends towards the expressive; the signs needed for the two types of relationship are composed in fundamentally different ways, even if in certain cases it is possible to effect an artistic discourse by means of signs usually used in the field of scientific communication or, on the contrary, to transmit a technical piece of information by means of signs that are not adapted to it (for example, iconic signs). This is not, perhaps, the moment to dwell at further length on this distinction, regarding which reference may be made to other studies that specifically focus upon the theme set out just above.[5] Ideographic writing is semantically weak as far as abstract and, more specifically, scientific discourse is concerned; it flourishes in civilizations that are culturally oriented towards the emancipation of thought and the free formulation of rational universes, but that are still rooted in a mythical humus and weighted down by the value of visual experience, as well as the habit of imaginative speculation.

IDEOGRAM AND CUTTING

A dog + a mouth = *to bark*; a mouth + a child = *to cry*; a mouth + a bird = *to sing;* a knife + a heart = *sorrow*, and so on. But this is – montage! Yes. It is exactly what we do in the cinema, combining shots that are depictive, single in meaning, neutral in content – into intellectual contexts and series.

Thus wrote S. M. Eisenstein[6] in 1929, noting with extraordinary percep-

[5]   Brandi (1960). The subject is also taken up by Mario Praz in an essay from *I volti del tempo* (Edizioni Scientifiche Italiane, 1964). See also Bettetini (1964).
[6]   Eisenstein (1951), 29.

tiveness the close link between the compositive moduli that lie behind
ideographic writing (in this case Japanese) and those that lie behind
cinematographic narration.

In reality, just as in the formation of the compound hieroglyph, the
sign synthesis takes on a meaning that does not derive from the sum of
those belonging to the component ideograms, but from their reciprocal
dynamic conditioning, from the metaphorical value of their juxtaposition; so in the process of cinematographic cutting the meaning of an
image is the fruit of the dynamic inter-reaction between the various shots,
rather than of the addition of their partial meanings. Eisenstein goes so
far as to call the shot the CELL of cutting (instead of the ELEMENT), because "...just as cells in their division form a phenemenon of another
order, the organism or the embryo, so on the other side of the dialectical
leap from the shot, there is montage".[7]

The language of the cinema is structured around iconic signs, and
can only tolerate a scientific orientation or, more generally, the attribution of a designative qualification to the relation between its images and
the reality that it is to represent with considerable difficulty. On the other
hand, the shot is linked to the reproduced object by its photographic
nature, by an almost specular similarity, so that the abstraction of its representative value from the contingent reality that has been photographed
is problematic and frequently unrealizable. The simple ideogram, even
though determined by an outwardly figurative relation with the signified
object, assumes a conventional value that allows it a reasonably widespread generalization (and thus a certain release from the represented
object): ideographic characters make up a writing instrument which is
intended as much for the graphic formulation of poetic compositions as
for the setting out of scientific texts. But on the other hand cinematographic
images are engendered without any tendency toward abstraction and
scientific speculation.

The signs of a script may be images of things and images of thoughts;
the signs in a film are only images of things, and are able to express
thought by means of juxtaposing shots, which always conserve their
contingent relation with the represented reality. Cinematographic cutting
may be assimilated to the functions of ideographic writing, above all
when considered in its compositive (or, to use Eisenstein's adjective,
copulative) phase, but it cannot tolerate any generalization, nor may it be
reduced to any convention. The cinematographic sign is the reproduction
of a certain reality that has been chosen by the director and translated

[7]   Eisenstein (1951), 37.

into images by virtue of a certain interpretative approach that has been adopted toward it, this latter being renewed at every contact between the lens and the representable world. The ideographic metaphor is born rooted in the partial realities from whose signs it is made up, but, "following objective lines of relations in nature herself" and grasping them in a rapid synthesis,[8] it attempts to abstract itself from its original determination – so that it is possible to read a hieroglyphic script by virtue of conventional and mnemonically exterior information as well, without the remotest concern about reconstructing all the mental processes that have determined the formation of the various signs.

As far as the cinema and its cutting is concerned none of this is possible, because its images refuse rational classification. Behind every one of its signs (despite the photographic and thus specular nature of its formation) lies a complex of subjective, apparently free, incoercible, and unrepeatable choices. With the cinema one cannot write a *précis*, nor can one invent stenographic formulae; like all the figurative arts, the cinema has no vocabulary, and even less an alphabet. The resultant image is expressively unique as far as the elements making it up are concerned and, as such, is not adapted to establishing an abstract idea, except by virtue of a complex relation that is analogical, symbolical, or at any rate metaphorical, and is specially created as a result of some felicitous inspiration on the author's part, making use of photographic reproduction.

FUNCTIONS OF CINEMATOGRAPHIC LANGUAGE

We have already dealt with the formation of the elementary cinematographic signs, the shots, in an earlier paragraph analyzing the technical situations and the types of operative adaption that allow the director to exercise a distorting influence, for expressive ends, upon the formal values of the reality in front of which the lens is placed. The iconic sign of the cinema, the image, has in itself a power for representation that is subordinate to the thing represented, the technique of shooting, and the relations established by the cutting. Whatever type of film one may choose to analyze, one will quickly realize that the phantasms evoked by the film on screen exercise a communicative function that is a far cry from all direct abstraction and instead aims to put forward a reality that may be identified with the image of the phenomenon or object that is fixed on film.

[8]   Fenellosa (1936), 26. See also, naturally, Aristotle's *Poetics*.

Of the two intellectual functions assigned by Suzanne Langer to language ("to fix the pre-eminent factors of experience, by giving them NAMES" and "to extract concepts of relationship, by talking about the named entities", the first having an essentially hypostatic character, the second an abstractive one), the cinema at times takes on the first, though not without a certain difficulty.[9] A certain type of cinema, naturally – because by exaggerating the integrative power of the sound-track without any criteria of linguistic essentiality one can, for example, produce a scientific, or philosophical, or technical, or at any rate rationally abstract discourse, even though using film – although its linguistic function has (in the better cases) to be contained within the strict limits of an iconographic documentation 'ad verbum', a more or less justified collection of pictures intended to illustrate visually a lecture given in the ambiguous guise of a documentary film.

Cinematographic language is not, therefore, simply a mode of discourse that has been brought down to essentials, and simplified until it reaches the boundaries of a generalizing convention; it involves within its expressive evolution the author's and the audience's powers of imagination, their cultural commitments, and all of the re-creative energy that they are able to focus upon the world, and the things and ideas that make it up. The cinematographic sign can never be directly related to an abstract idea or a 'name': in the cinema, there aren't any signs for 'goodness', 'charity', or 'ambiguity', but only ambiguous images of phenomena that imply these abstractions in the way developed or evaluated. In the same way, this hypothetical and impossible film vocabulary will not, in fact, possess generic signs for 'car', 'house', or 'glass', but will instead have ones that are to be referred to concrete examples of these objects, shot according to certain technical criteria in a particular situation; the discourse that one can construct by virtue of their semantic contribution should be able to come to grips with universal generalization thanks to a series of relationships between the various images, the perception of which will stimulate in the spectator a sensory reaction and a certain type of intellectual activity, that between them will get him to make spontaneous use of his rational faculties, and thus arrive at a form of abstraction. The cinematographic author must not put forward any logical argumentation nor, even less, should he seek to rationally persuade and convince his hypothetical audience. Like the poet, he must lead the public into

---

[9] Suzanne Langer (*Feeling and Form* [London, Routledge and Kegan Paul, 1953] 236). She is here concerned with the two functions defined by Greimas (in reference to verbal language) as DENOMINATION and DEFINITION (which respectively correspond to con-

enjoying a fiction which has the power to make them relive the "virtual experience of a conviction or of its achievement".[10]

THE REPRODUCTIVE ASPECT

The cinematographic sign directly represents the thing, and may achieve an indirect significative relation with an idea by virtue of a metaphorical analogy or of some other rhetorical translation effected by means of cutting. But while grouping together the various shots and developing a certain expository proposition, by virtue of their semantic and rhythmic relations, the author of the film cannot leave their photographic reality completely out of account, nor can he sublimate it or force it beyond a certain semantic space.[11] The cinema came into being with the specific aim of reproducing reality as perfectly as possible, and the Lumière brothers were certainly not spurred on by artistic or, at any rate, autonomously linguistic considerations. They succeeded in constructing two pieces of apparatus which allowed one in one case to obtain and in the other to project a series of moving photographs, thus bringing to an effective con- clusion the technical process which had been developed from the dis- covery of the magic lantern, passing through a great variety of animatory procedures. The history of the cinema has often felt the effect of the medium's primitive (and fundamental) photographic tendencies, which have found frequent expression in linguistic movements and in the work of isolated authors who aimed to eliminate all the recreative power of the ideal film, and to reduce its communicative function to a detached and truthful documentation of the phenomenal reality that had taken place in front of the camera lens. But Dziga Vertoff, who was the first to assert the reproductive impartiality of the film, gradually discovered cutting and came to attribute so high a value to it that he forgot about the actual

---

densation and expression). Greimas (1966a) writes that a language is not a closed system: "...la dénomination tout aussi bien que la définition, s'y exercent à tout mo- ment et grâce à des procédures diverses et nombreuses."

[10] Langer (1953), 243. She adds that the "poet's 'argumentation' is the semblance of a thought process, and the strain, hesitation, frustration, or the swift subtlety of mental windings, or a sense of sudden revelation are more important elements in it than the conclusion".

[11] I use the expression 'semantic space' in the simplest of its etymological senses, leaving aside the analyses and specifications that have been devoted to it by Charles E. Osgood, G. J. Suci and P. H. Tannenbaum in *The Measurement of Meaning* (Urbana, 1957). (See also Gombrich[1960]).

content of the shots: "...parti du réalisme le plus brutal, on tombe maintenant dans l'art abstrait".[12]

The authors of Cinéma-Vérité have already abandoned their original intentions (and their works have almost always acted as a partial disavowal of their theoretical principles) for a more evident methodology of interpreted information. The cinematographic image is the fruit of a complex of choices (which have already been analyzed in a previous paragraph), and the subsequent cutting of the filmed material makes the various shots even more open to the expressive intentions of the director. The cinematic sign's ambiguity is both considerable and complex; the film image consists, essentially, of an iconic representation linked by specular similarity to the object represented, yet at the same time it acquires extraordinarily complex powers of signification by virtue of a series of rhythmic and figurative relations that are able to attribute to its representative function (through the dialectical collision between the various shots) new values and new realities (that are at times in themselves ambiguous and rationally indefinable).[13] The author of the film makes up his narration out of images, arriving at the conquest of a certain generic quality (in regard to theme, subject, or language) by means of signs that are closely linked to the represented object and therefore may not in themselves be generalized (and certainly not conventionalized). The photograph of a phenomenon becomes, in the cinema, an element of expression that goes beyond the object represented, although the author can intervene subjectively in the reproduction of reality using a definite (and limited) number of technical instruments.

The film may be created to document something in the most impersonal and objective of ways, or it may be intended to bring a certain dramatic situation to fictional life, but in both cases its signs will bear meanings that are much more complex than those implicit in the original, simple iconic relation. It is not by chance that one of the cultural and productive movements best adapted to the aesthetic and linguistic characteristics of the film medium has, perhaps, been Neo-Realism, with its determination to perceive the reality of things by presenting them in the most simple and direct ways, photographing their fictitious reconstruction, their carefully judged reviviscence, in the most analytically immediate form. The skill of Rossellini, De Sica, and Visconti in his *Ossessione* and *La terra trema*, consisted in creating an interplay of scenes which possessed the characteristics of a fictitious spontaneity and naturalness that was not

[12] Amédée Ayfre, *Conversion aux images?* (Paris, Cerf, 1964), 210.
[13] For an analysis of the AMBIGUOUS SIGN see Bettetini (1964), 177 et seg.

to be invalidated by any analytical approach. Their films gave the impression of a casual recording on film of real and unconditioned events, and of an impersonal and objective view of things.[14]

The paradox of the cinematographic sign, almost identical with the thing represented and yet, despite this, able to free itself from this ironic slavery, was put to brilliant use by the Neo-Realists using a direct action upon observed reality that, in itself, could not be distorted, but that could be put forward again in episodic reconstructions (and was therefore open to selective criticism). Other directors have instead preferred to act by virtue of a direct distortion of the photographic phenomenon, or by means of a transcriptive deformation derived from the system's optical techniques, or else (as in the majority of cases) they have conserved ambiguous positions, turning to various forms of modal integration.

CUTTING AND THE AUTHOR'S INTENTIONS

Cinematographic cutting thus consists of the composition of iconic material effected in anticipation of a partial or total renunciation of its direct representative values and oriented towards the acquisition of new sign potential. This work of re-elaboration, which confers upon the image a reality of its own, independently of its reproductive origins, may be critically analyzed according to two of the basic parameters of human communication: that which makes out in the transmitter's behaviour an explicit INFORMATIVE intentionality and that which, on the other hand, stresses a mode of behaviour explicitly oriented towards EXPRESSIVE creativity. In both cases, and not as might be thought only in the second, one can never leave out of account an INTERPRETIVE component that is inherent in the very nature of the communicative medium. The documentary film is a typical example of a work in which the author intends to elaborate a discourse with a basically designative character, offering to the spectator anxious to inform himself a series of signs so coordinated as to represent on screen a certain reality. The audience watching a documentary knows that beyond the phantasm on screen there exists an object with which they enter into indirect contact, and that the communicator ought to offer them an image of what he has analyzed with the camera that is as impersonal and as near to reality as possible.

---

[14] With regard to Neorealism and its possible relation to Husserl's phenomenology, see Amédée Ayfre's interesting essay, "Néo-Réalisme et Phénoménologie", in Ayfre (1964), 209.

The average viewer of the documentary image thus adopts an attitude of open-minded trust regarding the signs placed in front of him, an immediate and almost automatic transposition of the values perceived by virtue of the communicative exchange onto a level of implied reality. The average spectator attributes an almost scientifically informative designative function to the documentary film, unconsciously leaving out of consideration the possibility of a critical integration on the transmitter's part. This attitude of passive trust (which is also to be found in the case of non-documentary films, if they are shot with an apparently documentary technique) cannot possibly find an honest response on the part of the director who, as has already been noted a number of times, can never construct a purely scientific discourse using the cinema – his exposition will always be invaded by elements of an evaluative, prescriptive, or formative nature that are ingrained in the work of selection from which the cinematographic work springs and in the methods of cutting, which cast the shadow of the author's personality upon the composition of the film in increasing measure.[15]

THE DOCUMENTARY FILM

But if this instrument is one that does not allow the director to reproduce anything faithfully and if, starting from this apparent limitation, he is thus in a position to achieve an original linguistic form, it will be necessary to make the use of the medium conform to the basic aims of the communication. Although the result is entirely conditioned by the author's personal contribution, he must assume the modest function of a truthful narrator, as far as possible looking for basically unambiguous signs and putting them together in a cutting process which produces an image of reality that is almost monovalent from the semantic point of view. If the film is only there to inform, profiting by the spontaneous credibility that moving iconic signs enjoy in the cinema, then the director should never allow himself any license in his cutting that might let elements of evaluation, stimulus, or organization creep into the sign values being proposed on screen. The communication would in such cases lose its intentionally reproductive and scientifically designative structure, introducing instead ambiguous and morally dubious aspects that function in a way designed to stimulate the imagination or to prescribe rules.

[15]   In this instance, I refer to Morris' terminology, which I consider particularly suitable and clear (Morris [1971], 123 et seg.).

Although one may well appreciate the definition of so detached and sincerely committed an attitude, it must all the same be admitted that its value is, quite simply, theoretical, and that it only makes sense to consider it on an abstractly scientific level. The director's choices are never merely linguistic and are not simply to be referred to a hypothetical narrative methodology; they always involve the ethical, critical, political, religious, and mythical aspects of their author's character as well. A scientific discourse made up of signs from the verbal language contains a certain number of assertions, negations, and observations that must be interpreted by the listener in a single and clearly defined sense without any possible ambiguity and without the presence of any act of subjective integration. Scientific discourse thus resorts to signs that, by convention, possess a single meaning known to both the agents of the communication. As a result, technical and scientific vocabulary continues to become more specialized and richer in neologisms that are able to concentrate within the simple microcosm of a word the idea of an entire physical or chemical process, or the presence of some more or less complex piece of equipment.

A gradual process of primitive symbolization (effected with straightforwardly constitutive aims) thus occurs in a sector of human communication that ought, apparently, to structure all its messages around values appropriate to a purely representative sign function.[16] But when the author of a scientific communication (or an informative one in the widest sense of the word) has to resort to the signs of the cinema, which are so self-sufficient and, at the same time, so closely bound to the thing they reproduce as to be unable to guarantee it a monovalent meaning, the exact correspondence that he may intend to establish among the values of the analyzed phenomenon, those of the analytical operation and those of the receptor's perception, threatens to become compromised from the first, primitive photographic operation onwards. But the effort to transmit to the spectator a particular interpretation of the event or phenomenon being presented may also turn out to be compromised when one omits the sign redundancy of the moving image, and the enormous powers of imaginative integration that the public may make use of when confronted by it. Not only, therefore, is the iconic-kinetic sign one of the least adapted to the transmission in mirror-like reproduction of a certain reality, but it is not even able to bear the weight of a single significative direction, an explicit interpretation; it couldn't even signify a certain position adopted by the director in relation to what he is com-

[16]   See the "Provisional Conclusion" to Bettetini (1964).

municating, even if his attitude were reduced to that of confirming an honest and passive receptive openness with respect to the events and things that make up the object of the information.

In reality, a disenchanted and careful analysis of cinematographic communication could reveal the author's intentions in every case – but how many people are aware of the fundamental rules of this type of approach to the film? How many people are able to separate, at first sight, the images' informative contribution from their cultural integration and from the particular psycho-physical situation in which they are perceived? And, finally, how many directors are aware of the laws and values of audio-visual communication, and put together their images with an explicitly informative aim, giving up falsely emotive elements, debatable effects, and expositions whose ambiguity derives precisely from the context into which they are inserted? The study of cinematographic language, and generally of every form of communication that makes use of moving audio-visual images, should become one of the more important themes of education in the future, if one wishes to avoid leaving these extraordinary informative media in the hands of inspired dilettantes who are only capable of fortuitous contributions to systematic progress in this sector.

And yet even when everything were clearly and organically structured within the limits of an inexhaustible scientific becoming, the moving image would always conserve a basic ambiguity, paradoxically inherent in the photographic richness of its composition and, more obviously, in the modalities that govern the joints in the cutting. The authors of documentaries and filmed inquiries are aware of this, above all those who use the instruments of the film for the television screen, and thus for a public that could hardly be more heterogeneous and culturally indefinable. Sometimes a spectator has only to make out a certain marginal element in the communication as being particularly pertinent to his social circumstances or his personal experience in order to integrate himself almost automatically with that (possibly fortuitous) component of the message, thus distorting its basic sense and turning the transmitter's intentions upside down. One must thus add to the natural ambiguity of the iconic-kinetic language the inadequacy of the reception and, at times, a certain degree of confusion in the author's methods of composition; so that the result is a communication with little designative value, in which the purely informative elements are mixed with others involving appreciation, opinion, belief, mythology, and illusion, thus generating a depreciation of the sign values at stake.

Up to this point, our analysis has been limited to those aspects of the film in which the relation between the thing that is the object of the representation and the representation itself takes on a particularly basic importance, above and beyond all considerations of a strictly technical or linguistic nature. We have, that is, been concerned with those cases in which the specular reproductiveness that stands at the very heart of the cinematographic phenomenon is used as the principal vehicle of the communication, in a relation between transmitter and receiver that is characterized by the desire to bring into play the greatest possible number of qualitative and quantitative data about the reality translated into images by the film camera. In the documentary film the thing reproduced, be it an event, a phenomenon, a person, or an object, conditions its representation image by image, and all the director's efforts should be directed towards continually adjusting his informative exposition to the reality of what happened in front of the camera lens, although he knows quite well that the result of his transposition will always be partially independent of the way in which 'the thing' really manifested itself. In this instance, the content of a cinematographic image, considered as a straightforward "material representation",[17] coincides with the content of the image when considered on the level of "significant representation", because the aim of its author (that is, of whoever attributes a signified to it) is only that of using it as the reproductive phantasm of what has been recorded on the film.

As for the spectator's activity, it should be reduced to an interpretation of what the screen offers him, constructed around a factual analysis of what is happening on screen and a series of interpretive acts which, as Panofsky says,[18] would oscillate between pre-iconographic description (identification of pure forms, relations, events, certain modes of expressiveness) and iconic description (the exact semantic insertion of what is seen on the screen into the appropriate historical, cultural, and political universe), according to his own particular level of erudition. In both cases, however, his receptive behaviour ought not to be drawn, by the material that he is watching, towards attitudes of an 'iconological' nature (that is, the attributing of symbolical values), nor towards the discovery of a meaning inherent in the communication as such – it ought not to be subject, that is, to the imposition of a critical slant or an interpretive distortion.

---

[17]   Taddei (1963) (see note 70 in part 1), 34 et seg.
[18]   Panofsky (1955), 26.

THE FILM AS EXPRESSION

As soon as one leaves the restricted field of the filmed chronicle, enquiry, or documentary, the relations are turned upside down: the objective reality that lay behind the formation of the image loses a considerable amount of its interest as an object of study, and the cinematographic phantasm's signification acquires a value that is independent of its three-dimensional matrix and only subordinate to the director's expressive intentions. If the film renounces all claim to the direct provision of information, and instead tends to address itself to the spectator's sensibility and intellect by means of a series of messages that aim to move him aesthetically, then its elementary sign must perforce possess that complexity on the level of its signifieds which is typical of the artistic sign. We are thus no longer concerned with signs that are monovalent and defined by a single significative relation, but with signs that are open to various interpretative integrations, even though all of them may conform to the same poetic aims. The cinematographic sign used for artistic purposes, that is the image which is capable of signifying something above and beyond the material object represented, elevates its linguistic position to a quota of expository autonomy that is so cut off from the original specular relationship as to allow the resultant communication a meaning based on the author's poetical world and the public's receptive capacities alone. It is often reality that yields to the demands of the intentionally expressive cinema, with the use of tricks and of pre-arrangement of the scene; equally often it is the techniques of shooting and cutting that alter the coordinates and the *raison d'etre* of the kinetic and optic centre of attention making out of it an image that has some degree of significant function.

But poetic speech does not renounce all its potentially informative aims *a priori*; instead, it integrates and enriches them by finding a place for them within its own sphere. This means that the cinematographic image can retain a certain basic link with the reality that it presents, but its meaning cannot be reduced to the straightforward representation of this reality so that, basing itself upon its mediated form, it rises above it, giving birth to the values that the author had intended to communicate. A film that refers to a concrete and historical episode, for example, ought never to alter the exact description of the facts, which is the crowning achievement of such a work, in order to arrive at a tendentious distortion that may be useful for the expressive quality of its narrative development. The author of such a film ought to respect the informative aspect of his exposition, bringing to bear upon it a precise sociological awareness, and should enrich it with all the integrative elements that his artistic inspiration, his ideological formation, and the ethical conception that he has of his role as a communicator suggest to him. The signs of his film will not have a univocal meaning, but neither will they be in a position to neglect their coherent and straightforwardly designative signification. This will be the first and most obvious stage of their revelation as poetic elements, but it is one that they will not be able to avoid, above all in cases where the work inclines by intention towards a scientifically known and defined sphere (be it on the technical or the systematical level, or on that of historical awareness).

Thus films such as Rossellini's *Paisà* or Rosi's *Salvatore Giuliano* construct the sequence of their events within several historical situations, respecting their phenomenal development, and engendering a poetic atmosphere that tends towards an interpretive function, as indeed it is the author's right that it should. (Rosi, in fact, transforms his search for historical truth into poetic exposition.) But, on the other hand, many of the films stemming from Socialist Realism or Italian Fascism have deliberately distorted the historical coordinates of a certain event that framed the events of their plot, thus compromising their hypothetically informative qualities for reasons of propaganda. And on another level, science-fiction films that take no account of scientific and technical verisimilitude, and pay no attention to concreteness and credibility in regard to the ideation of the magical circumstances in which their heroes are involved, neglect one of the basic aspects of their communicative function and, apart from anything else, risk producing an unconvincing exposition.

Thus cinematographic images always possess an elementary meaning that may be directly related to the object represented, and, in cases where a documentary orientation is not the only or the most important element in the communicative context, their meaning is further enriched by aspects transcending the original 'thing' which are present in all the polyvalence of their sign function. It could be suggested in response to this statement that there do exist completely metaphorical films in which the primitive and spontaneous signifieds of all the individual images must in themselves be neglected and only used as elements of a sign transposition, so as to be able to deduce from them their real iconological meaning. In this instance Alain Resnais's *L'année dernière à Marienbad* might be a significant example, as could be Jean-Luc Godard's *Alphaville*.

But to turn back from the metaphorical sign[19] to its intentional meaning, the author must clearly perceive its primitive representative relationship in all its elementary and specular reality. The exact perception of this instrumental signified is an indispensable element for the complete understanding of the message, just as, at the other end of the chain, the elements making up the metaphorical narration must be chosen with care and precision, by virtue of a univocal relation between the final meaning and the sign reality that supports its primitive linguistic formation. When the poetic idea or, at any rate, the communicative urge that stimulates the author of the film is valid, strong, and unconfused, there should be no possibility of elasticity in the choice of the initial iconic material, because the idea and the vehicle by means of which it is presented in the film ought to be so closely inter-linked that any change in the latter would compromise the nature of the former.

Galvano della Volpe, developing a penetrating critique of the poetic image along materialist and historicist lines, defines LITERARY BANALITY (or, that is, the truly UNPOETICAL) not as a phenomenon to be attributed to

...a POVERTY of IMAGINATIVE RESOURCE or of IMAGES, but rather to an imagination or to images that have not been PROVIDED with sufficient STRUCTURE or INTELLECTUALITY to avoid the generic and casual qualities that affect their SIGNIFIED and THUS their very capacity as IMAGES.[20]

He thus attributes the fundamental cause of poetic mediocrity to a lack of rational clarity, to the images' confused contribution to cognition when considered in their primary conceptual meaning. One can extrapolate from the literary sphere to the cinematographic one by virtue of an almost automatic series of translations. Della Volpe himself points out that the metaphor is "indispensable as a mental, intellectual, and cognitive instrument",[21] defining its concept as a relation of similarity-dissimilarity (concrete intellectuality), and retaining the attributes of rationality, truth, and awareness of the truthful for poetry even when it resorts to metaphorical images. Therefore, if the verbal signs of a poetic composition must be analyzed and evaluated in their primitive function as conceptual designators, and if the poem's poetic sense may only be perceived through a careful and precise consideration of the increases in intellectual awareness with which the words from which it is composed

---

[19] "A sign is METAPHORICAL if in a particular instance of its occurence it is used to denote an object which it does not literally denote in virtue of its signification, but which has some properties which its genuine denotata have" (Morris [1971], 136).

[20] Della Volpe (1967), 72.

[21] Della Volpe (1967), 74 et seg.

enrich the reader, then one may also extend the same type of critical reserve (and, naturally, of poetic attitude) to the universe of moving audiovisual images. The photographic nature of their primitive sign relation favours a mode of reflection that does not leave out of account the object represented and its reality as an intermediary vehicle of communication, even if it is inserted into a chain of significative relations that tend to end up on expressive levels that transcend the original reality.

After all, the recent success of a number of films structured around the objectual evaluation of certain aspects of technology and interior decoration in contemporary society (films that do not add anything cinematographically to the representative content of their images, and are shot with what is apparently documentary technique) may undoubtedly be attributed to a fashion following upon the Pop Art phenomenon that has by now extended to all levels of communication, but, at the same time, it reveals how the cinema has spontaneously adapted itself to the public's latest demands by means of an original compromise whose validity is already inherent in its nature. In this respect, the cinema has disregarded the capacities for expression and autonomous distortion possessed by its instruments of reproductive narration, attributing 'cinematographic' qualities to the objects that are to be photographed, and entirely shifting its 'fictional' activity into the world outside the camera, and the apparently informative effectiveness of its presentation; thus films such as the James Bond series or Marco Vicario's surprising *7 uomini d'oro* resort to no cinematic tricks in their exposition, but photograph mysterious and exceptional technical realities, specially constructed for the shooting (and functioning just as the film shows them to).

The image in this type of film constructs its message by freely putting together photographic fragments of a pre-arranged reality, whose primary meaning is simply designative and reproductive, and whose interpretation on an elementary level is well-nigh essential for an exact understanding of its context.

The primary interpretation of the cinematographic image thus consists in deciphering its direct sign relation with the reality represented, this being indispensable for the acquisition of all its other signifieds but, at the same time, insufficient for the perception of its expressive intentionality, in the cases where this exists. At successive levels of critical interpretation the image reveals its various meanings in their entirety, and communicates with all the ambiguity that its poetic origins confer upon it. The cinematographic sign communicates the represented object, its signifieds, and the signifieds that it adds to it by virtue of its own powers of recreative distortion,[22] thus producing a continuous entanglement among designative and connotative relations, interpretive suggestions, and critical conditioning; one cannot put forward a synthetic summary of a cinematographic image's meanings with any great degree of rational certainty, above all in cases where the authors make reference to the natural ambiguity of this sign vehicle in order to enrich its expressive effect.[23] Perhaps one ought to talk of the 'polyvalency' of a sign, rather than of its 'ambiguity', since the latter, as commonly understood, involves a "connotation of shrewdness and deception" which is no great help to a potential critic approaching the study of the cinema and its problems.

Furthermore, the metaphor of 'valency', taken from chemistry, is very suggestive because it denotes the cinematographic sign's adaptability (different in every case) to the various cognitive integrations that may be effected at different levels of interpretation. The director may thus directly lift the sign function of his image into the realm of symbolic representation, conferring upon it a greater power of signification than that of the primitive, directly designative relation. On a symbolic level, he can communicate both the represented reality and an idea, an intuition, or at any rate another reality, for which the one that generated the image is already a spontaneous or conventional sign in itself. In the first case, he will have to translate the object destined to produce its own symbol into an image that conventionally suggests a symbolical evaluation of what is directly represented, using well-chosen shooting techniques and an approach to cutting specially adapted to this end (that is, as long as the reality represented does not already in itself possess a potential symbolic evaluation, such as a flag, a sculpture, or a coat of arms).

In Fellini's *8½* and *Giulietta degli spiriti*, the scenes showing the two young protagonists at their respective schools, run in one case by priests and in the other by nuns, are already provided with a symbolic evaluation of their signifieds, quite apart from the accentuation of this element that is then produced by the method of filming: the sets, costumes, actors' faces and gestures, voices, and music in themselves already make up a reality that is interpreted in a certain way and reconstructed with the evident intention of completely substituting the mnemonic model for the objective data (a symbolic procedure). What is more, the selection and composition effected by the cinematographic instruments definitely establish the symbolic representation of mistaken propaedeutic restriction, and

---

[22]   Taddei (1963), 231 et seg.
[23]   William Empson, *Seven Types of Ambiguity* (London, Chatto & Windus, 1930), p. 1.

the obtuse imposition of empty rules, backed up by a terrifying nightmare atmosphere.[24]

In Godard's *Alphaville*, on the other hand, along with the process of rendering a certain reality as cinematographic symbol (the concrete reality of a modern city, which is, however, photographed with clear interpretive aims in view, and recreated along the lines of obvious and highly effective science-fiction models), there is a continuous effort in the direction of transignification, so that the film's images acquire a large number of sign aspects, and succeed in implying the values of universal problems or, at any rate, ones which exceed the limits of a direct and contingent symbolism between object and representation. The endless tracking shots that precede the protagonist's movements in the corridors of the mysterious hotel where he is staying (for the narration acquires its mystery through its cinematographic structure and the cutting techniques used for it, rather than through any of the natural qualities of the environment) may be subjected to symbolic evaluation on two different principal levels: that of signifying the strange, hostile, obsessive, and indefinable atmosphere in which the cosmic city is immersed (primary symbolic meaning), and that of suggesting a painful existential awareness that may be related to the unchanging archetypes of coercion, limitation, the mysterious, tyrannical, and overwhelming power of the unknown god (in this case an electronic brain that coordinates and governs an entire state).[25]

So that attributing (by way of an approximation that will, in this particular instance, suffice) a value of symbolic signification to a sign relation that goes beyond the simple representation or individuation of a certain phenomenon to involve realities that transcend the phenomenal manifestation of the thing that gives birth to the image, one may assert that the iconic-kinetic language communicates on three principal levels of semantic integration:

(a) on a level of linear, direct representation of a certain reality which, although distorted and interpreted, is reproduced by the cinematographic sign and used as a potential generator of successive acts of communication. In this instance, the relationship does not involve any considerations of a symbolic nature, as long as the object translated into images may not of itself be conventionally referred to symbolic evaluations;

(b) on a level of direct sublimation of the original reality in a symbolic

---

[24]   *8½* and *Giulietta degli spiriti* by Federico Fellini; both films were produced by Angelo Rizzoli, the first in 1963, the second in 1965.
[25]   *Alphaville, une étrange aventure de Lemmy Caution*, by Jean-Luc Godard (1965).

universe of a linguistic nature, in which the relationship between a thing and its image loses a good part of its communicative interest, and the image already acquires a significative autonomy of its own, which is as detached from the thing in question as a photographic sign can be. One could talk of primary symbolization in this case, making it correspond, from a critical point of view, with the phase of iconographic interpretation that we singled out above;

(c) on a level of symbolic transposition into a poetic universe, where the image as sign is deliberately charged with a polyvalency conferred upon it by the scenario, the shooting, the acting, and above all by the cutting – the juxtaposition and dialectical synthesis of various shots, which this determining technical operation involves, is responsible for a large part of the film's symbolic potential, transforming the image into an autonomous and independent vehicle of communication. This is a process of total symbolization of the sign relation, which almost always involves substituting the original referent or translating it from the realm of the phenomenal to that of the idea, from the world of objects as they are in their contingent reality to the one in which they are arranged according to relational terms that involve them above and beyond their material limits. Interpretation on an expressive level such as this involves an attitude of iconological nature (see above).

CUTTING FOR TELEVISION

As far as television is concerned, the study of cutting is not subjected to any notable technical modifications as compared with its application to the cinema. Television communication, whether it derives from film techniques or is the result of the continuous and simultaneous working of electronic cameras, always turns out as a succession of moving audiovisual images, flattened onto a two-dimensional screen. Thus, in theory, television cutting can develop along the same linguistic lines as cinema cutting, subordinating the differentiated choices that may be involved to the type of audience envisaged and the social and cultural characteristics of the message (and also, naturally, to the process of its transmission and reception). In reality, the dimensions of the screen and the conditions in which one normally watches a program notably impinge upon the formation of the image and the choice of relationships in cutting, so that a consideration of some of the technical and psychological aspects of the relation between communicator and receiver in television programs leads one to differentiate them from their equivalents within the ambit of the film.[26] If, furthermore, the broadcast is being done with television cameras, the inertia of the medium, the limited number of viewpoints, and the slow and awkward varying of their positions enormously limit the producer's creative freedom, and oblige him to adopt a type of cutting that is not only contemporary with the evolution of the action in space-time, not only adapted to the translation into images of a dynamic reality caught at the moment in which it happens, but also placed in descriptive subjection to the durations, volumes, and rhythms of whatever moves and exists in front of the television camera. The cutting of a transmission using television cameras is thus connected to the general reproductive process that typifies the formation of the images; it is reality which, in these cases, dictates the spatial and temporal aspects of its manifestation on the screen and which in itself impregnates the succession of reproductive images (quite apart from any interpretive or conditioning intervention).

There is also a margin of independence and recreative liberty for the television producer – and this margin is often a relevant one, all the more so when every part of the broadcast can be foreseen and controlled with some degree of precision – but he will almost always find himself obliged to work on the reality that ends up in front of the cameras (scenographic devices, the actors' movements, a shrewd use of lighting, etc.), rather than trust to the powers of semantic transfiguration possessed by the television cameras and simultaneous cutting; in such cases, it is indeed the photographed object which possesses signifieds and connotations going beyond a hypothetical and straightforward representation of reality in its crude, material state, unformed by the producer's expressive intentions. Thus televised drama, despite the image that interposes between the television studio and the receiver, is often much closer to the forms of a theatrical performance translated into moving pictures and distributed to a mass audience than it is to those of an original audio-visual form of communication in which words and images integrate themselves in a complementary function that reveals their mutual incompleteness and their necessary tendency towards an expressive synthesis.[27]

Using film instruments for television reduces these inconveniences and in theory restores to television cutting the same possibilities for linguistic autonomy that the cinema enjoys; but in reality shooting and cutting

[26]   For all of these questions, and for others that are here given in outline, the reader is referred to Bettetini (1965).

[27]   Roland Barthes gives the name "*rélais*" to this type of relation between image and verbal integration, distinguishing it from the relation of "*ancrage*" which will be analyzed further on (Barthes [1964b]).

must always be performed in the light of the psychological and sociological techniques known to be suitable for television viewing, since the instrument that forms the message (cine-camera or television camera) has nothing to do with its reception. Substituting one operative vehicle for another doesn't in the slightest alter the conditions in which the result is viewed.[28] Recording the message on cinematographic film does potentially allow one to compose the various shots in accordance with those rapid and linear forms of cutting which the dimensions of the screen and the consequent reduction in the time needed to appreciate the image (relative to the time normally needed for a cinema image) demand, and which a production using television cameras always achieves with some difficulty, or at any rate through a series of frequently evident compromises.

The use of the television camera hardly ever allows the image that recreative liberty in relation to the object which is one of the basic prerogatives of film cutting; the use of the cine-camera must, in turn, subordinate itself to an analytical interpretation of reality that is always more descriptive and 'diegetic' than would be a free reconstruction of that reality in forms suited to the cinema screen. Considering the problem from a theoretical and linguistic point of view, the image is much more heavily conditioned by reality in television than it is in the cinema, no matter what instrument one constructs the iconic message with. In general, the television film does not allow itself the expressive freedom that it could technically have, limiting itself to an emphasis upon the rhythm with which the various shots follow one another, as compared to a hypothetical translation into images achieved with the use of television cameras.[29]

From the sociological point of view, the television medium appears, under analysis, to conform to co-ordinates that are on the whole in agreement with its linguistic characteristics. In fact, television is more a complex and extraordinary information machine, geared to cultural and scientific vulgarization, than it is an instrument for autonomous expression and artistic communication. Its fundamental contribution to society consists in the amount of news and organized knowledge that it communicates to the average viewer. Whatever the nature of the program may be, those watching it always find themselves in a more or less conscious state

[28]   Bettetini (1965), 63 et seg.
[29]   Naturally, these observations only seek to establish a norm, and do not exclude the possibility of fairly numerous exceptions; they refer back, that is, to everything that has been achieved in television up to now, without in any way wishing to commit themselves in regard to the future, except within the limits of a forecast that may be scientifically checked.

of '*apprentissage*' regarding the message that arrives in their homes, and the broadcast's iconic emphasis will condition them to choose of their own accord forms of behaviour and mental attitudes suggested to them by the television screen, either explicitly or else by implicit connotation. The sets, furnishings, objects, and persons whose images make up the television shots can easily be absorbed by the public as models for personal and collective imitation, as stimuli to interior choices and exterior actions – in other words, as real sources of social culture. The informative and notional connotations of a medium communicating by means of audio-visual moving images are also typical of the cinema; but film-goers (or at any rate, most of them) are aware of the spectacle's fictional qualities, and know that they are participating in a collective game whose ritual value is decidedly lower than the levels achieved in analogous theatrical experiences, since those involve going to the place where the film is shown, choosing the type of film one wants to see, and all the other social norms that usually go with a visit to the cinema. Television viewers, on the other hand, are naturally without these ritual aspects and, although they are faced with an overt 'fiction', tend to analyze what the screen offers them and to extract from the image-content such truthful or credible elements as will be useful to them in their particular circumstances, rather than projecting themselves passively into the universe that the images open up before their eyes.

In 1961 the Stanford University Press published, in one volume, an exhaustive analysis of television broadcasting. After three years of work and "the observation of details provided by over 6,000 children and over 2,300 parents, teachers and educators", the three authors, Wilbur Schramm, Jack Lyle, and Edwin Parker, pessimistically stated that, among other things, "...television, considered in terms of its current programs, may bring new cognitive interests; but it would be unable to stimulate and bring to life new and creative intellectual activities".[30] Television would, that is, be an excellent instrument for stimulation on a notional level, and for empirical divulgation, but it would not stand up to being used for autonomous expression that was capable of involving the 'poetic' activity of the spectator himself (or at least would not have stood up to it in the social area analyzed, and up to the time at which the research took place). In countries that have been using it long enough to be able to draw some reasonably generalized conclusions, television is always seen more as a support for various other languages than as a language in itself, as a useful dispenser of image-objects rather than as an instrument for free

[30]   Adriano Belloto, *La televisione inutile* (Milano, ed. di Comunità, 1962,) 109-112.

recreation. Its transmissions have come to adopt an increasingly accentuated level of denotation and of documentation that is better adapted to stimulate in the spectator a critical interest in the phenomenal reality presented by means of simple, reproductive images, than it is to present him with a poetic act, or at any rate with one that is, by tendency, interpretive. Thus televised theatre will tend to regard its divulgation as being all the more efficient, the less the production distorts the text's original dramatic dimension; examples of autonomous play writing find their most concrete form in the dramatized documentary, one of whose basic elements is a need for substantial documentation, and thus for a translation into images that is impersonal and entirely faithful to the object.

Every form of spectacle in which television tried to achieve dimensions of autonomous expressiveness has only lasted a short while, and has never succeeded in arousing a sufficiently positive response from the public. When the small screen offers images of a fictitious reality, or one that is cut off from any concrete relation with the every-day world of the viewer, public interest is greatly reduced, and becomes concentrated within a group exceptionally predisposed to the message, whose potential elevation into an important cultural élite can hardly justify the neglect of all the other television users. Adriano Bellotto writes

The MESSAGE of the TV must not try to convert or to persuade, but must limit itself to ensuring that the spectator be provided with sufficient elements to start him thinking about questions that are the concern of everybody. The most stimulating definition of the television viewer, in this sense, is the following: a person who accepts being disturbed, a man moved to ask himself questions. And if you think about it a moment, what distinguishes good from bad television, apart from formal and linguistic values, is precisely its capacity to be INTERROGATIVE.[31]

To really disturb, to give rise to concrete and substantial questions in the spectator's mind, television must convince him of the existence of a phenomenon or a reality that touches upon his existence, or stands at its very heart, brushing past it, or conditioning it.

We are here concerned with a continuous process of screen didactics which is all the more effective, the more that it offers material which is designative, descriptive, and only subject to the ways in which the object naturally manifests itself. This does not mean that an original television language cannot exist, but that the search for its forms must be pursued within the limited sphere of specular reproduction, of a reconstruction through images, of the perception and reconstitution of a rhythm which

[31]   Bellotto (1962), 55-56.

will tend to be that of the phenomenon and not that of one of its possible interpretations – all of which naturally comes within the limits of that subjectivity, inherent in the medium (or rather, in its use), that marks any communicative or expressive act whose sign-vehicle is represented by audio-visual moving images.[32]

The popularizing, didactically reproductive, and informative nature of the television instrument is thus revealed by considering its technical characteristics, the linguistic arguments that derive from it, and the psycho-social situation in which the viewer usually finds himself. One might suggest that television cutting tries to make the image adhere to the object not only by virtue of the inertia of the medium and its spontaneous adherence to the reproduced events, but also, and above all, by virtue of the receptive awareness of the average spectator and the function that television performs in a social community; so that it is possible to resort to film techniques even when preparing television spectacles, but it is not necessary (often quite the opposite, in fact) to cut the material provided by the takes in such a way as to take advantage of all the creative liberty that the Movieola allows. The transmission's background, its author's communicative intentions, and the many technical operations through which it is realized should always tend towards an objectual analysis of reality, and consequently towards a faithful reproduction of whatever it is in them that constitutes the focus of its viewers' sociological, political, scientific, and, more generally, gnosiological attention.

THE DECLINE OF CUTTING AS A SPECIFIC COMPONENT

Now, analyzing the progress of cinema production during the last few years – that is, in the period which coincides with the establishment of television in almost all countries of the world – one notes with ever greater frequency how the infatuation of directors for cutting, which they considered as the component specifically determining the form of the work, has become completely consumed by new cultural exigencies and new expressive tendencies. Cutting, as codified and lauded by the theoreticians of the silent film and by those who painstakingly attempted to bring the sound film into conformity with its principles, is strongly on the decline and unless directions of thought and of formal research[33] that are nowadays

---

[32] For several investigations into the language of television, see once more Bettetini (1965).
[33] See Part 1 of this book.

limited to a few exceptional instances become re-established, the near future would not seem to hold out much hope of bringing it back to life. After all, theories about cutting as a specific have always involved, at the roots of the cultural orientation that determined their development, a contempt for the object, or a consideration of reality limited to its instrumental value and its destined expressive transfiguration, and, on the other hand, an unlimited faith in the linguistically autonomous possibilities of this latter passage from object to image. Hardly any films, not even the most committed ones (which best reveal the personality of the man responsible for them), resort to narrative techniques in which cutting imposes itself as the basic element for structuring and forming the images' poetic reality. Nowadays cinematic narration is accomplished by means of shots that are almost always very long and are able to sustain consistent narrative fragments and concentrate more than one linguistic unit in their audio-visual exposition, so that cutting is often reduced to the additive connecting of different parts whose signifieds have already been made almost entirely evident.

Eisenstein, in putting forward his theories about intellectual cutting and deducing from them a methodology that aimed at the explicit formulation of ideas by means of the cinematographic image ("conflict-juxtaposition of accompanying intellectual affects"),[34] showed a decided contempt for cinematographic naturalism, for the objective representation of reality.[35] The cinema, born as an instrument of specular reproduction, underwent a revolutionary and unpredictable theoretical re-orientation: from a tautological instrument of narration (tautology is always implicit in the primary denotations of a moving photographic image) it transformed itself into a language whose syntactic procedures may be codified, but not its lexical manifestations, which are not easily conceived of, even at the height of creative enthusiasm.

Analogical cutting, so skillfully used by the Russian director, was only able to take a secure and concrete linguistic direction within the ambit of the silent film, because the spontaneous detachment from objective manifestations of reality that was implicit in the reproductive incompleteness of the medium (the lack of words and sounds) ensured that the public adopted an attitude more of interpretation than of passive projection when faced with the images. It was easier, that is, to conceive processes of symbolic abstraction by virtue of the juxtaposition of entirely free silent images, than it was to apply the same cutting procedures to reproductions

[34] Eisenstein (1951), 82.
[35] Metz (1964), 53.

of the object that were also capable of including its sonic features. It has already been noted[36] how the discovery of new technical means in the film world, all of them aiming at a reproduction of reality that corresponded ever more evocatively to reality and could thus be substituted for it, in a communicative exchange designed to create epidermic sensations rather than an effective, cognitive approach, coincided with a distinct decline in the importance of the most autonomous and recreative of narrative operations – cutting. But here, faced with contemporary cinematographic production, we find ourselves in a very different situation. Cutting disappears without there being any innovatory presence, from the technical point of view, within the complex reproductive machine of the cinema.

The classical conception of cutting vacillates because a large number of directors, after the experiences of Neorealism in Italy, act upon reality by means of a series of selective interventions, which are then assembled into a unity by simply juxtaposing the various parts. So this is not a matter of a stylistic and linguistic orientation being favoured by technical pressures, but of a real and problematic choice which carries cinematographic expression back to its origins, without neglecting the finest moments of its history. Nowadays the director is a meticulous and inspired researcher rather than a creator of magical illusions; he is still free, but within the limits of a respect for the object that is under the continuous control of the medium's photographically reproductive nature and of his fictitious creation's intentional adherence to the reality represented.

A comparison between the two following examples might prove illuminating in this respect: in 1941 Orson Welles made *Citizen Kane*, a zestful denunciation of several of the social evils that plague a capitalist country, embodied in the parabolical story of a despotic giant of the American press, rich and desperately egoistic; in 1964, Franco Rosi made *Le mani sulla città*, a biting condemnation of the methods of low politics and of the men involved in them, embodied in the realistic narration of the affairs of an unscrupulous building contractor with connections in the Mafia. Welles made use of cutting as one of the many, entirely free components of his creative work – all of them controlled by his imaginative inspiration, his whimsical taste, and his aristocratic contempt for everyday reality (a contempt that forces him to distort everything represented into a baroque and evocatively magniloquent dimension). The film's opening sequence is a rather good example in this case (it is then discovered that this is a documentary on the life of the great Mr. Kane), because the shots in it have a greatly reduced average duration, and follow one another with an insis-

[36]   See Part 2 of this book.

tent and emotively beguiling rhythm. Franco Rosi, on the other hand, has put together his shots according to the rules of a type of cutting that shows an objective respect for external reality, this latter being reconstructed in a realistic dimension that is in itself convincingly credible, and without resorting to suggestions alien to its own presence, to its value as object, and as a phenomenon belonging to our lives and our history. Orson Welles replaces the object with his own mental representation, and cutting serves him as the basic technical operation for manipulating reality; Rosi reproduces reality, intervening in its composition only as far as natural verisimilitude allows – but the result is always, obviously, a personal model of reality, because the filter of the director-author can never be eliminated, nor can it be constricted within the limits of a set of clearly defined theories; yet this REPRESENTATION of the object belongs to a different poetic (and thus cultural, social, and human) universe from the one in which Welles' images are rooted. C. Metz writes

Comme le souligne R. Barthes, cette reconstruction [of the model of an object] n'a pas pour but de représenter le réel, ce n'est pas une REPRODUCTION, elle n'essaie pas d'imiter le visage concret de l'objet initial, elle n'est pas 'poiésis' ou 'pseudo-physis'; c'est une simulation, un produit de la 'téchné'. En somme: le résultat d'une manipulation. Squelette structural de l'objet érigé en un second objet, c'est toujours une sorte de prothèse. Voilà ce qu'Eisenstein aurait voulu faire, voilà ce dont il a rêvé sans cesse... A Rossellini qui s'écriait: "Les choses sont là. Pourquoi les manipuler?", le Soviétique aurait pu répondre: "Les choses sont là. Il faut les manipuler."[37]

And Welles shoots his films making reference to Eisenstein, although he doesn't do it explicitly, and the ideological connotations involved are different; Rosi, on the other hand, shoots his films making reference to Rossellini and the Neorealist school.

One could at this point assert that the cinema is an instrument of audiovisual communication that is better used in conformity with one or the other of these two theoretical positions: but arguments about specific components are always ambiguous and risky, because there exist completely successful and valid films in the productive history of both types of creative approach and, above all, because if the cinema is a language that adheres greatly to reality, by virtue of its photographically reproduceable nature, this external reality is not merely made up of physical objects, and of men fatally characterized by a fully mapped-out destiny, a 'character's' existential heredity. The cinema photographs man, his actions, the things involved in his physical behaviour, and, at the same time, the motives that

[37] Metz (1964), 56.

justify his acts and his choices (or at a limit, as in the case of Godard, his lack of motives) and, at any rate, the social, psychological, and cultural atmosphere within which the various characters develop. It thus comes about that anything within the cinematographic sign that involves an act of denotation for a certain spectator on a determined historical occasion can rise to the level of connotation for other spectators at different points in time.[38] At the same time, it can happen that a certain cultural atmosphere is recorded in all its simplicity on film, thus involving a complex of connotations that were already implicit in the reality that is the object of analysis, and that may therefore elude the observation of a spectator distanced from them by time and lack of preparation or of a mentality suited to their interpretation. One may impose a sense upon things by using them as instruments, recreating them within a poetical atmosphere, and one may equally discover their natural sense and help it to blossom forth of its own accord – but even in this second case one can talk in terms of poetry, and of cinema (for the cinema can, in fact, construct and describe by means of direct representation).

THE LINGUISTIC REVOLUTION BROUGHT ABOUT BY SOUND

When the sound-track arrived to complete the cinematographic image, the esteem in which cutting was held, as the principal formative instrument of the cinema, suffered a humiliating defeat. The talking image (with voices, sounds, and music) naturally lost that complex of symbolic meanings which a certain detachment from the represented reality, such as that found in the silent film, had frequently, and equally naturally, bestowed upon it. As has already been noted, sound increased the cinematographic instrument's reproductive powers in relation to reality, and consequently reduced its capacity for imaginative recreation and symbolical expression. Film production, despite a large number of attempts to revalue classical forms of cutting and to restore their former power, oriented itself increasingly towards displays of reproductive realism, and left to cutting the simple technical concern of joining the lengthy shots together. This does not mean that the cinema has irretrievably commited itself to a poetic

[38]   It can rise to the level of true connotation – but that does not mean that the denotation in itself already involves connotative elements. This is quite another matter: the clothes of the travellers and those who have come to meet them at the station in *Arrivée d'un train* denote for the spectator of 1895 a differentiation between the sexes and a certain aspect of contemporary fashion; for an alert spectator today, those clothes are much more important, and connote a certain *ambience*, a style, an epoch.

recomposition of reality in which the liberty of those that contribute to its making is reduced to a choice and a more or less consequential grouping of its elements. Even if in the present social and cultural climate one can make out these dominant characteristics, it must however be recognized that they are distinctly in evidence in other sectors of human expression, above all the literary one.

After all, the manipulation of things suggested by Eisenstein is no more than a natural consequence of taking up a clearly defined ideological position with regard to the things themselves and to the world, no more than the result of taking a careful look at society and at reality in its entirety, and then setting them out again in a structural *impasto* of their modes of manifestation. From a certain point of view, one could assert that Eisenstein shot his films just as Balzac wrote his novels – in fact, the latter thought of his works as models rather than mirrors; writing "à la lumière de deux grands principes, la monarchie et la religion", he believed himself capable of discovering the sense of things, "la raison du mouvement".[39] And thus the Russian director, thinking about and shooting his films in the light of two other principles, Bolshevik popular government and Marxism, proposed to his public an attempt at "building a synthesis of science, art, and class militancy",[40] a model for interpreting contemporary life and history – with all the well-known vicissitudes the assumption of these two models brought to his work.

However, the techniques and styles of writing to be found in the novel have undergone some notable changes, and the weakening grip of cultural models that have guided humanity from Balzac's time to ours has enabled the various styles of literary writing to transform language from "a privileged area to a sufficient sign of ideological commitment",[41] in cases where the writer makes way for the intellectual, and finally from a sign of ideological commitment to a univocal sign of the author's personality, committed to a cruel process of laying bare the subjective self in a fragmentary and almost always illogical series of relations with things and with other men. Thus the modern novel tends to express only the subjectivity of its author, as revealed in what Robbe-Grillet would call "the movement of

---

[39] On this subject, see Bernard Pingaud's interesting essay "Nouveau roman et nouveau cinéma", *Cahiers du Cinéma* 185 (1966).

[40] Eisenstein (1951), 83.

[41] See Roland Barthes' intelligent study, *Le degré zéro de l'écriture* (Paris, éd. du Seuil, 1953). English translation: *Writing Degree Zero*, trans. Annette Lavers and Colin Smith (London, Cape Editions 4, 1967), 32.

[42] A. Robbe-Grillet, *Nouveau roman, homme nouveau*, 129. English translation in: *Snapshots and Towards a New Novel* (London, Calder & Boyars, 1965), 146. One is

the description'':[42] no more cultural, ideological, or behavioural models, no more descriptions, but instead sensations and the communication of internal experiences.[43] The cinema naturally lies on the same level, but since it does not have at its disposition a linguistic instrument, such as the word that may always be referred to abstract entities, and thus has to resort to objectual representations of reality, it ends up by turning its authors' subjectivity to account in precisely those rare instances where film production still makes use of cutting and imaginative recreation, otherwise setting out a series of careful selections from reality in films that abandon the principle of the dominance of cutting and that therefore do not propose to display any definite cultural or sociological model.

Thus, paradoxically, the cinema shows traces of the same basic cultural position as has been taken up by contemporary literary activity, but translates its stimuli into works with connotations inversely proportional to those produced by written work. In literature, the encounter with an object and with a disconnected fragment of reality is transformed into a sign for the author's subjective nature (as revealed by a certain way of writing). In the cinema, the specular representation of objects and of their chaotic universe reveals the presence of their physical nature, their existence in a certain manner, and can only take on the role of a subjective sign by virtue of a resolutely formative mode of cutting – the type of cutting, that is, which has been abandoned precisely in order not to interfere with the ordering of reality. From this point of view, the films of Godard and Resnais provide the best examples for an experimental analysis of the two opposed creative attitudes.

Godard reproduces reality in apparently clashing fragments, put together in what is at times a disconcertingly casual manner; Resnais edits his film material according to the continuous and highly personal series of choices and syntheses that accompany the development of the work, and to his own way of looking at the elements of reality that surround him. But of Godard and Resnais, nowadays, it is in fact the latter who represents the exception. Only films dealing with the supernatural and the out-of-the-ordinary still make use of cutting as a means of autonomous expression, as do thrillers, or rather any films characterized by a certain degree of suspense within their narrative evolution.

---

here concerned with that "movement of description" that always threatens to disappear in the film or television version of a novel.

[43] Pingaud (1966), considers contemporary poetry and certain aspects of contemporary prose (Robbe-Grillet, for example) as being without meanings, and able to identify their form with the 'sense' tout-court. The author uses the meaning-sense antimony that derives from Sartre.

Alfred Hitchcock, for example, is well aware of how to make use of cutting so as to produce highly effective results; he plays with his shots, expanding them and contracting them according to his creative whim and to the sensation of violence, of slowly mounting tension, or of mystery that he wishes to communicate to the spectator. He thus passes with ease from the single, extremely long shot that makes up the whole of *The Rope* (1943) to the 70 different camera positions used while shooting the scene from *Psycho* (1960) in which Janet Leigh is killed, which, when projected on screen, lasts 45 seconds.

Le tournage en a duré sept jours et il y a eu soixante-dix positions de caméra pour quarante-cinq secondes de film... On ne voit jamais une partie tabou du corps de la femme car nous filmions certains plans au ralenti pour éviter d'avoir les seins dans l'image. Les plans filmés au ralenti n'ont pas été accélérés par la suite, car leur insertion dans le montage donne l'impression de vitesse normale.

This is the reply that Hitchcock gave when interviewed by François Truffaut,[44] thus revealing the two components of his technical slight of hand in this violent scene, and also his great ability in using several slow motion shots, for reasons of typical Anglo-Saxon prudery, without then varying their projection speed because their brief appearances on screen do not allow one to perceive their temporally exceptional nature. But the thriller, whether it be by Hitchcock or another director, has a very different aim from that of the contemporary narrative, literary or cinematographic.

The thriller is always presented as a closed universe, clearly determined and defined in all its parts, and the spectator is drawn towards perceiving the final solution via the richest possible series of surprises and violent emotions;[45] but the emotive interplay that the cutting of the film produces is counterfeit and without any existential meaning, because one already knows quite clearly what is going to happen before the projector begins to turn. The same thing happens for the thriller film as happens for the detective story,[46] so that the more the cutting complicates the narration, and the more it induces in the spectator a 'voyeuristic' attitude (the possibility of observing the way in which other people behave and live, regarding this as the one and only source of the clues necessary for understanding what is going on) with respect to the reality on the screen, the more one gets the impression of a game, unfolding according to its own rules.

---

[44] "Le cinéma selon Alfred Hitchcock" by François Trauffaut, *Cahiers du Cinéma* 184 (Nov. 1966), 55-56.
[45] Pingaud (1966), 28.
[46] Pingaud (1966), 28.

Against the works of Alain Resnais and, although they occupy an entirely different dimension, the group of productions that may be generically classified as 'thrillers', the contemporary cinema places the work of Ingmar Bergman (who resolves the mixed content of *Through a Glass Darkly* with the long speech of the writer, Gunnar Björnstrand, responsible for his daughter's grave and final crisis, to his young son, Lars Passgard – the theme of love and of the possibility of hope is thus inserted by virtue of the sound-track's contribution, the image acting as an integrative visual complement);[47] of Michelangelo Antonioni, in which dialogue often complements visual image, but in a dimension of reciprocal indispensability in which a sign function sometimes prevails; of Luchino Visconti (the long and ideologically programmed final dialogue from *Rocco e i suoi fratelli*);[48] of Jean-Luc Godard (the long speech made by the alienated protagonist, Bruno Forestier-Michel Subor, about his ideological disengagement in *Le petit soldat*, and the long account that the crazy victim of an amorous fixation gives of his situation to Belmondo in *Pierrot le fou*);[49] also the work of Fellini who, although resorting to magniloquent compositions in which his creative inspiration and a natural sense of how to magically deform reality are brought together and leaving to the brilliant merry-go-round of images no mean part of the communicative fascination of his works, attends to the spoken elements within his cinematographic universe with meticulous seriousness, in order to present the spectator with a code that will suffice for deciphering and interpreting the message on the screen. The examples are innumerable, and all of them agree in presenting a cinematographic image that is made up equally of sonic and visual elements, and is almost entirely free from the binding laws of a golden age in which cutting seemed to represent everything that the film stood for.

THE CIVILIZATION OF THE TALKING IMAGE

In reality, a visual image without the integration of verbal language is nowadays perhaps inconceivable; the cinema, by virtue of its productive nature, which is of a purely industrial order, brings out works aimed at reaching the widest possible public. The film comes into existence as a

[47]   *Sasom i en spegel*, by Ingmar Bergman, dates from 1961.
[48]   *Rocco e i suoi fratelli*, by Luchino Visconti, 1960.
[49]   *Le petit soldat* and *Pierrot le fou*, by Jean-Luc Godard, date respectively from 1960 and 1965.

product of cultural mass reproduction, and however high its level may be, however inspired the poetic aura in which it originated, it cannot neglect giving the spectator a few keys to aid his interpretation. Visual images then undergo a process of codification and semantic curvature by virtue of their contact with a few formations from verbal language; everything that the image shows of its own accord becomes specifically indicated by the words that accompany it[50] and restrict its sense to one or more meanings. On the other hand, what happens in the cinema also takes place in other spheres of mass communication where the visual image is employed as a vehicle: cartoons, television, advertising, and the press (in fact one can hardly imagine the presentation of a photograph in a paper or a rotogravure without a caption to specify and codify its interpretation). All of this has already been penetratingly analyzed by Roland Barthes in *Rhétorique de l'image*:[51]

Aujourd'hui, au niveau de communications de masse, il semble bien que le message linguistique soit présent dans toutes les images: comme titre, comme légende, comme article de presse, comme dialogue de film, comme *fumetto*; on voit par là qu'il n'est pas très juste de parler d'une civilisation de l'image: nous sommes encore et plus que jamais une civilisation de l'écriture, parce que l'écriture et la parole sont toujours des termes pleins de la structure informationelle.

Barthes undoubtedly hits the nail on the head and thus dissipates, for once and for all, the misty confusions engineered by the devotees of a total and direct language, by now destined to prevail in every social relationship and to condition all future communication on all levels. Visual publicity does not exist; one is rather concerned with a series of persuasive acts in which the verbal slogan is united with an image. Even trade-marks often have names or other writings worked into them and, when they are entirely without linguistic elements, aim at fixing themselves in one's memory (reiteration transforming itself into an indirect stimulus), rather than expressly setting out to convince one. Advertising is strictly conditioned by the necessity of specifying with precision the message's designations and of keeping all of its connotations well within the bounds of a clearly defined semantic universe; such a message has a fixed scope, and the social structure that produces it must limit its free activity as a significative agent and as a behavioural stimulus, codifying its interpretation with the help of verbal integration, of a linguistic element that is socially generic and situationally polyvalent. In the case of

---

[50] Pingaud (1966).
[51] Barthes (1964b), 40-51.

the cinema, matters do not proceed in the shadow of such utilitarian (and thus rationally expressible) aims, but in spite of this, the visual image and clarifying verbal integration coexist in the same way. The audio-visual image is indivisible, except at a very primitive stage of analysis; the words from which it is generally made up never constitute a corpus, separate from its structure, but are fundamental elements of both its reproductive and its significant nature.

R. Barthes, in the study cited above, distinguishes two functions of the linguistic message in relation to the iconic message: that of ANCHORAGE (*ancrage*) and that of RELAYING (*relais*). The first is denominative, fixes the possible senses of the object, and is transformed, on the level of the symbolic message, into a guide to the interpretation; the second is brought about by a complementary relation between word and image: the words appear as fragments of a more general syntagmatic unit (this is the case above all in satirical drawings and cartoons).[52]

Bien entendu, ailleurs que dans la publicité, l'ancrage peut être idéologique, et c'est même, sans doute, la fonction principal; le texte DIRIGE le lecteur entre les signifiés de l'image, lui en fait éviter certains et en recevoir d'autres; à travers un *dispatching* souvent subtil, il le téléguide vers un sens choisi à l'avance.[53]

The word pursues a parallel course to the visual image, conditioning the perceptor's approach to its sign potential, or immerses itself in the substance of the image itself, compounding a new synthesis which also necessitates a verbal exegesis in order to be perceived in its total significant function.

CINEMA AND LINGUISTICS

A scientifically based semiotics of the film will not be able to leave out of account the research results of the better established linguistic schools; it will have, of necessity, to make reference to the values there set out, not only from an analogical point of view, as was attempted in the first part of this book, but above all bearing in mind the continuously and indispensably complementary relation (in terms of meaning or structure) between the various families of signs that make up the vehicle of communication. In this instance, linguistics does not assume the role of a sacred monster whose historical evolution is by now scientifically defined, and to which a related discipline (that of a language structured around audio-visual images) refers for its primitive and empirical methodological researches.

[52]   Barthes (1964b), 45.
[53]   Barthes (1964b), 44.

Transposing the results of a by now classically defined complex of studies from the ambit of verbal language to that of cinematographic language is naturally aided by the presence of a 'spoken' element in the signs of the latter, and consequently by the uniformity of nature and of values to be found in the two spheres of communication.[54]

Of course, this approach does not in any way resolve the problem of the signs and language of the film in its entirety, because it must be integrated with a consideration of the iconic aspect of the message, the structural relations between its various components, the psychology of its reception upon a personal and a social level, and of all the other elements that contribute to its formation as active or as conditioning factors. It is a decidedly small part, and an entirely complementary one, that is reserved for linguistics within a general analysis of the film such as the one we are here formulating; but it is a part that belongs to it by natural right, and one that places it without strain among the other disciplines that contribute to a definition of the object.

After all, the FILMOLOGY defined by Christian Metz as a synthesis of researches carried out in the differing fields of psychology, psychiatry, sociology, pedagogics, and even biology, all of them applied to the art of the cinema – filmology preceded by history, criticism ("Il faut voir les films et ne pas trop embrouiller les dates, bien sûr"), and theory (Eisenstein, Béla Balàzs, André Bazin), and followed by LINGUISTICS – may seem like a simplistic hotch-potch, and may perhaps reveal the desire for an impossibly universal agreement, but it is a great deal more convincing, even from the scientific point of view, than are Morris's pretentious declarations about the metalanguage of semiotics that is, in theory, adapted to solving all problems connected with the analysis and study of any linguistic form.[55] The semiotics of the film is as complex as is its elementary sign; at present, the analyst must content himself with gathering together and developing the results of differing scientific disciplines that contribute to the phenomenon, in anticipation of a gnosiological synthesis that would not seem to lie within easy reach. The audio-visual syntagms of the cinema can always be decomposed analytically, but the function of 'ancrage' that the word develops in relation to the visual image ought to be absorbed into that of 'relais' which, according to the canons of an

[54] With reference to this, it is well-known that profound and mutual influences exist between the verbal language spoken in films and that spoken in certain social communities. See for example *Il cinema nella lingua e la lingua nel cinema*, by Alberto Menarini (Milano, Bocca, 1955). See also Francesco Dorigo, "Uso e funzione della lingua nel cinema italiano", *Bianco e nero* XXVII: 7-8 (July-August 1966), 37-59.

[55] Metz (1964), 89-90. For Morris on the subject, see Morris (1946), 179.

aesthetics of the cinema enamoured of a dangerous and useless taste for the specific, should have taken the role of principal function. In reality, the cases of an effective and complementary relation between the sign contributions of the visual aspect and those of the sonic (or rather spoken) aspect are extraordinarily eloquent as far as demonstrating the expressive power of the cinema is concerned, but they are in no way able to support the dangerous qualification of being linguistically unique; for if this were so, the examples given above, and most of the scenes that we have been presented with and continue to be presented with by film productions, would thus acquire the strange qualification of expressive ambiguity and inadequacy.

THE LINGUISTIC INFLUENCE OF TELEVISION

The match between aural and visual elements is particularly significant within the sphere of television because of the renouncing of the canons of traditional specifics that is continually implied there. When television uses electronic cameras, the reproductive medium adheres to reality in a far more inertially specular and passive manner than is usually the case with films; the image will thus have, on the average, a substantial reproductive component and very little of the type of imaginative recreation that the instruments used to form it could in theory permit. If the natural or fictitious reality to be translated into images also manifests itself in sonic phenomena, its image will tend to reproduce their forms as perfectly as possible, and it will not then be necessary to try and make out a hypothetical predominance of the visual components within the communication's definitive sign. When the transmission is concerned with current affairs and documentary reproduction, the visual image and the words that accompany it (whether they are already components of the original reality, or added to form a commentary to its development) can possess a communicative incidence far greater than that possessed by the visual component of the phenomenon itself. Such is the case, for example, in an interview, where the relevance of what is said is usually greater than the way in which the interviewer and the subject are visually portrayed. In this instance, the visual image may, furthermore, supply effective commentary and integration on a connotational level, revealing itself as a support (at times, indeed, a counterpoint) to the semantically simple denotations of the sound-track. Generally, when the small screen of the television is used for this type of program, the incidence of the auditory component in the reception of the message is particularly great, and this is as much the case when electronic instruments are used as when a film camera is responsible for translating the images.[56] In such cases it is the reality of the transcribed phenomenon that takes over the entire semantic space of the communication; and since the sound components of the phenomenon manifest a far stronger incidence in relation to the relevant elements of its space-time formation (and thus to its potential for visual translation), the audio-visual image's sound-track supports the basic weight of the communicative exchange.

Television programs almost always spring from requirements of a reproductive nature. Both in the specific sector of current affairs and in the opposing one of spectacles based upon total fiction, television cameras tend to form specular images and, all in all, a screen medium very similar to the object from which the communication originated. Even in the case of a director making use of a film-camera, the informative aims of the first creative outlook analyzed above involve the medium in basically re-productive work, so that the product, as a result, finds a place within the approach set out here. Excluded from such considerations would be spectacles that were put together making free use of cinematographic in-struments, the transmissions, that is, in which the film is not only a chemical support for the specular recording of certain events, either real or reconstructed – and this is the case, for example, in almost all American telefilms – but also an autonomous medium for imaginative recreation and expression. It is, however, a rare thing for television producers any-where in the world to concern themselves with the conception and com-position of messages of this type.[57]

In reality, television has accustomed its public, often with some effort, to a continuous contact with reality, an increasingly rich series of straight-forward reproductive images in which the entire content of the message is often reduced (at any rate in intentional appearance) to a purely desig-native level, to its direct, audio-visually iconic nature. Even if every televi-sion viewer grasps, at different levels of awareness, connotations that are implicit in the message offered him by the screen (connotations that may be notably different according to the receiver's personal phenomenology), the atmosphere that normally typifies a television program is conditioned by the attention that the transmission group and the generic mass of

[56] See two interesting essays on the interview in *Communications* 7 (Paris, Seuil, 1966): Pierre Dumayet, "L'interview télévisionnelle" and Edgar Morin, "L'interview dans les sciences sociales et à la radio-télévision".
[57] For a study in greater depth of the problems related to television transmission and for a justification of the statements set out here, see Bettetini (1965).

viewers both give to the reality that stands (or stood) beyond the communicative exchange taking place between the transmitting station and the home.

The weight of connotation that all messages carry, and that is implicit in every audio-visual message, demands a foundation on the level of the 'denotata' of the signs used in communication; one cannot neglect the interpretation of the primary and immediate communicative function of the sign and of the sign system to which it belongs if one wishes to investigate the significative sphere that lies beyond the concern of its connotative activities. Now, the system of connotations brought into play within every linguistic exchange involves ideological attitudes belonging to the society within which the exchange takes place, and thus shared by transmitters and receivers alike; this "domaine commun des signifiés de connotation"[58] is in fact that of ideology, which determines an entirely individual line of approach, even when choosing the simplest significative relations. It thus comes about that the connotations of the message, which are discontinuous and pregnant with symbolic life, can only be received by the perceptor if he is able to penetrate to the heart of the universe denotated by the message – in the case of audiovisual communication, only if he is able to perceive the entire structure of its codification and its conventionality, as well as its direct representation.

"C'est très exactement le syntagme du message dénoté qui NATURALISE le système du message connoté,"[59] Barthes acutely observes, and perhaps he means to go beyond a simple normative reference, and to involve, metaphorically, a process of nothing less than 'adopting' or 'assuming' the connotated values within the world of the expressable. The author's attempts at symbolic stimulation will thus be hidden within the relationships of the primary representation, establishing a quantitive inclination in favour of one or the other extreme of the message, in relation to the historical moment, the ideological characteristics of society, the ways in which the type of language assumed in the communication manifests itself, the typology of the author and, indeed, of the receiver of the message. In several films by Dreyer and Bergman, for example, a system of instrumental denotations is built up, these being entirely conditioned by the work's symbolical (and at times positively metaphysical) perspective; certain films by Rossellini, Truffaut, and Godard, on the other hand, are structured around the direct representation of aspects of reality (denotation) that are in themselves valid as objects of analysis, and therefore

[58]   Barthes (1964b), 49.
[59]   Barthes (1964b), 50.

already implicitly connotating an ideological universe that the director seeks to propose to his public. In the second case, the fact that denotation is used in this way is much less evident, because the work sticks to what the image represents, and does not refer the spectator beyond the object projected on screen; the connotation tends to come very close to the denotative procedures and, in one or two cases, the setting out of a cinematographic reality may be directly identified with the author's ideology (see Godard below).

Television is almost always the direct and 'total' sign of a reality because its communicative function is frequently characterized by aims of an informative or indeed didactic nature; even the 'closed' spectacle, whose every aspect has been worked out and tried out a number of times, is recorded by the cameras which follow the action as it happens, in a manner that inevitably includes certain aleatory elements provided by the physical manifestation of the action itself, and the successive technical acts involved in translating it into images. In all cases where an action is directly televised, the message that the small screen gives out is always based upon elements of direct signification, representation, and pure denotative documentation; at a limit, in cases of the most intense symbolical and expressive activity on the part of the audio-visual sign, this aspect of its communicative function may be concentrated within the way that the actors approach their parts, the physical presence of the environment, and the minor incidents that characterize the development of the spectacle (when the latter is considered as one of an infinite number of possible realizations). Even when its transmissions are filmed, television tends to respect the real – at times to the point of unjustified bad taste. Certain probing interviews in which the person concerned is analyzed by the film camera represent phenomena of undoubted linguistic value, but at the same time they raise many doubts as to the validity of the form that they take, above all if this is considered in relation to their aim (which hardly ever coincides with the revelation of an actual mode of behaviour, however falsified this may be by the obsessional presence of the film-camera, but with the discovery of a truth that can never be achieved by raw audio-visual photography).

The fact that the average viewer is accustomed to the filtering of reality through the television screen (and here reality means any identification of the television image with the object that forms it, any form of communicative synthesis between the instrument and the referent of the transmission) has undoubtedly encouraged, along with particular cultural and psychological premises, the spread of a type of film concerned with reality and direct denotation, and devoid of any specific linguistic properties as far as the classical outlook on cutting is concerned. And thus the cinema also analytically retrieves fragments of a pre-existing reality, natural or fictitious, and attempts to integrate it in a synthesis that is codified as little as possible by syntactic tradition.

Franco Rosi achieves a clear demonstration of artistic maturity with his *Salvatore Giuliano* – recomposing into a historicizing unity the direct documents of a reality that is reconstructed by virtue of a close investigation, dimensioned by a precise sociological choice – but loses his track in *Il momento della verità*, indiscriminately adding to the real and spontaneous document the recreated one, to the flash of the camera wandering around in search of 'its' bit of history the false and pre-arranged fragment, which is however always direct and apparently fortuitous. Gillo Pontecorvo made *La battaglia di Algeri* by reinventing one of the most dramatic political situations of our recent history in various phases of its development, but setting them all out as documentary fragments showing the actions and personalities involved in that complicated international crisis. Finally, there is Jean-Luc Godard, who from this point of view is perhaps the most programmatically significant author of all.

JEAN-LUC GODARD

Godard is, by nature, the standard bearer of a cinema of things, of that fragmentary objectuality which is to some extent the key to many aspects of contemporary culture. He singles out a discrete series of materials for cultural consumption within the world that surrounds him, fixes them on film, and then recomposes them in an attempt at a classicizing anthology, which finds its fundamental inspiration (and thus its attendant hazards) in the existential separation between the director and the objects chosen by him, which stands at the heart of the work.[60] In his films, with the clearly marked accentuations that reveal a publicist's sensibility, he places the gangster and the cartoon, torture and Vietnam, slogan-ridden advertising and various recently successful books, science fiction and a few quotations from high-school classics, the game of death (his characters really do die in a great game) and the delicious joke of ideological noncommitment. The objectual images of his work do not amount to a heterogeneous chaos, nor indeed do they seek to impose upon the spec-

---

[60]   J. Collet, *Jean-Luc Godard* (Paris, Séghers, 1963).

tator a series of realities abstracted from their natural context so as to
deliberately delude him as to the film's validity. Thus one is not concerned
with a phenomenon related to kitsch or midcult, as the purely designative
composition of the various messages might lead one to suppose, but with
a real and honest qualitative evaluation of the world, directly carried out
on reality itself by means of a number of choices that are unlikely to
complement one another.

Godard does not want to place his films on the classical level of the
work of art, so that a snobbish interpretation of his works is quite the
worst thing one can do when it comes to making an exact critical evaluation of the phenomenon. His output must be interpreted in the conviction of living through an original and unique experience of the restructuring of reality through its own elements; otherwise, one ends up searching
for a non-existent traditional structure, and accusing one of the sincerest
of contemporary directors of creative duplicity.[61] His films never contain
effects that aim to gain particular emotive results; instead, they exist
within the atmosphere of a primitive communicative exchange, which
frequently succeeds in creating a truly innocent relation between the
spectator and the work's image-reality – reality thus becoming baptized
anew, freed from its history, able to offer itself to every attempt at re-
discovery. Perhaps it is precisely because of this that Godard's films have
not had any great success among the bourgeois public that normally go to
film premières; they were not able to offer experiences capable of liberating the spectator from the anxieties and agitation[62] of a deviating and
alienated cultural quest that is projected onto models as false as they are
easily won.

Films like *A bout de souffle* or *Pierrot le fou* are not products of the
cultural industry, and they address the public according to entirely new
linguistic paradigms. The state of anxiety, to which the apparently committed cinema almost always brings satisfaction, thus further deflecting
the truthful element within the average spectator's cultural interests, is
here augmented, and thus may well condition a negative reaction to the
film. But Godard is not a 'committed' director, in the traditional sense of
the term: he declares, with great clarity, "As far as I'm concerned, my
ideology is making this film. That's all."[63] So that if one wanted to interpret his words according to Barthes's structuralist interpretation of the

[61]   Regarding the problem of Kitsch and Midcult, the reader is referred to Umberto
Eco's intelligent analysis in *Apocalittici e integrati* (Milano, Bompiani, 1964), 67-133.
[62]   Eco (1964), 83.
[63]   "Incontro con Jean-Luc Godard", edited by Maria A. Maciocchi, *Filmcritica*
XVII : 172 (November 1966).

concept of ideology, in the sense, that is, of a COMMON UNIVERSE OF CON-
NOTATIVE SIGNIFIEDS (see footnote 58), one would end up identifying the
director's poetic world (the connotational activity of his signs) with
photographed reality itself and, better still, with the image that slavishly
imitates it, and is faithfully equal to it (as far as the cinema allows) in its
space-time extension. In Godard's films the image really is sign and non-
sign at the same time, because it tends to identify itself so entirely with the
object that its linguistic function may be reduced to the classical rhetorical figure of the tautology.[64] The spectator is unable to pick up any
meaning above and beyond what is on the screen that is not already implicit in the original reality, so that the system of sign correlations that
constitutes the image's denotation tends to become identified with its
connotative activities, and thus with the author's ideological choices.[65]

Godard's non-committed ideology naturally translates itself into the
signifiers-cum-connotators of his films, in a process whose results are
always suspended between the nature of things, the reality of the objects
(and therefore the narrative structure of the work as well), and the
linguistic system that translates everything into audio-visual signals.
Driven on by the very nature of his poetic investigation (the isolating
fragmentariness of his choices), Godard puts together his narration
according to parabolical models, which allow him to re-insert within a
hypothetical but credible reality (Barthes would say that they allow him
to 'naturalize') the objectual and denaturalized fragments that are without
any social links because they are uprooted from the universe from within
which they were taken. His films avoid any realistic dimension, although
they are formed through the juxtaposition of autonomous segments of
reality. Analyzing them, one almost always finds oneself faced with a
display of situations lifted from newspaper reports, facts that have already
made their appearence in the headlines of the world press, which in his
films are brought to life in an exemplary dimension, avoiding all mytholo-
gizing processes but, at the same time, universalizing themselves by
affirming their own particular concreteness.

"Godard doit être un grand dévoreur de journaux: on peut retrouver
l'origine de ces deux films dans la presse des derniers mois", wrote Bernardo Bertolucci with reference to *Deux ou trois choses que je sais d'elle*

---

[64]   Barthes (1964b).
[65]   It does not seem necessary to dwell any further on the distinction between the two
modes of signifying, denotation and connotation, within the perspective that is our
concern here. On this subject, the reader is referred to Stephen Ullmann (1962), and
Roland Barthes (1964a), 91 et seg. (In the English edition [1967], 89 et seg.)

and *Made in U.S.A.*;[66] these fragments of world news, gathered together with the rapidity and timing of a journalist, are not subjected to any aesthetic revaluation, or restructuring within a different system from the one that produced them. They only recover a certain coherence and semantic unity when viewed as part of a narrative that is almost always made up by means of elements derived from real life through their similarity with the various ideological components that accompany the author's work – when viewed, that is, as a parable.

From this point of view, Godard may be placed alongside two Swiss-German authors whose theatrical and literary works have much in common with his films, and above all with his dialogues: Friedrich Dürrenmatt and Max Frisch. Dürrenmatt's Switzerland, as opaque and heavy as are the sauces for the meals that he has so well described,[67] is the same one that forms the background for Bruno Forestier's absurd Genevan adventure in *Le petit soldat*, and the basic ambiguity of *Stiller's* protagonist has its roots in the same soil as the protagonist's libertarian frenzy in *Pierrot le fou*. But the relation between Godard's creative work and that of the two scourges of Swiss neocapitalism goes far deeper than these simple references, because the motivations behind their respective poetic approaches are fundamentally the same. Their work stands out against the leaden sociological background of a nation that has made its political and ideological agnosticism into the main instrument of its fortune and wealth. The Swiss element in Godard's cultural formation is undoubtedly weak and has been deflected by his Parisian experiences, but for all that it is still alive and kicking. Frisch is a natural moralist, an intellectual who suffers and who seeks a possible order into which things may be put; Dürrenmatt wishes to rise above the moral chaos in which he places his parables about physicists and bourgeois with twisted lives, but his caustically destructive powers in which, at times, he takes a positive delight, are so violent that they finally carry the author off with them; both catch wind of the stench of a European society that is drenched through and through with bad faith and with "the ideological disguising of reality"[68] and take up the position of intelligently indicating a general situation that has reached a position of almost definitive jeopardy.

Godard gathers the same society into the living body of his dynamic

---

[66] "Versus Godard", *Cahiers du Cinéma* 186 (January 1967), 29.

[67] As, for example, in the final chapter of *Der Ritter und sein Henker* (Zürich-Köln, Einsiedeln, 1952). English translation: *The Judge and his Hangman*, trans. Cyrus Brooks (London, Cape, 1954).

[68] See the introduction to *Max Frisch, Il teatro*, edited by Enrico Filippini, trans. Aloisio Rendi and Enrico Filippini (Milano, Feltrinelli, 1962).

evolution, but does not involve himself in any moralistic restructuring of the fragments that he succeeds in removing from it. The ethical qualities that mark the approach of the two Swiss-German authors are transposed by them into the structure of their works, and thus into the subject of the events that they describe; Godard, on the other hand, transposes no moralistic suggestions into his films, but knows how to gather any number of them from the auto-significant presence of objects extricated from the world's every-day development by the film-camera. From this point of view, Godard's film work acquires a classical dimension that is not easily found in other manifestations of contemporary production; his films do not belong to linguistic systems that are alien to the norm established by the spontaneous way in which reality reveals itself, so that they are not subjects that may be 'contemplated' in the traditional sense of the word, but stimuli to the contemplation of reality that the director has chosen and set out in an ostensibly disheartened collage in which he would appear to want no part.

The parables of Frisch and Dürrenmatt are brought into being by calling upon the evidence of classical and exemplary incarnations: Don Giovanni, all the characters from *The Great Wall of China*, the old President of the Republic, Philipp Hotz, Biedermann, the old lady, Mississippi, the three physicists who are patients in a psychiatric clinic; but on the other hand Godard's parables are almost always brought into being by virtue of a process of exemplary extraction carried out within the meshes of the society and the world that surround his characters: Bruno Forestier and the Algiers war, the protagonists of *Bande à part* and crime-reporting, those of *Pierrot le fou* and Vietnam, those of *Deux ou trois choses que je sais d'elle* and prostitution within a certain bourgeois stratum of Parisian society, those of *Made in U.S.A.* and the Ben Barka affair. His parables are therefore a lot more violent and direct than are those of the two playwright-novelists mentioned above, even though they lack an explicit and systematic allusiveness, and an expressive orientation that would anyhow be translated into more indirect, and therefore more conventional, forms than those which he almost always makes use of. Even his parabolical inventions, like the operations that contribute to the composition of his films, are direct and immediate translations of his internal ideological energies. One could pursue analogous considerations with regard to the relations between Godard's films and the plays of two other 'parabolical' European playwrights: Jean Genet (see *Les bonnes, Les nègres, Le balcon*) and John Arden (see *Sergeant Musgrave's Dance*, suggested by British repression in Cyprus, and *Armstrong's Last Good-*

night, whose basic idea derives from a book by Conor Cruise O'Brien on the ONU and the Congo during Lumumba's time).

So Godard damps down on the cutting; the specific qualities of this classic instrument of film narration are watered down and, as far as all its fundamental qualities are concerned, destroyed. In his work, the cinematographic "*plan*"[69] takes on a richness of sign function that, until a few years before, was only to be found in certain successful television transmissions. For Godard, as for his more or less open followers, cinema is made up of shots and photographic fragments, and not of scenarios or precise previsions as to the composition of as yet unrealized pieces. And so

...les plans, qu'ils soient fixes, panoramiques ou sur travellings, sont autonomes, avec une résonance autonome et une beauté autonome, et... il ne faut pas trop se préoccuper de prévenir un montage, car de toute manière l'ordre naît automatiquement à partir du moment où nous les mettons l'un à la suite de l'autre, et... au fond un plan en vaut un autre (Rossellini le sait) qui s'ils ont une charge poétique, la relation naîtra malgré tout...[70]

No funeral rites for a particular poetic approach to the cinema could resort to crueller and less concessive words than these; from now on the film is no longer a discourse on reality, but is instead its truest and most evocatively representative phantasm. The author's ideological stimuli are translated into a choice of objects, rather than imaginative distortions and recreations of a material considered in its instrumental dimension alone. Since the ideological axes dear to contemporary intellectuals are frequently modified and oscillate between a variety of values, films shot according to the dictates of this creative attitude could well be doomed to a rapid exhaustion of their informative weight; their denotative powers are so subordinate to their connotative activities, that the exhaustion of the latter could compromise the entire communicative existence of the cinematographic sign, bringing into prominence its mere photographic formation, which amounts to little more than its shrivelled chrysalis. As a result, the passing of time could well render them far more cruelly banal than it does a film made up according to the classical rules of structural cutting. Which doesn't mean that everything must necessarily turn out as this pessimistic view would imply, nor that, even if it did, the path that the most astute directors are at present following is a mistaken and useless one. For the moment, however, a requiem for cutting is indicated.

[69] There being no satisfactory English equivalent for the terms *piano* and *piano-sequenza*, I have retained throughout this final section the original French terminology: *plan* and *plan-séquence* [Translator's note].

[70] Bertolucci (1967).

THE 'PLAN-SÉQUENCE'

The advent of the long-held shot and the tendency to move away from splitting up the action into fragments shot from different angles should not, however, be interpreted merely as a facile return to the reproductively designative origins of the film instrument. The *'plan-séquence'*[71] of Godard, Antonioni, Losey, Rosi, and Bertolucci does not (despite certain statements by these authors to the contrary, especially Godard) in any way abandon considering the image's representative powers from the point of view of its sign function, nor does it reduce its significant function to a simple and total identification with the object, which anyway cannot be accomplished. Cutting is above all brought into question as a fictional instrument, potentially capable of evocatively involving the spectator's attention, but the expressive and linguistic lesson that it offered has been re-absorbed into other dimensions of film composition. Camera movements and 'cinematographic' movements of reality (the ones, that is, that have been pre-arranged with their distorting translation onto a two-dimensional surface in mind) result in the cinematographic narration developing by virtue of a rich series of explicit connotations of a technical and linguistic nature, even when whole actions, whole scenes, or indeed whole sequences are absorbed into a single shot.

In the *plan-séquence*, reality is revealed according to parameters that appear to be rather more its own, and less invented than is the case in narrative situations codified by classical cutting – but even in this instance is one not, as always, concerned with a pre-arranged reality, or at any rate with one that has been selectively translated into images so as to signify something that invariably differentiates itself from its purely denotative aspect? Cutting revealed itself to be an inadequate cultural instrument once the attention of directors had become oriented towards a critical examination of the film's linguistic characteristics and, above all, once the urgent desire for truth that had been establishing itself throughout contemporary thought, anchoring its values to the physical aspects of reality and renouncing all possibility of re-elaborating them in some fanciful or mythical form, had impregnated the various types of research taking place in the sphere of audio-visual expression as well.

A film using the *plan-séquence* is still a communicative instrument that signifies on other levels as well as that of direct representation (which in

---

[71] See footnote 69. A *plan-séquence* indicates the use of a single shot, whether still or moving, for the entire duration of a section or scene [Translator's note].

itself is already incomplete and intentional); it is still a work in which the place occupied by the signifiers is the support and root of the place occupied by the signifieds, by the diegesis.[72] The *plan-séquence* of the contemporary cinema is therefore governed by expressive intentions that transcend the impersonal values of the continuous spatio-temporal photographing of a certain action or object. In informative films concerned with current affairs, the *plan-séquence* is often the natural way of translating reality into images – but there, as in the most normal television program, the sign on screen is attempting, in cases of considerable expressive richness, to connote the same connotations that are revealed by the direct manifestation of the object concerned, the hints of meaning that the phenomenon in front of the film camera itself gives rise to, irrespective of its translation onto film.

In the case of a film composed by virtue of a narrative fiction, on the other hand, the *plan-séquence* tends to increase the moving image's credibility (which is, by its very nature, already considerable), and hence the indirect persuasiveness of its dialectic positioning between the author and the receiver of the message. It also tends to lower the threshold of suggestivity beyond which the normal spectator finds his powers of critical reaction fade away. But one is always confronted by a significant fiction, by a deliberate representation of reality that is subordinated to creative, or at any rate interpretive, interests. Or rather one might say that the choice of a *plan-séquence* or of a type of cutting that makes use of shots of great length reveals a desire on the author's part to free himself and the spectator from the risk of projecting themselves into the film, the danger of a total identification between the perceptor's psychic existence and the action taking place on screen, which often implies the suffocating of such effective catharsis as may be derived from the perception of the work.

The *plan-séquence* ensures that the director will do without the various expressive tricks and effects that the medium offers him, and that, at the same time, his entire interest will be oriented towards setting out a sign, whose iconic nature may not be reduced to a simple figurative relation (or a relation between formal percepts), but also involves the whole spatio-temporal development of the phenomenon translated into images or of the action invented as the dramatic root of the event on screen. This expressive tendency can at times overcome straightforward reference

---

[72] Metz, "Le cinéma moderne et la narrativité", *Cahiers du Cinéma* 185 (December, 1966a).

to a natural or invented reality outside the camera; it can, that is, imply connotations as to the very way in which the cinematographic work is formed and the linguistic techniques that condition its realization. The director's 'realistic' interests are, in this case, directed towards the behaviour of film material, the actors' spontaneous reactions to a certain dramatic proposition, the dialectic between the interpreter and the scenery around him, the ephemeral and finalized life of all the elements that go to make up the shot, and on the other hand they lead him to consider the narrative development of the work as a simple heuristic pretense. Rather than concern himself with the truth of facts, he chooses to concentrate on the truth of the dramatic reactions determined by using them as the model for a certain situation; the only part of them that he makes use of is the stimulating function of a certain linguistic reality. So the *plan-séquence* presents itself as the ideal setting for this kind of research, as the semantic space within which the fortuitous, aleatory and accidental elements that may accompany the making up of the scene find room to expand naturally.

In such cases, the director's search for expressive means draws close to the principles that lay behind Bertolt Brecht's concern with creating an epic theatre, as revealed in all of his plays and productions. Openly displaying to the receiver of the film message the means by which the dramatic action has been structured does, in fact, tend to estrange him from any possibility of suggestion, revealing at every moment the presence of a dramatic fiction and a mediating instrument of communication. To gain this end, the cinema resorts to making the actor look straight into the camera lens (Bergman, Godard), inserting evidently documentary material (Brass, Godard, Straub in *Nicht Versöhnt*), a direct relation between actor and spectator (in the narrative form of an unseen voice, or in the more agressive one of apparent dialogue), sub-titles (Godard, Pasolini); but it can also resort to the well-calculated use of the *plan-séquence*, choosing from among the various takes those that make clearer the constructive and compositional effort lying behind the many elements that go to make up the film.

Once again, the example of Jean-Luc Godard is particularly interesting from this point of view: his films very frequently show traces of a certain degree of improvisation and of being made rather quickly. In his determination to "gather the definitive almost by chance", Godard does not attempt to put pressure on the actors in their interpretive game; he leaves them free and responsible for their own gestures, aiming more at the truth of their condition as actors than at that of the characters they represent.[73] When cutting, he often makes use of shots that have not turned out well, according to the traditional praxis of film expression, but which better reveal the elements discussed above. Godard is perhaps an extreme example of a linguistic game that may appear gratuitous, but that draws its *raison d'etre* from the necessity of re-thinking the ways in which the film message, supported and elaborated by the forms of cinematographic narration themselves, is put into effect.

Even in these apparent exceptions to contemporary production, however, one can always make out a signified that goes beyond the image's mere denotation, and that finds its place as a connotative element within a representation of reality which is rendered dialectic from its earliest stages by intentionally presenting an account of the linguistic elements that make it up. In the sequence of the domestic squabble between Angela (Anna Karina) and Emile (Jean-Claude Brialy) from *Une femme est une femme*, Godard resorts to lengthy shots, which reveal by direct representation a certain milieu, certain of the two characters' attitudes and modes of behaviour, a certain segment of the film's narrative evolution, and at the same time place before the spectators the two actors' efforts at interpretation, their uncertainty (the alternation of crying and laughing on Karina's face after she has dropped the eggs), and the ways in which their attempts to communicate with the public become established.[74] Introducing the spectator into the compository secrets of the film image in this manner has no purely informative and documentary aim; it is not an end in itself. On the contrary, it is precisely from the simultaneous and superimposed reception of the two narrative levels (the story and the data regarding its formation) that the spectator may deduce the complex meaning of the message: the director's critical attitude to a certain familiar reality, the sense of intellectual fun that pervades the whole work, a parodying glance at the Hollywood musical comedy.

So one can state that the use of the *plan-séquence* and the abandonment of cutting by the most interesting directors of the present generation do not in the slightest invalidate an approach to the cinematographic image in terms of its sign function. Apparently, the specular reproduction extolled by the latest techniques of film narration notably reduces the communicative space within which that OTHER THAN ITSELF to which every linguistic sign refers may find a place; apparently the ABSENCE, within whose field occurs the synthesis of perceiving the world ("whether one is

---

[73] Collet (1963), 41.
[74] *Une femme est une femme*, by Jean-Luc Godard, dates from 1961; prod. Rome-Paris Film (Georges de Beauregard, Carlo Ponti).

concerned with retention or projection") and at whose dissolution is aimed every one of man's cognitive activities, and therefore his acts of aesthetic contemplation, finds (within this mode of conceiving of the language of the film), as a motive for research, behind the message, the possibility of expanding within an indefinite totality and thus, ultimately, disappearing.[75] Apparently, because the director's imaginative elaboration and expressive aims are always present as a function of the work's specific significative nature, adapting themselves to the models, structures, and codes that condition the audio-visual communicative relationship, and at the same time recreating and recomposing them in a continuous exchange, a reciprocal enrichment between the sphere of personal stilemes and that of traditional codifications.

Perhaps the scholar's fear that the 'objectual' tendency of contemporary cinematographic language may reduce the possibilities of forming an autonomous semiology derives from an excessive subjection to the scientific approach characteristic of the study of verbal language – from that dependence which has already been analyzed and censured in the first part of this study. After all, film stylistics has always been content to trace within film material, and within the operative possibilities of the language connected to it, the same rhetorical figures that have been traditionally codified by the various types of discourse in verbal language. Even the research on the metaphorical and metonymical aspects of cinematographic narration, which refer back to Roman Jakobson's penetrating intuitions and to the work of Tzvetan Todorov, Roland Barthes, and Christian Metz, tries to establish a stylistic polarity deduced analogically from studies and instances that belong to a sector of human communication related to, and yet substantially differing from the cinema.

Methodological translation from one linguistic universe to another and the extrapolation of a few scientifically checked results are undoubtedly fascinating, but dangerous and, above all, too convenient. When studying the audio-visual language, it is necessary to develop an approach to the phenomenon and a perceptual attitude that are not conditioned by pre-fabricated models of behaviour, and adhere more closely to things, to their reality – in short, that are more prudent, in the Thomistic meaning of the word (prudence understood, precisely, as knowledge of reality, as adapting action to the real situation).[76] The film's iconic signs stimulate in the spectator spontaneous and apparently direct perceptive reactions; a

---

[75] Virgilio Melchiore, *La funzione dell'immaginario* (manuscript to be published shortly).

[76] With reference to which, see Josef Pieper's excellent study, *Traktat über die Klug-*

semiology of the film ought to base itself on the decomposition into elementary fragments of these perceptive situations and of the sign stimuli that give birth to them. Once one has established a limit for significant division of the film into large-scale syntagmatic units, one cannot stop at a global consideration of their form. The syntagm must be further broken down, analyzed, and subdivided into parts that are oriented according to different classifications from those favoured by traditional linguistics. This process of de-codification must be pursued right down to the elementary signs that make up the cinematographic image, to the figures within the shot.

One will be concerned with technical fragments that are univocally non-significant; but the possibility of grouping these elements in selectively oriented sets will favour a codification of audio-visual forms that is, perhaps, more rigid and more valid than one might be led to suppose by the apparent identity between image and object that is basic to film communication. It is the actors' gestures, their mimic expressions, their tricks, the lighting of the surroundings, the scenographic elements, and all of the objects that make up the shot (quite apart from the technical elements themselves that individuate it as such: cuts, angulation, camera movements, etc.) that enter into a mutual dialectical relationship, and make up the semantic value of the syntagm.

These "ultimate elements or units of the film", as Jakobson defines them, referring to Lev Kulesòv,[77] must constitute the research area of any well-based semiological attempt – the way towards the definition and comprehension of the iconeme, of the linguistic unit of the film, passes through a meticulous analysis of its component parts. At this point it is as yet difficult to maintain the priority of personal research, however enlightened. Any scientifically based attempt will not, at this juncture, be able to leave out of account an experimental and carefully organized form of research that has at its disposal all the film material that it may have need of. The figures of the film may tend to articulate themselves in codifiable groups; but only the meticulous analysis of a large number of works will be able to guarantee freedom from illusion or from confused intuition.

This is the moment for film libraries, specialized schools, and academic institutes. It is, above all, the moment for collective and direct research – in filmology as in almost every other scientific discipline.

---

heit (München, 1953). English translation: *Prudence* (London, Pantheon, 1959), 19.
[77] "Conversazione sul cinema con Roman Jakobson", edited by Adriano Aprà and Luigi Faccini, *Cinema e Film* I:2 (Spring 1967), 157-162.

APPENDIX

THE CINEMATOGRAPHIC SIGN AS AUTOSIGNIFICATION OF THE OBJECT

It was the writings of R. Jakobson that brought back into prominence St. Augustine's theory about certain modes of signifying things which make semantic reference to nothing apart from themselves. In *De Doctrina Christiana*, Augustine does in fact establish a fundamental distinction between objects that are USED to signify something other than themselves and those that are not USED for this purpose. To the first he gives the name SIGNS, and to the second, THINGS.[1] Things are known by means of signs, which are, in turn, things that make a certain impression on the senses, but that also in themselves bring to mind a further idea, 'something more': "aliud aliquid ex se faciens in cogitatione venire".[2] One immediately notes that the author wishes to make a clear distinction between the two types of objects by virtue of their particular USE, of the operative aims to which they are subordinated by the interpreter of the communication (and indeed by its author, if known). Sign objects can in themselves make known something more, something above and beyond what they themselves are, without having the slightest intention or desire to signify; in such cases they are defined as NATURAL signs. At the opposite extreme, Augustine distinguishes CONVENTIONAL signs, these being the results of subjective operations, the vehicles of those reciprocal exchanges that men use in order to show their state of mind – everything, that is, that they sense or think ("vel sensa, aut intellecta quaelibet").[3]

When, in *De Magistro*, he sets out the problems of education, and distinguishes between the method that makes use of verbal communica-

---

[1] Augustine, *De doctrina christina*, in *Le Magistère chrétien* (*Oeuvres de saint Augustin*, Iʳᵉ série, II) tr. et notes par G. Combès et J. Farges (Paris, Desclée de Brouwer et Cie, 1949), 183.
[2] Augustine (1949), 238.
[3] Augustine (1949), 240-241.

tion and the intuitive one, which involves placing the pupil in direct contact with things rather than with verbal signs, Augustine tends to give pride of place to the latter rather than the former, because words "…seeking to ascribe much [to them] …draw our attention to seeking out things, but do not show us them in order that we may know them".[4] Words make known only themselves, while knowing things also allows one to know words; "listening …to words alone, one does not even learn these".[5] Leaving aside the problem of a valuational differentiation between the two pedagogical methods, since this is not relevant to the argument in question (though one should remember, among other things, that Thomas Aquinas took up Augustine's arguments, modifying the evaluation they had previously received and pointing out the existence within language of "intelligible species that are necessary… for the formation of concepts"),[6] two aspects of Augustine's thought must nevertheless be considered: the fact that the distinction between objects as things and objects as signs is established by their USE, and the fact that words (verbal signs) only possess the faculty of concentrating the perceptor's attention on something above and beyond themselves, with respect to which they do no more than exercise an indicative function. Augustine does indeed admit to the existence of things that can be shown without signs – the ones that, when someone asks about them, can be put directly into effect, such as talking, or teaching, or (with all due caution, in view of the extreme contingency of the demonstration) any action that the person addressed may immediately and directly perform.

THE USE OF THE OBJECT'S SIGN FUNCTION AS A DISCRIMINATORY ELEMENT

This characteristic has already been singled out by Luigi Faccini, who bases his observations on Jakobson and Barthes.[7] Faccini substitutes the concept of SENSE for that of SIGNIFIED, justifying this by the film image's greater semantic richness when compared to the simple relationship joining concept to linguistic sign. The sense of the cinematographic sign is "the reference to the socio-cultural FUNCTION or USE of the object as its own sign" and is "actively manifested by an analogical 'visual-acoustic image' that motivates it and shows itself as such immediately".[8] The inter-

---

[4] Augustine, *De Magistro*, edited by Mario Casotti, VI ed. (Brescia, La Scuola, 1968), 89.
[5] Augustine (1968), 90.
[6] See Casotti's excellent introduction to Augustine (1968).
[7] Faccini, "La letteratura come spazio critico", *Cinema e Film* I:4 (Autumn, 1967), 398-415.
[8] Faccini (1967), 409.

pretation of Augustine's thought put forward here does, however, seem rather forced, because the function or use of the object to which reference is made is the one that typifies its history within a particular society and epoch, whereas the use to which the definitions of *De doctrina christiana* refer is nothing more than the contingent situation in which the object happens to be (through the wish to communicate or by accident) in relation to the interpreter. One could establish an identification between the same concept's two modes of existence in the case of an object, used in reality as a sign, being photographed as such, or in the opposite case of an object, used as a thing, being represented in this function. We should thus be faced with an object-image that would respectively be the sign of a sign and of a thing, and would be able to impose the original contribution of a sign function upon its link with the object (by means of technical interventions and contextual relationships).

When Jakobson states that St. Augustine imagines, in his classification, "a system of signs in which the object becomes a sign of itself",[9] and then proceeds to define him paradoxically as the first theorist of the cinema, perhaps he is mixing up the sign's objectual nature with the thing's, since the objects that become signs of themselves are simply things, which are different from film images despite all the specular links between them. One could then consider the film image as an object that is its own sign and is therefore, to adopt Augustine's approach once more, only fit to be enjoyed (*frui*) or used (*uti*). But, in one case as much as the other, the resultant argument would be a far cry from the semiological outlook on which these notes are based. The concept of 'use' proposed by Augustine is valid when it is employed to discriminate within an area of study that stands at a more basic level than the formation of the film image itself, and that limits itself to an analysis of the relationship between reality and its audiovisual transcription. The USE to which Augustine refers occurs within the concrete reality of the objects; the one implied by Faccini is already the referent of a message that can have within it a type of function that exceeds the socio-cultural employment of the represented object.

SIGNS AS 'INDICATORY' AGENTS WITH RESPECT TO THE OBJECTS SIGNIFIED

In this field, Augustine's argument refers to verbal signs, and, as has already been noted, these considerations inspire in him a certain degree of diffidence as far as the cognitive data acquired by recourse to the linguistic logos alone are concerned. But in the case of cinematographic signs, one

---

[9]   Aprà and Faccini, *Cinema e Film* (1967), 257-162.

is faced with images that in representing the object concentrate the perceptor's attention upon it, and that show the object in all its significative weight (use → thing or use → sign). The cinematographic language would then overcome the antinomy between the values of a verbalistic pedagogy and those of an intuitive (objective) method, concentrating the perceptor's denotative attention upon the things represented, and therefore indicating them by means of the signs that reproduce them. And since "not only things and their qualities can be directly shown, but also actions",[10] one can understand how the various segments that make up a film (and that can almost all be reduced, broadly speaking, to the value of ACTIONS) are naturally very similar to the category of objects that Augustine defines by virtue of the property of being able to be shown without signs. It is indeed possible to avoid or reduce, within the corpus of cinematographic language, the risk of extreme contingency indicated in *De Magistro* with regard to such 'shown' objects, since the interpretation of a film can do without conceptual abstractions, and must remain firmly attached to the image's concrete data – and thus to the contingency of the objects that make up its content with their representations.

The sign does not produce knowledge of things, it presupposes it – in the sense that either knowledge "is already there, in which case the sign says something, or it isn't, in which case the sign remains incomprehensible".[11] However, in the case of the cinematographic image the sign does not limit itself to indication, but also shows a reality which, even in cases where the perceptor doesn't know about it beforehand, seems to him to be directly represented, and therefore intuitively perceptible. So that for cinematographic signs one could propose the theory of a communicative activity that above all aims at OBJECTIVELY SHOWING something, at an indirect exposition of the object that solicits its perception upon a fundamentally INTUITIVE level. Armed with this working hypothesis, one could turn to the analyses carried out in this area of human communication by two American authors to whom semiological research owes a great deal: Charles S. Peirce and Charles Morris.

THE CINEMATOGRAPHIC SIGN AS 'ICON'

The first of these two, a brilliant, disorderly man, proposes the well-known division of sign typology into three parts, considering the ele-

[10] See footnote 6.
[11] See footnote 6.

mentary sign in relation to its own object, and thus leaving out of account its material and the nature of its interpreter.[12] Peirce's sign is "something which stands to somebody for something in some aspect or capacity" (*Collected Papers*, 2, 228).[13] The SOMETHING (else) is, precisely, the object of the sign and, according to the type of relation that is established with it, one finds oneself faced by an ICON, an INDEX, or a SYMBOL. The ICON signifies passively, and by resemblance; the INDEX by organic connection; the SYMBOL, however, does not signify by means of an intrinsic relation, but by convention.

Peirce proposes as examples of the icon a mental or specular image, a painting, a formula, a diagram, a metaphor. These are thus completely motivated signs, but ones that do not have a "dynamic" relation with the object – they convey its formal aspect, and nothing else except its pure logical possibility. At this point, analogical considerations might tempt one to write that the cinematographic image could be considered on a level with Peirce's icon, but the matter is decidedly more complex than might appear, so that it is well worth examining the other aspects of Peirce's tripartite division before drawing conclusions. The INDEX (examples: a graduated scale, a signal, a shout, a demonstrative pronoun) forms an organic coupling with the object, connected by a link that the perceptor's mind must, of necessity, recognize. Indices direct "the attention to their objects by blind compulsion" (*Collected Papers* 2, 306).[14] They possess the capacity to make us distinguish reality from imagination, but are entirely blind to the character of the denoted reality. The sign with an 'indexical' function takes us back to the arguments of Augustine, R. Jakobson, and Faccini: the subject's powers of attention are, in fact, also sensitized in relation to the signified object in this instance. The SYMBOL has no intrinsic relation with the object, but it is a type, a model linked to it by means of a relation governed by a normative convention, a law "which operates to cause the Symbol to be interpreted as referring to that

---

[12] For an ordered account of the argument, see Ninfa Bosco, *La filosofia pragmatica di C. S. Peirce* (Torino, Edizioni di Filosofia, 1959), 70-90, from which the following analysis of Peirce's ideas on the sign has been drawn. See also Umberto Eco, *La struttura assente* (Milano, Bompiani, 1968). (To be published in English as *The Semiotic Landscape* by Mouton and Co.)

Bosco's book attempts to set in order the "vast and chaotic amount of material" in the *Collected Papers of Charles Sanders Peirce*, collected into 6 volumes by Charles Hartshorne and Paul Weiss (Cambridge, Harvard University Press, 1931, 1936). See also N. Salanitro, *Peirce e i problemi dell'interpretazione* (Roma, Silva, 1969).

[13] Bosco (1959), 73.

[14] Bosco (1959), 79.

Object" (*Collected Papers* 2, 249).[15] That law is the signified of the symbol, which is the only sign to have as its signified a universal element.

The way in which Peirce approached semiological problems is undoubtedly less 'scientific', but more totalizing and comprehensive than Saussure's methods. It was in fact Roman Jakobson who pointed out that, while for the Genevan linguist completely arbitrary signs realized better than any others the ideal semiological process, Peirce considered that the greatest perfection in a sign would be obtained where the three typical aspects (iconic, indexical, and symbolical) were "amalgamated, almost, if possible, in equal proportions".[16] In verbal language, symbolic components predominate, although one can also make out iconic and indexical ones, above all when one considers its poetic dimension or the use of words. In the cinematographic language, on the other hand, iconic and indexical components predominate, but the symbolic level also finds its place (Russell talks of a "submerged dimension"). So perhaps cinematographic signs turn out to be the richest, from Peirce's point of view, since it is difficult to find the same trivalency of sign function in other areas of human communication. In every film, the three modes of signifying analyzed above are simultaneously present, but in the form of a stratified combination, a functional intersection, rather than in that of an alternation or an elementary juxtaposition. So that, except in one or two cases, it will not be possible to make a precise distinction between the icons, the indices, and the symbols amongst the signs in a film, but one can instead point to the prevalence of one of these modes of signification on the level of elementary units, or on that of syntagms, or on that of signs, or on that of sequences, or on that of the whole work. This stress on the functional aspect does not rule out the presence of other significative activities that must be perceived and interpreted in order to complete one's awareness of the image on screen, within the sign under analysis.

Lee Russell attempts an interesting demonstration of the presence throughout the history of film of Peirce's three dimensions, which are shown to function in a mutual exchange of sign functions that brings them to conditions of reciprocal predominance. Thus the works of J. von Sternberg (who went so far as to paint trees and scenery with aluminium, applying make-up to nature as well as to human faces) and Max Ophuls (who painted the trees gold and the streets red in *Lola Montez*) tend to occupy an expressive dimension that may be placed beyond any repro-

[15]   Bosco (1959), 80.
[16]   L. Russell, "Cinema-Code and Image", *New Left Review* 9 (May-June 1968), 76.

ductive realism but that, at the same time, does not get to the point of displaying symbolic intentions – an iconic dimension, in fact.[17] To these one might add the names of Alain Resnais (*L'année dernière à Marienbad*), Michelangelo Antonioni (*L'eclisse* and *Il deserto rosso*), Franco Rosi (*Il momento della verità*), and Elio Petri (the debatable *Un tranquillo posto di campagna*), without, of course, forgetting the works of the 'underground' cinema, which often aims at an instrumental conception of the film-camera fairly close to that of painting implements (Gregory J. Markopoulos, Andy Warhol, Luca Patella, Mario Schifano, Ettore Rosbosch, et al.). The works of Flaherty, Murnau, von Stroheim, Renoir, Welles, Wyler, Rossellini, and all the Italian Neorealists may instead be referred, according to Russell, to a predominantly indexical dimension, to a significative activity that tends to urge the perceptor's attention towards the object. This is a cinema of designation, in which the image offers a mirror version of reality rather than an enigmatic one. Finally, the symbolic dimension may above all be traced in Eisenstein's films, where the image is used as a cellular element within a more complex structure, which imposes upon the reproduction of the object a formative law that is often alien to the object itself – and this law, as was noted above, is the signified of the cinematographic sign. To his name one might add those of Resnais, Pasolini, and, with reference to certain aspects of his work, Godard.

So the history of the cinema reveals differing attitudes to film communication; attitudes that do not exclude the use of other modes of sign activity that are also present within the form that the work adopts, and that, above all, intersect with the level singled out by the author for preferential treatment. Above and beyond Peirce's tripartite division, the film sign is always photographically rooted in reality, and has an intrinsically iconic relation with the object – which is thus attached to it by a motivational link. This iconic element must, however, be understood in terms of the sign's characteristic property of acting as an icon and as an index at one and the same time. The cinematographic image re-unites within it the properties of the first two types of sign codified by Peirce, since it directs that perceptor's attention by means of an impulse that is not completely blind, but structured around a resemblance.

The cinematographic sign indicates the object by means of a phantasm that reproduces it and that is therefore motivated in a different way, and at two different levels. The iconic motivation (in Peirce's sense) is almost complete, because the sign is constructed around the object in a deeply analogical relationship. In fact, the iconic aspect has almost always been

17   Russell (1968), 74-75.

overlooked by semiological studies, because its structures are not easily distinguished and generalized. On the other hand, the indexical motivation is subordinate to the object's physical nature and to the laws that are revealed within it, but it is also reduced by the technical choices that condition the reproduction of the object itself, subordinating it to the author's 'indicative' intention: angulation, the way the shot is cut, illumination, figurative composition, rhythmic relations, internal and external dynamic considerations – in fact, the whole complex of expressive factors that allow the director to show the spectator certain aspects of reality and not others, or to reveal them in a certain way, without as yet intervening with a profound expressive restructuring of reality.

The iconic aspect of the cinematographic sign is thus not easily codified but it exists and one cannot leave it out of account. One could attempt to establish an iconographic schematization for it (as recommended by Russell but questioned by Panofsky himself), which would seem to be particularly useful and effective when limited to the study of a precise type of cinematographic production, within a clearly defined period, and with reference to a limited number of authors (or, naturally, when dealing with one particular author, historical period, or movement of expression).[18] The points of reference that one could thus arrive at would be the fruit of wide-spread analytical research, aimed at discovering the formal schemes and the psychological, sociological, and ideological motivations that originated their crystallization within repeated episodes. The intervention of an enumeration of the iconographic possibilities would, however, involve raising the level on which the signs were interpreted, so as to include the values of a primitive form of symbolization, and thus the perception of a law that goes beyond the forms of the sign (the applied iconographical principle) and yet is embodied in the resemblance to the object that entirely pervades it.

It is easier to codify the behaviour of the cinematographic sign from an indexical point of view, despite the motivations that condition its communicative activity. It is precisely its way of setting out to indicate and reveal to the attention a certain reality that lends itself to schematization and organization, even though, as has already been pointed out, this rhetoric on the level of small units (for it is to this that indexical codification reduces itself) is weak systematically, and inefficient historically; it can, that is, be easily overcome by the author himself (see, for example,

---

[18]   Russell (1968), 77. See also Panofsky, "Style and Medium in the Motion Pictures", from *Film: An Anthology*, edited by Daniel Talbot (University of California Press, 1966). The essay dates from 1934.

Ingmar Bergman's varying stylistic choices with regard to the sound-track, or Tony Richardson's as regards the cross-fade) or by the history of the cinema, which at times moves faster than do the discoveries of theorists.

Finally, the symbolic function of the cinematographic sign is the one that is most difficult to distinguish within the history of the cinema, but at the same time is also the most easily codified, and adapted to any attempt at organization. After all Peirce's symbol takes possession of that abstract and partially unmotivated area which we have seen to distinguish the ambit of connotation – a space within which almost all theories of the cinema (which have always tried to reduce the cinematographic sign to its symbolic aspect) have found a place, including, recently, Metz's syntagmatic research, with all of its rhetorical implications on the level of large-scale units. The symbolic area of the cinematographic sign is above all that of cutting, which should be understood in its widest sense, as an instrument of film 'writing'. If, along with Roland Barthes, we accept the field of writing as that of the author's entire commitment, as the zone within which he makes his choice as to tone and ethos (writing as an "act of historical solidarity")[19] and therefore, in the case of the cinema, as the area within which the director chooses his way of filming, his language, and his public (not as one possible set of aims among many, which would be the equivalent of a detached, antihistorical, and reactionary choice, but as moral involvement and totalizing personal commitment), then in the moment of cutting we witness the hypostasis of a man within the forms of a fictitious object that magically aims to reflect reality within itself. Whether the director undertakes the cutting of his shots so as to give strong ideological weight to their composition, or denies cutting its function as sovereign recreator of the object, he always arrives at the formation of a model of reality, in constructing which he reveals his artistic commitments.

So it is possible to state that Metz's semiological analysis on a syntagmatic level covers the symbolic dimension of the cinematographic sign, just as the imposition of a rhetorical schema (of whatever type it may be), which also extends in part (on the level of small units) to the indexical one, makes reference to it as well. The iconic dimension remains uncovered, not being sufficiently defined by an iconographic systematics. It is in precisely this area of the cinema that the critic feels the lack of a methodology, and that his approach to the work becomes personal, total, and dangerously adventurous;[20] but it is only at this point, after the spec-

[19] Barthes (1953).
[20] Russell (1968), 80.

ulative *iter* suggested to him by the approaches codified above (and by other possible ones), that he will be able to give himself up freely to the work in a communicative exchange that can produce that metalinguistic reinvention to which every analysis and every evaluation of a film should reduce itself.

Cinematographic images may be considered to be icons that indicate values or aspects of the represented object and that are able to single out within it a symbolic aura, or make up a symbolic meaning by virtue of their iconic and indexical functions. The signified of the film sign then appears as both more and less than the 'concept' that Faccini deduces from R. Jakobson's musings upon Augustine (concept as "reference to the socio-cultural function or use of the object as sign of itself");[21] it appears as making continuous reference back to differing levels of meaning, each of them incomplete and contained within the other, classifiable according to three angles of investigation that interfere mutually with one another and condition more or less codifiable procedures of a semiological type.

More particularly, the interpretation of a film will reveal a paradigmatic structure and a syntagmatic one on the level of symbolical interpretation; it will only single out an analogous possibility for schematization within certain elements of the indexical interpretation (which anyway makes reference to the parameters of reality above all, thus involving the whole of Pasolini's argument about the film being the product of an intervention that restructures the linguistics of the object within a personal and subjective dimension – film as '*parole*' of reality); and finally it will make reference to preventive classifications within the ambit of iconic interpretation, but only by virtue of iconographically established relationships and presences. For the moment, the iconic dimension is the most difficult to codify.

Proposing this method of interpretation, deduced from Peirce's triadic conception and from other considerations concerning the activity of stimulating the perceptor's attention in relation to the represented object, as established in the cinematographic sign, does not imply a judgement upon the value of the work according to the greater or lesser complexity of its sign functions. The three functions examined there are always present in the film, whatever the nature and destination of the messages sent out may be, but in differing proportions and with differing reciprocal values, subordinated to the director's expressive intentions. The films that best conform to this schematically tripartite division and that best satisfy its

[21]   Faccini (1967), 409.

powers of classification are undoubtedly those directed towards imposing upon the material offered by reality a formal structuring of trans-significant realism, those that aim to discover within things values and senses that transcend them without excessively straining their linguistic resources and without resorting to evident distortion: such are the films of Jean Renoir, Luchino Visconti, and John Ford, the most significant examples of a narrative tradition that tends towards the recovery of an 'internal' expressive originality, in spite of the drawbacks implicit in accepting obsolete schemata derived from other areas of human communication.

The suggestions stimulated by Peirce's intuitions naturally find further possibilities for development within the arguments of Morris, whose sensitive interest in those aspects of meaning that have a certain relation with the indexical function analyzed above and with the attention paid to the object in St. Augustine's writings is of particular concern to us here. In fact Morris talks of signs that signify localizations in space and time, and that "direct behaviour towards a certain region of the environment".[22] These are IDENTIFIORS which, because of being able to exist in contexts that differ regarding the objects involved in them, are subdivided into three types: the INDICATORS, which are "non-language signals" (a gesture, a face, a weather-vane),[23] the DESCRIPTORS, which describe a localization, and the NAMORS, which are linguistic symbols. The film image is always an iconic indicator and can be an iconic descriptor; it may, just possibly, in itself give birth to a naming activity. But in developing an argument on Morris' indicators, one would find oneself repeating considerations analogous to the ones that have already been pursued with reference to Peirce's indexes, to which the reader is referred.

THE SENSE OF THE FILM

The invention of the film message's sense is not only, therefore, a complex operation that frequently lacks homogeneity within its various phases, but also one that always finds its definitive form, its internal method, and its structure in contact with the communicating object; it is the film that, with its unique and unrepeatable way of presenting itself to the spectator, stimulates a specific analytical approach that is equally unrepeatable. But, at the same time, a study of the signs that have made their contribution to film communication during a hundred years of experimentation and

[22]   Morris (1946), 66.
[23]   Morris (1946), 67.

production allows one to infer modes of approach, mental schemas, and operative attitudes that may be cautiously generalized, even if not rigidly codified. One will then be able to absorb film interpretation into a process of progressively paring down the signs from which it is composed to the values of their symbolical activity. From this could spring a semantic conception of the cinema which, while being sufficiently functional, would only be applicable to those works that base their communicative behaviour upon reference to a universe of signifieds that may be rationally formulated, and that transcend the objectual nature of the iconic contents. One could maintain, in support of this hypothesis, that within the film image's semantic space one can always find an arbitrary and unmotivated component, and therefore a mode of signifying that may be referred to symbolical paradigms; but the history of the cinema, as we have already had occasion to observe, is rich in examples that contradict this type of assertion. Only in the case of films whose sign structures possess considerable symbolic functions could one lay stress upon this interpretive schema, paradoxically viewing the iconic and indexical aspects of their images almost as if they were the author's personal and subjective interventions (the *parole* aspects) in the formation of his language, which would make reference to a *langue* of ideological symbols that might be metalinguistically translated into the forms of the spoken language. The iconic and indexical functions would thus have to be overcome in critical interpretation, so as to arrive at the abstractive consideration of a codified universe of symbols, values, and emblems associatively governed by the ideology of the work.

The film would simply be a way of revealing the abstract principles embodied in it and its sense, a complex of conceptual signifieds. Such an interpretation would have to take into account the three levels of approach to the figurative object described by Panofsky, defining their results and deducing from them a symbolic codification which one could hypothetically view as immanent within the entire structure of the film. For the films which cannot be referred to this type of semiological approach (and they are the majority), the interpretive models that may be proposed are much more ephemeral and episodic: in general terms, one could consider an attempt at synthesis between the symbolical and iconographic codification that, by dialectically interfering with reality's spontaneous manifestations (indexical attention), could aid the composition of a sense, understanding this as a formative idea, a cultural choice that in itself impregnates the film object's entire material.

At this point theoretical argument comes to an end, and a wide area to be devoted to verification on individual films opens up – a complex area whose outlines are not easily foreseen. Such verification will have to deal with historical and productive phases that were principally concerned with only one of the three sign functions listed above, but it must not ever leave aside films belonging to the narrative tradition, which at times provide the most obvious examples of a polymorphous complexity of sign function. To get out of the structuralist *impasse*, hypotheses have been put forward that resort to some of the oldest theories in the semiological field – one might well get the feeling of having pushed the investigation towards regressive areas of cultural involution; but the nature of audio-visual phenomena and the history of linguistic speculation and of the science of signs during the last few years confirm the validity of the operation, giving sufficient guarantees of scientific coherence. Returning to the origins of the problem is, after all, justified by the scarce attention accorded by scholars to its profoundest aspects, and by the sterility that has always typified convenient attempts at *a priori* solutions by means of analogy or methodological deduction. It is the film itself that reveals the laws of its interpretation.

REFERENCES

Argan, G. C.
  1964   *Salvezza e caduta nell'arte moderna* (Milano, Il Saggiatore).
Aprà, Adriano
  1966   "Premessa a 'A proposita dell'impressione di realtà al cinema' di Ch. Metz",
          Filmcritica 17:163, 19-21.
Aprà, Adriano and Luigi Faccini
  1967   "Conversazione sul cinema con Roman Jakobson", *Cinema e Film* 1: 2,
          157-162.
Aristarco, Guido
  1961   "Senza passato né prospettiva l'oro' di Marienbad", *Cinema Nuovo* 10: 153.
Arnheim, Rudolph
  1958   *Film as Art* (London, Faber and Faber).
Augustine
  1949   *De doctrina christiana* in *Le Magistère chrétien* (=*Oeuvres de Saint Augustin*,
          Iʳᵉ série, II) G. Combès et J. Farges (eds.) (Paris, Desclée de Brouwer et Cie.).
  1968   *De Magistro*, Mario Casotti, ed. (Brescia, La Scuola, VI ed.).
Ayfre, Amédée
  1964   *Conversion aux Images?* (Paris, Cerf).

Ballo, Guido
  1960   "Linguaggio e dinamica del colore", *Cornigliano* 4:4.
  1966   *Occhio critico* (Milano, Longanesi). English translation: *The Critical Eye*,
          R. H. Boothroyd, trans. (London, Heineman, 1969).
Barthes, Roland
  1953   *Le degré zéro de l'écriture* (Paris, Seuil). English translation: *Writing Degree
          Zero*, Annette Lavers and Colin Smith, trans. (London, Cape, 1967).
  1964a "Éléments de sémiologie", *Communications* 4. English translation: *Elements
          of Semiology*, Annette Lavers and Colin Smith, trans.(London, Cape, 1967).
  1964b "Rhétorique de l'image", *Communications* 4.
  1966a "Critique et vérité", *Collection "Tel Quel"* (Paris, Seuil).
  1966b "Introduction à l'analyse structurale des récits", *Communications* 8.
Bellotto, Adriano
  1962   *La televisione inutile* (Milano, Communità).
Benjamin, Walter
  1965a *Schriften* (Frankfurt, Suhrkamp).
  1965b *Das Kunstwerk im Zeitalter seiner technischen Reproduzierbarkeit, Schriften*
          (Frankfurt, Suhrkamp). English translation: *The Work of Art in the Age of
          Mechanical Reproduction*, H. Zohn, trans. (London, Cape).
Bergman, Ingmar
  1961   *4 Film di Bergman*, Bruno Fonzi and Giacomo Oreglia, trans. (Torino, Ein-
          audi).

194   REFERENCES

Bertolucci, Bernardo
    1967   "Versus Godard", *Cahiers du Cinéma* 186.
Bettetini, Gianfranco
    1964   *Il segno, dalla magia fino al cinema* (Milano).
    1965   *La regio televisiva* (Brescia, La Scuola).
    1966   "La regio teatrale alla T.V.", *La rivista del cinematografo.*
    1967   "Immagine cinematographica e immagine televisiva", *I problemi dell'informazione e della cultura di massa.*
Bontemps, Jacques, Jean-Louis Comolli, Michel Delahaye and Jean Narboni
    1967   "Lutter sur deux fronts", *Cahiers du Cinéma* 194.
Bosco, Ninfa
    1959   *La filosofia pragmatica di Ch. S. Peirce* (Torino, Edizioni di filosofia).
Brandi, Cesare
    1960   *Segno e immagine* (Milano, Il Saggiatore).
Bremond, Claude
    1964   "Le message narratif", *Communications* 4.
    1966   "La logique des possibles narratifs", *Communications* 8.
Bruno, Edoardo
    1966   "Prospettive del cinema diretto in relazione al inguaggio filmico", *Filmcritica* 163.

Cassirer, Ernst
    1922   *Philosophie der Symbolischen Formen, I: Die Sprache* (Oxford). English translation: *The Philosophy of Symbolic Form*, Ralph Manheim, trans. (Yale University Press, 1953).
Chiaretti, Rommaso (ed.)
    n.d.   *"L'avventura" di Michelangelo Antonioni* (Bologna, Cappelli).
Ciaureli, M.
    1954   "Della forma figurativa del film", *Il mestiere di regista* (Milano-Roma, Bocca).
Collet, J.
    1963   *Jean-Luc Godard* (Paris, Séghers).

Debrix, Jean R.
    1960   *Les fondements de l'art cinématographique* (Paris, Cerf).
della Volpe, Galvano
    1962   "Il verosimile filmico", *Filmcritica* 121.
    1964   *Critica del gusto* (Milano, Feltrinelli, 2nd ed.).
    1967   Round Table Conference of the III Mostra Internazionale di Pesaro del Cinema Libero.
de Saussure, Ferdinand
    1955   *Cours de linguistique générale* (Paris, 5th ed.). English translation: *Course in General Linguistics*, Wade Baskin, trans. (London, Peter Owen).
di Giammatteo, Fernaldo
    1947   *Essenza del film* (Torino, SET).
    1966   "Chi non conosce il basso bretone", *Bianco e Nero* 27: 7-8, 1-36.
Dorfles, Gilllo
    1966   "Soggettività Socialità Semanticità nell'inchiesta filmata", *VII Premio dei Colli for Cinema Reporting* (Este).
Dorigo, Francesco
    1966   "Uso e funzione della lingue nel cinema italiano", *Bianco e Nero* 27: 7-8, 37-59.
Dumayet, Pierre
    1966   "L'interview télévisionnelle", *Communications* 7.

Dürrenmatt, Friedrich
1952 *Der Ritter and sein Henker* (Zürich-Köln, Einsiedeln). English translation: *The Judge and his Hangman*, Cyrus Brooks, trans. (London, Cape).

Eco, Umberto
1964 *Apocalittici e integrati* (Milano, Bompiani).
1967a *Appunti per una semiologia delle comunicazioni visive* (Milano, Bompiani).
1967b III Mostra Internazionel di Pesaro del Cinema Libero.
1968 *La struttura assenta* (Milano, Bompiani). (To be published in English as *The Semiotic Landscape* by Mouton and Co.)
1971 "A semiotic approach to semantics", *Versus* 1.

Eisenstein, Sergei M.
1935 "Soggetto e sceneggiatura", *L'Italia Letteraria*.
1942 *The Film Sense* (London, Faber and Faber).
1951 *Film Form*, Jay Leyda, trans. (London, Dobson).
1959 *Notes of a Film Director* (London, Lawrence and Wishart).

Eliot, T. S.
1954 *Selected Poems* (London, Faber and Faber).

Empson, William
1930 *Seven Types of Ambiguity* (London, Chatto and Windus).

Fabro, Cornelio
1961 *La fenomenologia della percezione* (Brescia, Morcelliana).

Faccini, Luigi
1967 "La letteratura come spazio critico", *Cinema e Film* 1 : 4.

Fenellosa, E.
1936 *The Chinese Written Character as a Medium for Poetry*, Ezra Pound, ed. (London, Nott).

Fergusson, Francis
1949 *The Idea of a Theater* (Princeton University Press).

Filippini, Enrico (ed.)
1962 *Max Frisch, Il teatro*, trans. Alois Rendi and Enrico Filippini (Milano, Feltrinelli).

Foucault, M.
1966 "Entretien", *La Quinzaine Littéraire* (May).

Gardiner, A. H.
1922 *The British Journal of Psychology* XII, part 4.

Garroni, Emilio
1967a "Popolarità e comunicazione nel cinema", *Filmcritica illustrata* 175.
1967b Round Table Conference of the III Mostra Internazionale di Pesaro del Cinema Libero.

Gherassimov, S.
1954 "Il mestiere di regista cinematografico", *Il mestiere di regista* (Milano-Roma, Bocca).

Gombrich, Ernst H.
1960 *Art and Illusion* (New York, Pantheon).

Greimas, A. J.
1964 *Cours de Sémantique* in *Cahiers ronéotypés par l'École Normale supérieure de Saint-Cloud* (Paris).
1966a *Sémantique structurale* (Paris, Larousse).
1966b "Éléments pour une théorie de l'interpretation du récit mythique", *Communications* 8.

Hodeir, André
1960 "An Analysis of Alain Resnais' Film *Hiroshima Mon Amour*", trans. R. Howard, *Evergreen Review* 12.

Jakobson, Roman
1963 *Essais de linguistique générale* (Paris, Minuit).
Jespersen, Otto
1925 *Mankind, Nation and Individual from a Linguistic Point of View* (Oslo).

Koffka, Kurt
1921 *Die psychische Entwicklung des Kindes.*
Kracauer, Siegfried
1961 "Lo Spettatore", *Film.*

Langer, Suzanne
1953 *Feeling and Form* (London, Routledge and Kegan Paul).
Lefebvre, Henri
1966 *Le langage et la société* (Paris, Gallimard).
Lévi-Strauss, Claude
1962 *La Pensée sauvage* (Paris, Librairie Plon). English translation: *The Savage Mind*, trans. (London, Weidenfield and Nicolson, 1966).
Leydi, Roberto (ed.)
1959 *La Piazza* (Milano, Avanti).

Maciocchi, Maria A. (ed.)
1966 "Incontro con Jean-Luc Godard", *Filmcritica* 17: 172.
Majoux, Jean-Jacques
1960 *Vivant piliers – Le roman anglo-saxon et les symboles* (Paris, Juilliard, Les Lettres Nouvelles).
Manvell, Roger and John Huntley
1957 *The Technique of Film Music* (London, Focal Press).
Marois, Pierre
1950 "Art réligieus, art sacré", *La Vie Intellectuelle* (March), 309-321.
Martinet, André
1960 *Éléments de linguistique générale* (Paris, A. Colin). English translation: *Elements of General Linguistics*, trans. Elisabeth Palmer (London, Faber and Faber, 1964).
1962 *A Functional View of Language* (Oxford).
Masure, E.
1954 *Le Signe* (Paris, Blond et Gay).
Melchiore, Virgilio
La Funzione dell'immaginario (in press).
Menarini, Alberto
1955 *Il cinema nella lingua e la lingua nel cinema* (Milano, Bocca).
Metz, Christian
1964 "Le cinéma langue ou langage?", *Communications* 4.
1965 "À propos de l'impression de réalité au cinéma", *Cahiers du Cinéma* 166-167.
1966a "Le cinéma moderne et la narrativité", *Cahiers du Cinéma* 185.
1966b "La grande syntagmatique du film narratif", *Communications* 8.
1967a "Problemi di denotazione nel film di finzione: contributo a una semiologia del cinema", *Cinema e film* 177.
1967b "Un problème de sémiologie du cinéma", *Image et son* 201.
1967c "Problèmes actuels de théorie du cinéma, *Revue d'esthétique* 2-3.

Mitry, Jean
1965   *Esthétique et psychologie du cinéma* (Paris, Ed. Universitaires). Vol. II: *Les formes.*
1967   "D'un langage sans signes", *Revue d'Esthétique* 2-3.
Morin, Edgar
1966   "L'interview dans les sciences sociales et à la radio-télévision", *Communications* 7.
Morris, Charles
1946   *Signs, Language and Behaviour* (New York). Reprinted in Charles Morris, *Writings on the General Theory of Signs* (= *Approaches to Semiotics* 16) (The Hague, Mouton, 1971).
Moussinac, Léon
1925   *Naissance du cinéma* (Paris, J. Povolozky).
Musatti, Cesare L.
1967   "La visione oltre lo schermo", *I problemi dell'informazione e della cultura di massa* (Istituto A. Gemelli).

Ogden, C. K. and I. A. Richards
1923   *The Meaning of Meaning* (London, Routledge and Kegan Paul).
Osgood, Charles E., G. J. Suci and P. H. Tannenbaum
1957   *The Measurement of Meaning* (Urbana).

Pagliarani, Elio
1960   *La ragazza Carla* (= *Il Menabò* 2) (Torino, Einaudi).
Pagliaro, Antonio
1957   *La parola e l'immagine* (Napoli, Edizioni Scientifiche Italiane).
Palmieri, E. F.
1959   "Cinema, dalla baracca alle salle", in Roberto Leydi, ed., *La Piazza.*
Panofsky, Erwin
1939   *Studies in Iconology* (Oxford University Press).
1955   *Meaning in the Visual Arts* (New York, Doubleday).
1966   "Style and Medium in the Motion Pictures", *Film: An Anthology*, Daniel Talbot, ed. (University of California Press).
Pasolini, Pier Paolo
1965   "Critica e nuovo cinema" (Round Table Conference of the Prima mostra internazionale del Nuovo Cinema, Pesaro), (Roma, Instituto Nazionale dello Spettacolo) (text cyclostyled by the Print Office).
1966a   "In calce al 'cinema di Poesia'", *Filmcritica* 17.
1966b   "Lingua scritta dell'azione", *Nuovi Argomenti.*
1967   Round Table Conference of the III Mostra Internazionale di Pesaro del Cinema Libero.
Peirce, Charles Sanders
1936   *Collected Papers*, eds. Charles Hartshorne and Paul Weiss (Harvard University Press).
Pieper, Josef
1953   *Traktat über die Klugheit* (München). English translation: *Prudence* (London, Pantheon).
Pierce, J. R.
1961   *Symbols, Signals, and Noise* (New York).
Pingaud, Bernard
1966   "Nouveau roman et nouveau cinéma", *Cahiers du Cinéma* 185.
Praz, Mario
1964   *I volti del tempo* (Napoli, Edizione Scientifiche Italiane).

Prieto, Luis J.
1964 *Principes de noologie* (The Hague, Mouton).
1966 *Messages et signaux* (Paris, P.U.F.).
Propp, Vladimir
1918 Morfologija skaski (Leningrad, Academia). English translation: *Morphology of the Folk-tale* (= *Indiana University Research Center in Anthropology, Folklore, and Linguistics Publications* 10) (Bloomington, University of Indiana Press, 1958).
Pudovkin, V.
1954 "Il lavoro dell'attore nel cinema e il sistema di Stanislavskij", *Il mestiere di regista* (Milano-Roma, Bocca).

Robbe-Grillet, Alain
1965 *Snapshots and Towards a New Novel* (London, Calder and Boyars).
Russell, L.
1968 "Cinema-Code and Image", *New Left Review* 9.

Sadoul, Georges
n.d. *Les Merveilles du cinéma* (Paris, Les Editeurs Français Réunis).
Salanitro, N.
1964 *Peirce e i problemi dell'interpretazione* (Roma, Silva).
Santayana, George
1896 *The Sense of Beauty, being the outlines of aesthetic theory* (London, Norwood, Mass., Black).
1927 *The Realm of Essence* (= *The Realms of Being*, book 1) (London, Constable).
1930 *The Realm of Matter* (= *The Realms of Being*, book 2) (London, Constable).
Schick, Carla
1960 *Il linguaggio. Natura, struttura, storicità del fatto linguistico* (Torino, Einaudi).
Simon, Pierre-Henri
1959 *Théâtre et Destin* (Paris, Libraire Armand Collet).
Szondi, Peter
1956 *Theorie des modernen Dramas* (Frankfurt, Suhrkamp).

Taddei, Nazareno
1963 *Trattato di teoria cinematografica. I. L'immagine* (Milano).
Todorov, Tzvetan
1964 "La description de la signification en littérature", *Communications* 4.
1966 "Les catégories du récit littéraire", *Communications* 8.
Truffaut, François
1966 "Le cinéma selon Alfred Hitchcock", *Cahiers du Cinéma* 184.

Ullmann, Stephen
1962 *Semantics: An Introduction to the Science of Meaning* (Oxford, Basil Blackwell and Mott).

Weiner, Norbert
1961 *Cybernetics*, 2nd ed. (Cambridge, M.I.T. Press and New York, Wiley).
Wollenberg, H. H.
1947 *Anatomy of the Film, an illustrated guide to film appreciation* (London, Marsland).

INDEX OF FILMS CITED

INDEX OF NAMES